CONVERSATION ANALYSIS AND EARLY CHILDHOOD EDUCATION

Directions in Ethnomethodology and Conversation Analysis

Series Editors:
Stephen Hester, Honorary Senior Research Fellow, Bangor University, UK
Dave Francis, Department of Sociology, Manchester Metropolitan University, UK

Ethnomethodology and Conversation Analysis are cognate approaches to the study of social action that together comprise a major perspective within the contemporary human sciences. Ethnomethodology focuses upon the production of situated and ordered social action of all kinds, whilst Conversation Analysis has a more specific focus on the production and organisation of talk-in-interaction. Of course, given that so much social action is conducted in and through talk, there are substantive as well theoretical continuities between the two approaches. Focusing on social activities as situated human productions, these approaches seek to analyse the intelligibility and accountability of social activities 'from within' those activities themselves, using methods that can be analysed and described. Such methods amount to aptitudes, skills, knowledge and competencies that members of society use, rely upon and take for granted in conducting their affairs across the whole range of social life.

As a result of the methodological rewards consequent upon their unique analytic approach and attention to the detailed orderliness of social life, Ethnomethodology and Conversation Analysis have ramified across a wide range of human science disciplines throughout the world, including anthropology, social psychology, linguistics, communication studies and social studies of science and technology.

This series is dedicated to publishing the latest work in these two fields, including research monographs, edited collections and theoretical treatises. As such, its volumes are essential reading for those concerned with the study of human conduct and aptitudes, the (re)production of social orderliness and the methods and aspirations of the social sciences.

Other titles in this series

Respecifying Lab Ethnography
An Ethnomethodological Study of Experimental Physics
Philippe Sormani
ISBN 978-1-4094-6586-7

Ethnomethodology at Play
Edited by Peter Tolmie and Mark Rouncefield
ISBN 978-1-4094-3755-0

Conversation Analysis and Early Childhood Education
The Co-Production of Knowledge and Relationships

AMANDA BATEMAN
Waikato University, New Zealand

LONDON AND NEW YORK

First published 2015 by Ashgate Publishing

Published 2016 by Routledge
2 Park Square, Milton Park, Abingdon, Oxon OX14 4RN
711 Third Avenue, New York, NY 10017, USA

First issued in paperback 2018

Routledge is an imprint of the Taylor & Francis Group, an informa business

Copyright © Amanda Bateman 2015

Amanda Bateman has asserted her right under the Copyright, Designs and Patents Act, 1988, to be identified as the author of this work.

All rights reserved. No part of this book may be reprinted or reproduced or utilised in any form or by any electronic, mechanical, or other means, now known or hereafter invented, including photocopying and recording, or in any information storage or retrieval system, without permission in writing from the publishers.

Notice:
Product or corporate names may be trademarks or registered trademarks, and are used only for identification and explanation without intent to infringe.

British Library Cataloguing in Publication Data
A catalogue record for this book is available from the British Library.

Library of Congress Cataloging-in-Publication Data
Bateman, Amanda.
  Conversation analysis and early childhood education : the co-production of knowledge and relationships / by Amanda Bateman.
    pages cm. – (Directions in ethnomethodology and conversation analysis)
  Includes bibliographical references and index.
  ISBN 978-1-4724-2532-4 (hardback : alk. paper)
  1. Early childhood education–Social aspects.
  2. Conversation analysis. I. Title.
  LB1139.23. B3797 2015
  372.21–dc23

2015006526

ISBN 13: 978-1-138-60277-9 (pbk)
ISBN 13: 978-1-4724-2532-4 (hbk)

Contents

Acknowledgements   *vii*

1   Investigating Teacher and Child Interactions   1

2   Teaching and Learning as a Social Process   11

3   The Research Project   31

4   Doing Pretend Play   41

5   Relationships and Knowledge in Disputes   67

6   Learning Outside   101

7   Managing Illness: A Single Case Analysis   131

8   Knowledge and Relationships in Early Childhood Education   153

Appendix: CA Transcription Conventions   *161*
References   *163*
Index   *179*

Acknowledgements

It is imperative to begin these acknowledgements by thanking Stephen Hester for his insightful contribution to MCA work, raising its profile in an often CA dominated arena. His analytical prowess inspired a growing interest in MCA and offers solid foundations for current and future academics. He will be greatly missed.

Thanks to Amelia Church for introducing me to the world of CA at Swansea University; my life was forever changed! Thanks go to my peers and friends for supporting me in my writing of this book through engaging in academic discussion and feedback on earlier drafts and analysis. In particular I would like to thank Dr Amelia Church, Dr Jane Waters, Dr Carly Butler, Professor Margaret Carr, Dr Richard Fitzgerald, Professor Susan Danby and Dr Maryanne Theobald. I would also like to thank Neil Jordan for his correspondence and support throughout this process.

I would like to thank New Zealand's Teaching and Learning Research Initiative for funding this research project; the support has provided me with the wonderful opportunity to learn from the real life experiences of the teachers and young children who were involved in the project. Thank you to the centre director, teachers, children and families who were involved in the project; I learnt so much from you. Thank you to the Michael King family and Waikato University Faculty of Education for providing a much needed and tranquil retreat for finishing this book.

As always, special thanks go to my husband Justin and children Keira and Tate for continuing to inspire me and helping me to keep grounded and maintain a good sense of humour!

Chapter 1
Investigating Teacher and Child Interactions

This book presents and discusses findings from a study that investigated the everyday teaching and learning interactions between young children and their teachers in an early childhood education setting in New Zealand. The central aim of the project was to further understand how knowledge exchange occurred during the process of everyday communications between teachers and young children within the framework of the New Zealand early childhood curriculum, *Te Whāriki* (Ministry of Education [MoE], 1996). As *Te Whāriki* is a world-renowned document (Waller, 2005) that has recently prompted several countries to revise or develop their early childhood curricula, it was regarded as important to investigate how it guides pedagogy *in situ*. The presentation and analysis of these findings in this book offer an ethnomethodological insight into the mundane activities engaged in by teachers and young children during their daily routine, offering a unique and detailed insight into everyday interactions that the participants themselves orient to as important. This line of inquiry revealed how both knowledge and relationships were being co-produced between children aged two and half years up to five years and their early childhood teachers. This book highlights the importance of understanding further how the youngest members of society contribute to the co-production of an early education institution with their teachers from a very young age, demonstrating their social competencies as they work to co-create their social worlds.

It is important to note at the very beginning of this book that the observations included here are intended to contribute to the growing body of work regarding how teaching and learning is locally managed between teachers and young children, they are not chosen to provide examples of 'best teaching practice'. Through discussing examples of *everyday* teaching and learning interactions, this book aims to demonstrate the usefulness and relevance of using an ethnomethodological approach to such investigations and the significant findings it can reveal. In particular, the findings presented in this book demonstrate how an ethnomethodological investigation into teacher-child interactions can reveal how the participants made relevant the co-production of knowledge and relationships within their *everyday* interactions with one another in situ.

This book aims to extend research in ethnomethodology, conversation analysis, membership categorisation analysis, early childhood studies and pedagogy. With regard to ethnomethodology (EM), conversation analysis (CA) and membership categorisation analysis (MCA), this book provides new knowledge about the interactional features of the mundane activities engaged in between early childhood teachers and young children. Likewise, through investigating child-teacher interactions using both CA and MCA, the research presented here also offers a unique insight into early childhood education for teachers and early childhood researchers. The empirical chapters of this book (Chapters 4, 5, 6 and 7) examine episodes of teacher-child interaction during pretend play (Chapter 4), in dispute episodes (Chapter 5), when talking about environmental surroundings in the early childhood centre and New Zealand bush land (Chapter 6), and during a single-case analysis of managing illness (Chapter 7).

These findings demonstrate the complexity of interactions between young children and their teachers through their systematic turns at talk where they display saliency in managing category membership. The analysis of mundane activities engaged in by early childhood teachers and young children provide new understandings by revealing how the participants attend to sharing knowledge whilst also orienting to emotional and relational exchanges during their interactions.

A Rationale for the Project: An Early Childhood Education Perspective

The work involved in this book has grown from the shift in thinking from a psychological, deficit view of the child to an increasing awareness that children are capable and competent members of society. In New Zealand the early childhood curriculum acknowledges that children bring wisdom with them to their early childhood centres where the 'starting point is the learner and the knowledge, skills, and attitudes that the child brings to their experiences' (MoE, 1996, p. 9). Of interest then is how children actively contribute in the process of a teaching and learning episode with their teachers, and how teachers manage opportunities for collaborative knowledge exchange with young children.

The New Zealand curriculum, *Te Whāriki,* promotes teaching and learning as a collaborative activity that is guided by its framework. *Te Whāriki* is recognised as a metaphorical 'mat' that is woven by the members of each early childhood setting, 'The early childhood curriculum has been envisaged as a whāriki, or mat, woven from the principles, strands, and goals defined in this document' (MoE, 1996, p. 11). This emphasis of a framework to guide teachers, rather than a checklist of outcomes that could be perceived as restrictive, recognises the different types of learning possibilities that occur within centres in New Zealand; an intentional approach to ensure that the diversity of the members within each setting is valued.

The perspective that teaching and learning is context specific and dependant on the individual members present in each location sits well with CA methods where it is recognised that the turn-taking actions of each person works to co-produce the context. Likewise, the systematic and reciprocal co-production of interaction that is acknowledged in CA is also evident in *Te Whāriki* where it states, 'This curriculum emphasises the critical role of socially and culturally mediated learning and of reciprocal and responsive relationships for children with people, places, and things' (MoE, 1996, p. 9).

In New Zealand qualified early childhood teachers are educated to degree level where they are guided in the proficiency of noticing a child's interests during everyday activity, recognising opportunities for teaching and learning within that interest, and responding in a way which extends and builds knowledge (MoE, 1996). The skills involved in such teaching approaches are a requirement for effective pedagogy where a shared understanding between child and teacher are co-produced. This shared understanding is affirmed in literature exploring effective pedagogy in New Zealand where the research findings revealed:

> Effective pedagogy is linked to teachers/educators who are involved, responsive and cognitively demanding, and who encourage 'sustained shared thinking' where adults and children co-construct an idea or skill. (Mitchell and Cubey, 2003, p. pviii)

What can be unclear to teachers though is how everyday interactions and conversations can effectively develop children's learning in practical and non-intrusive ways (Carr, 2007; Davis and Peters, 2008). Prior New Zealand projects, including a project by Davis and Peters (2008), 'Moments of wonder, everyday events: How are young children theorising and making sense of their world?' revealed some issues with regard to the dimensions of implementing effective pedagogy under the *Te Whāriki* framework. Within this project it was found that teachers were interested in learning more about what types of children's actions they should respond to and how they should respond to them (Peters and Davis, 2011). Of particular interest was how to respond to children's questions without unintentionally 'hijacking' children's progressive working theories rather than actively listen to their development (Peters and Davis, 2011). The project was essential in revealing these interests with regard to the practical implementation of the New Zealand early childhood curriculum on an everyday basis. The findings suggested that, although the importance of *Te Whāriki* is acknowledged both nationally and internationally, the implementation of effective pedagogy through its framework could remain somewhat elusive for some early childhood teachers.

The research presented in this book also builds on a New Zealand based early years project by Carr (2007) titled 'Learning Wisdom', which focused on 'knowing why, when and how to engage with learning opportunities'. One of the project findings revealed that the participating teachers used a range of conversational strategies in their practice to maximise learning and teaching opportunities (Carr, 2011). As a way of demonstrating the discussed strategies, the author used transcriptions of conversations between the teachers and children. Although not as detailed as CA transcriptions, this way of presenting the data showed the rich information that can be gained from a close investigation into the verbal interactions between teachers and children in everyday teaching practice. Also of interest to the current project was the finding that 'teachers deliberately used "identity"' (Carr, 2011, p. 268) to refer to children's competencies. The use of membership categories in the turn-taking of everyday conversations is also relevant in CA, where the identities of the people present can be made observable by all members through the talk that is used. The use of membership categorisation analysis lends itself well to exploring further the use of such identity categories in the co-production of teaching and learning episodes.

These valuable New Zealand projects demonstrate that further investigation into the variety of conversations that occur every day in early childhood centres would be beneficial in order to build on the already established information. The study discussed in this book therefore aimed to do just that, where it hoped to provide further insight into teaching and learning in early childhood education in New Zealand under the framework of *Te Whāriki*. The findings in this book offer early childhood teachers the opportunity to take a closer look at the teaching and learning moments that occur in a systematic and orderly way through various everyday activities between teachers and young children. In turn, the findings will help to answer questions posed by teachers in prior New Zealand research projects (Carr et al. 2008; Davis and Peters, 2008).

From an international perspective, the findings from the current research project contribute to a growing body of research investigating teaching and learning in early childhood education where a greater focus on reciprocal conversations between children and teachers has been initiated in order to gain a clearer insight into the co-construction of pedagogical moments (see Durden and Dangel, 2008 for an overview). Within this arena there have been discussions concerning how teachers can practically extend children's learning through conversations that are 'cognitively challenging talk' (Durden and Dangel, 2008, p. 253). The study and its findings discussed here also hold implications for international research, such as the Effective Provision of Preschool Education (EPPE) study where guidance has been offered regarding quality interactions between early childhood teachers and young children, including the promotion of interactions that consist of sustained and shared thinking episodes (Sylva, Melhuish, Sammons, Siraj-Blatchford and Taggart, 2010)

The EPPE study, developed in the UK, suggests that 'sustained shared thinking' is an effective way of implementing early childhood pedagogy where the concept of 'sustained shared thinking' is explained as:

> 'Sustained shared thinking' occurs when two or more individuals 'work together' in an intellectual way to solve a problem, clarify a concept, evaluate an activity, extend a narrative etc. Both parties must contribute to the thinking and it must develop and extend the understanding. (Sylva et al., 2004, p. 6)

This definition acknowledges the collaborative achievement of teaching and learning moments through reciprocal interaction when engaging in and around a task problem or activity, and therefore aligning well to a CA approach to investigating the social processes of collaborative achievement of shared understandings in everyday interactions.

The work of the EPPE study was further continued through the Researching Effective Pedagogy in the Early Years (REPEY) study (Siraj-Blatchford et al. 2002; 2003) which discussed the use of adults' questioning for effective pedagogy. The use of conversational strategies for promoting teaching and learning were explored in this research whereby the teachers' specific use of questions were employed in order to stimulate 'possibility thinking' (Siraj-Blatchford and Manni, 2008, p. 267). The importance of specific types of questions in children's learning were identified; open-ended questions were found to stimulate possibility thinking and exploration whereas closed type questions did not. This international research indicates that, although open-ended questions were promoted in early childhood education to encourage cognitive stimulation, these types of questions were not used very often in everyday practice, and there was ambiguity as to what an open-ended question might look like by the teachers involved (Siraj-Blatchford and Manni, 2008).

These findings suggest that, as with the national research in the area of teacher-child pedagogy, early childhood teachers are interested in learning more about how to implement teachable moments in their everyday conversational practice. Through the synthesis of national and international research, the project findings discussed in this book offer further understanding into moments of teaching and learning through everyday conversations, as the need for such an investigation is clearly apparent.

The Usefulness of Ethnomethodology, Conversation Analysis and Membership Categorisation Analysis for Studying Teacher-Child Interactions

The project used an ethnomethodological approach using a data-driven line of inquiry where findings emanate from the observations of the participants during their everyday interactions with one another; using an ethnomethodological approach to teaching and learning interactions identifies how pedagogy happens in everyday situations. The turn-by-turn verbal and non-verbal interactions between teachers and children were observable during transcription using CA where they revealed the systematic process that was made relevant by the participants. MCA added further depth to the analysis by revealing the membership categories that the teachers and children co-produced during their talk-in-interaction. Approaching early childhood pedagogy using EM, CA and MCA provides answers to the questions raised by the teachers involved in the valuable prior national and international studies.

The initial line of inquiry was to investigate, very broadly, how knowledge was exchanged during teaching and learning episodes in the co-production of everyday interactions between teachers and young children in an early childhood education environment. A CA approach to such a study requires *unmotivated looking* (discussed further in Chapter 2), allowing insight into the ways in which a shared understanding is achieved that might otherwise be overlooked. Through providing a broad and data-driven investigation into teacher–child interactions, the identification of moments of shared understanding could be revealed as a members matter.

This interest in how shared understandings are co-produced aligns with prior ethnomethodological research where it is recognised as 'how separate individuals are able to know or act within a common world' (Goodwin and Duranti, 1992, p. 27). The co-production of this shared understanding is made observable in everyday interaction during the process of the turn-by-turn co-construction of an interaction, and is imperative for successful teaching and learning episodes (MoE, 1996). Teaching and learning moments are co-produced through conversations between children and teachers where verbal and non-verbal interactions are the point where all learning takes place. This encourages a view where the co-construction of moments of shared understanding is an essential element of educational practice.

This present study was concerned with investigating children's and adults' interactions through their use of verbal and non-verbal actions, with an interest in 'how participants deal with and understand each other in social situations; how agreement is achieved in collaboration with others ... that such agreement is not a static state of knowledge, but an interactive process that stretches across different parties' (Aarsand and Aronsson, 2009, p. 1559). It was thought that, as conversations are the point at which knowledge exchange takes place, they are a crucial aspect of pedagogy and needed investigating in much greater depth in order to reveal what is important to the members during these exchanges. The findings subsequently revealed that the co-production of knowledge between teachers and young children could not be separated from their co-production of relational, emotional activities.

The synthesis of conversation analysis and early childhood education in New Zealand complement each other well as both align with the socially competent view of the child. The following quotation from Harvey Sacks, co-founder of CA, shows a perceptive understanding of the child as knowledgeable and capable in their ability to initiate, maintain and terminate their own social activities where he acknowledges them as active in co-producing their own unique cultures:

> There are, of course, real problems that adults have to come to terms with about children, most of which are completely unknown, and fantastic in their character. One is, for example, that there is, in a perfectly good sense, a children's culture, with its artifacts, songs, games, etc., that is unbelievably stable. (Sacks, 1992a, p. 398)

Subsequent CA work that investigates aspects of young children's interactions demonstrates the usefulness of the approach and the importance of exploring these investigations in such a way in order to engage with the everydayness of the activities (e.g., Butler 2008; Butler and Weatherall, 2006; Church, 2007, 2009; Cobb-Moore, Danby and Farrell, 2008; Cromdal, 2001, 2009; Danby, 2002, 2009; Evaldsson, 2005, 2007; Filipi, 2009; Goodwin, 1990, 1998, 2002,

2006; Goodwin and Goodwin, 1987; Goodwin and Kyratzis, 2007; Hester and Hester, 2012; Kidwell and Zimmerman, 2007; Mashford-Scott and Church, 2011; Theobald, 2013; Theobald and Danby, 2012). The growing body of research using an ethnomethodological approach to the field of early childhood education is new and innovative and is becoming increasingly more available as its effectiveness for informing practice is realised.

One example of this is provided by Mashford-Scott and Church (2011) who discuss how the relevance of children's talk is determined by the type of response given by the teacher; the teacher-child interactions were analysed using conversation analysis in order to clarify the types of response offered by the teachers during children's story time. The findings revealed varying levels of response to children's talk in child-teacher interactions that ranged from ignoring being the least amount of response, to expansion as the most responsive. The implications for early childhood teachers from this study suggested that story time afforded an opportunity for extending children's knowledge if the teacher responded to the children's comments in a particular way.

This book aims to contribute to this growing body of research by demonstrating the usefulness of EM and CA in the area of early childhood education, revealing how children and teachers interact during their everyday dealings together in their educational setting. It proposes to extend international research as it builds on findings to explicitly reveal what types of everyday interactions teachers and young children are involved in together. This is achieved through demonstrating the detailed turn-by-turn contributions of each participant within their sustained and shared thinking episodes. EM, CA and MCA enable a close and detailed look at what pedagogical practices look like in everyday interactions with children. In providing such an approach, this book is concerned with the proper organisation and interactional sequences engaged in by teachers and young children in an educational setting.

It draws on the early work of Sacks' 'An initial investigation of the usability of conversational data for doing sociology' (1972) (discussed further in Chapter 2), where calls for help to a suicide prevention call centre were analysed and revealed the callers use of Relationship categories (collection 'R') and Knowledge categories (collection 'K'). The focus of this book is to explore and discuss how collection K and collection R became observable in the interactions between young children and their teachers throughout the project recordings. The book builds on Sacks' collection R and collection K categories to reveal how the teachers and children locally produced knowledge and relationships in the orderly turn-taking processes of everyday interaction. The findings in this book suggest that child and teacher interactions can belong to either of these categories and that it is the talk-in-interaction that initiates and maintains such categories.

An Overview of the Book

Chapter 2 will offer an overview of early childhood literature discussing a sociocultural approach to teacher-child interactions in education and also provide insight into the relatively underexplored literature of relational, emotional aspects of teacher-child interactions. Aspects of EM, CA and MCA relevant to the empirical chapters 4, 5, 6 and 7 are then discussed. The empirical chapters work to build on each other to increasingly reveal the ways in which relational activities are co-produced by teachers and children.

Chapter 3 describes the research process in detail and includes accounts of ethical procedures, where the research took place, the participants and the role of the researcher. A description of how teaching and learning episodes were identified for transcription from everyday mundane interactions from a data-driven approach are presented.

Chapter 4 is the first of the empirical chapters and examines teacher-child interactions during pretend play. This chapter discusses how affiliation and alignment (Stivers, 2008) are co-produced during pretend play (Butler, 2008) through features of verbal and non-verbal interactions (Filipi, 2009) between adults and children. In order to reveal how knowledge and relationships are co-constructed, this chapter demonstrates how pretend play is negotiated between adults and young children, through the initial mapping of the play, and through the teacher either engaging fully in the play to achieve affiliation or not. How issues of safety and well-being are attended to as a matter of importance over the ongoing pretend play activity is then presented at the end of the chapter.

Chapter 5 presents episodes of dispute interactions that are attended to by teachers as they respond to children's cries as interactional devices (Harris, 2006) and subsequently seek knowledge from the children about the incident that caused the trouble. This is followed by episodes where children actively seek out a teacher with an emotional upset and set about sharing their knowledge about the situation with them. Finally, episodes of teachers asserting a relational activity to re-establish the social equilibrium in the early childhood centre are presented. These episodes work to demonstrate how emotional upsets are responded to as priority items within the everyday activities in an early childhood centre.

Chapter 6 demonstrates how the environment is oriented to and utilised (Bateman, 2011; Cromdal, 2009; Heritage, 1978) in knowledge exchange by teachers and children in their production of talk-in-interaction, as well as how relational activities are co-produced around the environment when its features are attended to as problematic. These aspects will be revealed though transcriptions of observations taken in the early childhood outdoor area and from the weekly trip to the natural New Zealand bush.

Chapter 7 will provide unique insight into how caring for an ill child is managed by early childhood teachers and how being an ill child is played out. This is demonstrated through the transcription of a single case analysis during morning teatime in the early childhood centre. The chapter will reveal how silence and close body contact are used by the child to communicate a problem to the teacher and the attempts made by the teacher to gain knowledge about how she is feeling through a series of questions. An analysis of how the interaction progresses to the teacher gaining medical knowledge through the use of a thermometer and approaching a fellow teacher is presented, as well as presenting how the child communicates being ill through her non-verbal actions. This chapter demonstrates how the teacher attends to a child's illness as taking precedence over her other 'educational' interactions with the surrounding children, and how Sacks' collection R is observable as omni-relevant and having priority.

The concluding chapter, Chapter 8, will join together the findings of the book that discuss the mundane activities early childhood teachers and children engage in during everyday interactions. It will give an overview of how knowledge is co-produced between members who are more and less knowledgeable, and highlights the overriding importance that relational activities have in everyday interactions between children and teachers in early childhood education. The chapter concludes by arguing that, although there is a move to employ more formal approaches to early childhood teaching through literacy and numeracy strategies, a holistic curriculum framework (as in NZ) affords teachers and children opportunities to engage in multifaceted, personal and emotional interactions where each members' interests are attended to during the co-construction of everyday interactions. In relation to this, there is also a call for the recognition of the complex work of young children and early childhood teachers.

Chapter 2
Teaching and Learning as a Social Process

This chapter presents an overview of prior literature and research related to the issues of teaching and learning in early childhood discussed throughout this book. It is deemed important here to consider both the wider sociological literature related to early childhood teaching and learning as well as work in the area of conversation analysis (CA) and membership categorisation analysis (MCA) in order to respectfully engage with the research context. Through offering a broad knowledge base, a greater understanding of the area can be gained and gaps in the existing research can be identified. The beginning of the chapter will offer an overview of literature discussing a sociological approach to teacher-child interactions from an early childhood perspective. This will then be followed with insights into teacher-child interactions from conversation analysis studies that offer a specific focus on aspects relevant to the analysis and discussion in the empirical Chapters 4, 5, 6 and 7. A particular focus on Sacks' (1972) paper 'An initial investigation of the usability of conversational data for doing sociology' is provided towards the end of the chapter to introduce relational and knowledge category collections prior to the empirical chapters.

Teacher-Child Interactions from an Early Childhood Perspective

The social interactions of young children have long been studied from both psychological and sociological perspectives where the latter approach is relatively new in comparison (Bateman, 2010). The move towards a sociological approach of understanding children's lives acknowledges children as 'not a naturally given phenomenon, but the result of social processes of discourse, definition and interaction' (Maynard and Thomas, 2004, p. 2). Through a sociological lens, children are perceived as active participants in their interactions with others where they 'both affect and are affected by society' (Corsaro, 1997, p. 5). Where children were once seen as individuals who were independent of their culture, it is now suggested that a holistic and socio-cultural understanding of early childhood is imperative to fully realise the social worlds of children (Rogoff, 2003).

Offering alignment to the work of Bronfenbrenner and Vygotsky, Rogoff (2003) suggests that children's interactions should be studied in context rather than investigating a child's actions as independent of their environment as 'together, the interpersonal, personal, and cultural-institutional aspects of the event constitute the activity. No aspect exists or can be studied in isolation from the others' (p. 58). Through this perspective an alternative image of children is afforded that differs to prior perspectives of children being potential threats to society until they are socialised by more powerful adults (Corsaro, 2014). This is important as the deficit model of the child underestimates their abilities and strengthens social imbalance between children and their caregivers, whereas acknowledging that children actively contribute to their social worlds recognises them as competent participants in society.

With regard to teacher-child interactions, early childhood teachers enforce which actions are acceptable in the culture of their specific school environment through engaging in an exchange of actions with the child (Rogoff, 2003). This offers potential for the management of the co-construction of context where teachers have a choice whether to intervene in a child's actions or not. Likewise, children also work to co-construct their own peer cultures in childhood through their interactions with other children and teachers (Corsaro, 1985a, 2014). Whilst these turn-by-turn interactions unfold, the teacher and child's roles in the process of the initiation and maintenance of the immediate context are being established.

The concept of co-construction is defined as 'the joint creation of a form, interpretation, stance, action, activity, identity, institution, skill, ideology, emotion or other culturally meaningful reality' (Jacoby and Ochs, 1995, p. 171). 'Co-construction' acknowledges each person as contributing to the production of the social environment. Language plays an integral part in the co-construction of social worlds, as it is the systematic communicative exchanges that demonstrate each participant's intentions where each utterance is systematically built on in the development of individual social situations. Children are active participants in the co-construction of their own worlds in this way where they negotiate meaning and interactions through their everyday co-construction of conversation with a range of people (Corsaro, 1979, 1985a, 1997).

This perspective of children being actively involved in the co-construction of their own lives and the lives of others has implications for teacher-child relationships where each member has an equal skill in contributing to the establishment of the teaching and learning environment. Through the verbal and non-verbal turn-by-turn actions in everyday social occurrences, children and adults co-construct the social organisation that creates reality. The co-construction of an interaction involves sequences of actions through the participants' immediate interpretation of a prior turn at talk, where they demonstrate a mutual understanding of an event, or not.

The reciprocal nature of the co-construction of meaning and reality is evident between teachers and children in early childhood education research where 'each party engages with the understanding of the other and learning is achieved through a process of reflexive "co-construction"' (Siraj-Blatchford et al., 2002, p. 34). The co-construction of knowledge is well known in educational arenas where sociocultural approaches to teaching and learning acknowledge the social and cultural contexts of the participants in individual situations (Berk and Winsler, 1995). In a socio-cultural approach to co-construction, each member of the interaction contributes equally to co-produce the teaching and learning situation.

Asymmetries of knowledge are also present in teacher-child interactions, as identified in the concept of scaffolding (Wood and Middleton, 1975; Wood, Bruner and Ross, 1976) where one member has more knowledge than the other and support for the specific child's learning is offered by a more knowledgeable other. Possible differences in conversational features that produce co-construction and scaffolding in outdoor teaching and learning situations in Wales and New Zealand have been identified with a view to investigating the role of the environment during teacher and learning interactions in early years education (Bateman and Waters, 2013; Waters and Bateman, 2013a).

The cultural differences evident in teacher-child interactions are important to consider when investigating teaching and learning in a range of countries, as was evident in the renowned comparative study that involved three preschools in three different countries by Tobin, Wu and Davidson (1989). The study involved observations of children aged between three and six years in preschools in China, Japan and the United States of America and revealed that each preschool enforced acceptable social rules relevant to their own particular culture, indicating that the provision of care was unique to each country. A second study (Tobin, Hsueh and Karasawa, 2009) revealed that teachers from each country intervened in conflict situations between children differently, as what was perceived as acceptable behaviour in one preschool was not acceptable in another. These studies of teacher-child interactions demonstrate how the rules of each preschool were co-constructed between the participants through everyday occurrences to create their own unique cultures within their unique contexts.

Further research investigating politeness in Japanese preschool settings reveals how teachers use verbal prompting and non-verbal embodied positioning of children as strategies to encourage politeness routines (Burdelski, 2010). This co-construction of social rules of conduct between teachers and children is also explored in prior research where it was found that teachers who co-constructed classroom rules with the attending children had more success in enforcing the rules as the children were bound through their own rules to behave appropriately (Mooij, 1999a, 1999b).

The social processes involved in early childhood education teaching and learning have also been acknowledged in the large scale UK Effective Provision of Preschool Education (EPPE) and subsequent Researching Effective Pedagogy in the Early Years (REPEY) study where *sustained shared thinking* episodes between children and teachers were acknowledged as good quality educational interactions (Siraj-Blatchford and Manni 2008; Sylva et al., 2010). Through such interactions teachers and children work together so that each participant contributes to the problem solving activity in a shared and sustained way. Findings from the EPPE and REPEY studies suggest that teachers' open-ended questions are particularly effective in facilitating the building of knowledge as they afford a broader range of answers from the children rather than the simple 'yes' or 'no' response that is prompted by 'closed' questions. Question-answer sequences have been explored in prior research investigating teacher-child interactions and knowledge exchange where the initiation-response-evaluation (IRE) (Mehan, 1979) and initiation–response–feedback (IRF) (Sinclair and Coulthard, 1975) techniques were found as teaching strategies.

However, it has also been suggested that teachers should pay significant attention to the child's answer in response to the teacher's initiation of a question, and respond appropriately to ensure that they are listening to the child and following their interest rather than asking a series of open-ended questions (Bateman, 2013). Further issues with the practical implementation of a socio-cultural approach to co-constructing and scaffolding teaching and learning episodes have been identified in New Zealand research (Peters and Davis, 2011; Carr, 2007). The findings in these projects suggest that teachers can be unsure of when to intervene in children's activities to offer scaffolding support or to initiate a co-construction of knowledge. In these situations, early childhood teachers are cautious of interrupting children's developing working theories, where children work out task problems independently, as they are aware that they may misjudge the situation and unintentionally hijack the learning episode (Peters and Davis, 2011).

Relational Care in Early Childhood Education

Although the primary focus of early childhood education is to provide an educationally stimulating environment for the activity of knowledge exchange in teaching and learning episodes guided by government policy, the importance of emotional attachments in early education is becoming increasingly more recognised (Page and Elfer, 2013), as evidenced in UK policy documents (Elfer, 2013). An acknowledgement of the link between emotion and reasoning is evident in literature from David (1996) who writes:

> I would argue that the field of early childhood and those who work with small children have always had problems with nature of rationality, because early childhood involves so much more openly the imperatives of emotions. (p. 95)

The connection between early childhood teaching and emotion is evident in research where young children are perceived as 'agentic partners in the learning, social and emotional interactions they experience in group settings' (Stephen, 2010, p. 15). Furthermore, the early childhood centres that were rated as being within the highest quality in the EPPE study were those where 'adult-child relations are warm, caring and respectful, and where the adults are sympathetic in response to any children being hurt, upset or angry' (Siraj-Blatchford and Sylva, 2004, p. 719).

The educational and emotional needs of the youngest children from birth are often met by assigning an individual teacher to a specific child so that attachments can be maintained and a knowledge of the individual needs of each infant can be supported by a teacher who has an in-depth knowledge about the child they are caring for. However, it is suggested that there are tensions surrounding members of staff working with specific infants in the role of key worker, as it limits the social interactions that infants and toddlers would have with a wider range of people (Page and Elfer, 2013). A study exploring teachers' opinions of attachment based pedagogy revealed that teachers of children aged 0–3 years found their work emotionally challenging where 'emotions should be seen as an inevitable aspect of this part of the work and not as an indication of professional or personal failure' (Page and Elfer, 2013, p. 564).

Furthermore, research exploring the notion of love in early childhood education between teachers and children aged 0–3 years reveals that the complexities of loving relationships in this context are often oversimplified and underestimated (Page, 2008), leading to the important identification of 'professional love' (Page, 2011, p. 313). Although emotional relationships are occasionally discussed in early childhood education research, there is a dearth of literature linking the importance of emotional relationships to teaching and learning episodes and this is an area identified as needing more academic attention (Stephen, 2012).

In New Zealand, where the current study took place, qualified early childhood teachers are educated to degree level and there is a national curriculum framework, *Te Whāriki*, in place. Within the national curriculum document, there is a deliberate emphasis on the importance of supporting relationships as well as knowledge exchange in educational settings, demonstrated through the identification of 'Relationships' as one of its four principles, along with 'Holistic Development', 'Empowerment' and 'Family and Community'. These four principles are woven together with five strands: 'Belonging', 'Contribution', 'Communication', 'Exploration' and 'Well-being' to create the early childhood curriculum framework. *Te Whāriki* was created as a bicultural document in order to support the children and families of both Maōri and Western descent in response to the specific social context of New Zealand (MoE, 1996). *Te Whāriki* was groundbreaking in acknowledging the inseparable link between educational teaching and learning, well-being and relationships in early childhood education, and provided a national curriculum that truly realised holistic, socio-cultural teaching and learning in practice.

Teacher-Child Interactions in Conversation Analysis

The prior research and literature discussed in this chapter indicates how teaching and learning in the early years can recognise the unfolding of knowledge exchange as a social process between the participants involved in that interaction, and the growing awareness of the importance of acknowledging emotions and relationships in early childhood education contexts. This view of teaching and learning as a social process is mirrored in ethnomethodology (EM), conversation analysis (CA) and membership categorisation analysis (MCA) where insights into social worlds from an insider's perspective through analysing aspects of interactions which the members themselves orient to in their verbal and non-verbal communications is afforded (Sacks, 1992a, 1992b).

Investigating teacher-child interactions through analysing the detailed sequences of talk between the participants offers insight into the everyday mundane activities attended to by the participants. This is particularly useful as it affords, 'the perspective from within the sequential environment in which the social action was performed' (Seedhouse, 2005a, p. 252). By employing EM, CA and MCA to investigate the social worlds of teachers and children, an important insight into the aspects of interactions which the participants themselves find important is made observable. Therefore an overview of aspects of EM, CA and MCA that are relevant to the analysis and discussion in Chapters 4, 5, 6 and 7 now follows in order to make these familiar prior to the presentation and analysis of the empirical chapters.

Studying Early Childhood Education as its Own Culture – Ethnomethodology

The work of Schutz, Goffman and Mead demonstrated an interest in the study of everyday social interaction (Atewell, 1974; Hassard, 1990). Goffman's work became specifically interested in how everyday activities were produced through the syntactic organisation of human behaviour (Pomerantz and Fehr, 1997) and these ideas were progressed by Garfinkel (1967) through encouraging an understanding of social organisation through the systematic way people engaged with one another.

> Garfinkel posed the question – if norms and values were indeed relevant in accounting for social action, then how are persons able [to] recognise in any particular instance their relevance for conduct. (Hester and Francis, 2000, p. 2)

Ethnomethodology is a tool that is useful for revealing how people make sense of their everyday interactions with one another through analysing their actions-in-context (Garfinkel, 1967). An ethnomethodological underpinning has been pivotal in CA research in order to make visible these systematic processes of talk-in-interaction in a diverse range of everyday situations.

The usefulness of an ethnomethodological approach to the study of social worlds is acknowledged in a special issue of the Australian Journal of Communication (see Butler, Fitzgerald and Gardner, 2009), which provides an insightful contribution to the field of ethnomethodology, CA and MCA research. In the special issue, the contributing authors provide illuminating perspectives of the usefulness of ethnomethodology, CA and MCA for the study of social order and interactions between members of society.

> EM is not so much interested in the notion of communication as the transmission of messages, but rather ... how people *interact* with others in society. That is, what people say and how they say it is understood in terms of the activities accomplished in and through *interaction*. (Butler et al., 2009, p. 2–3)

The usefulness of using an ethnomethodological approach to the study of children's interactions with their teachers is evident as it affords the opportunity to see what the members themselves orient to as important through their actions, and how they make and find those actions accountable through their subsequent actions. Ethnomethodology helps to make observable these matters during everyday interactions, providing a true representative of the co-production of a culture as it unfolds and offering an understanding of how everyday events are locally managed. It reveals members' methods of doing real life activities with the people, places and things they engage with in their everyday lives in situ, as ethnomethodology values the observation of real life for understanding the mundane, ordinary lives of people.

The Turns at Talk that Co-produce the Culture of Early Childhood Education – Conversation Analysis

This section does not aspire to provide a thorough review of CA as it has a wide range of elements in its framework (see Emmison, forthcoming, 2015; Hutchby and Woofitt, 1998; Schegloff, 2007a; Sidnell, 2010 for introductions); it sets out key features of CA that are relevant to the study of interactions between teachers and children in early childhood education, and to the empirical Chapters 4, 5, 6 and 7.

Approaching some interesting social phenomena through CA affords the opportunity 'to take singular sequences of conversation and tear them apart in such a way as to find rules, techniques, procedures, methods ... that can be used to generate the orderly features' (Sacks, 1984a, p. 413). This approach reveals how social interactions are co-produced during everyday, mundane social situations through conversation turn-taking where a first pair part (FPP) utterance from one person prompts a second pair part (SPP) utterance from another (Sacks, Schegloff and Jefferson, 1974). Through their verbal and non-verbal turns at talk, people make observable the issues that are important to them, at that time in that place and with those people.

The turn taking process in verbal and non-verbal interactions co-produce the social situation and it is this systematic co-production of context that is the underpinning of conversation analysis where, preferably, one person speaks at a time and openings and closings of conversations are observable (Sacks, Schegloff and Jefferson, 1974). Conversation turn-taking sequences that people engage in every day are initiated through conversation openings (Schegloff, 1968). In relation to children's conversational openings, Sacks (1992a) suggests that children 'have restricted rights to talk' (p. 256) and so they often open an interaction with an adult by asking a question such as 'guess what' as this requires a sequential action from the adult, usually in the form of another question 'what?' The child is then required to speak a second time; therefore successfully securing an interaction. Children's use of question-answer sequences encourage an interaction, as a question requires an answer; a FPP produced in the shape of a question is more likely to provoke an

SPP in the form of an answer (Schegloff, 2007a). When a question is not responded to its absence is noticeable, leading the questioner to repeat their question until the recipient provides an adequate answer (Sacks and Schegloff, 1979).

With regard to teaching and learning situations, the concept of knowledge exchange and shared understandings between participants is key in CA where the success of the systematic process of everyday interaction relies on the participants understanding each other. Within the domain of CA, there is a large body of literature that explores knowledge in interaction as it is the foundational underpinning from which all interactions can build; with a shared knowledge and understanding in interaction between participants the interaction can progress more efficiently then if repairs were needed (Schegloff, 2007a). With regard to knowledge exchange in CA, but not specifically to early childhood education, Heritage (1984, 2011, 2012a, 2012b, 2013) has provided much insight into the systematic ways in which knowledge is co-produced in everyday talk. Within interactions each person designs their turn to account for the knowledge of their recipient, so to avoid telling someone something they already know and make their utterance newsworthy (Goodwin, 1979; Heritage, 1984; Sacks, 1973). Heritage suggests that speakers can make observable their knowledge positions in their turns at talk where they 'occupy different positions on an epistemic gradient (more knowledgeable [K+] or less knowledgeable [K−])' (Heritage, 2012b, p. 32).

This occurs where a shared focus and understanding is present in interaction between people. Where there is a failure of understanding, or miscommunication, the participants make it observable through their marking of a repair sequence (Schegloff, 1992a). Conversation repair is evident in the organisation of talk whereby one member of the interaction initiates the repair sequence by orienting to the trouble source, otherwise known as the repairable (Schegloff, 1992a, 2007). This application of conversational repair is referred to as 'Error Correction Format' (Jefferson, 1974, p. 188) where the repairer initiates their self-correction by cutting off their sentence and reorganising their words. Self-initiated repair is the preferred form of correction over other-initiated repair as it is less disruptive to the progress of the ongoing conversation (Schegloff, Jefferson and Sacks, 1977). Children have shown their competence of understanding the rules of repair in their everyday interactions with their peers in conflict situations (Bateman, 2012b; Bjork-Willen, 2012; Church, 2009; Danby, 2005; Deniz-Tarum and Kyratzis, 2012) and even very young children through their non-verbal use of gaze with adults (Filipi, 2009).

Recent research in a special volume of Journal of Pragmatics titled 'Understanding understanding in action' (January, 2011) has revealed themes that emerged from a CA approach to knowledge exchange. A number of papers in the collection investigated older students learning in the classroom where focus was given to the social process of teaching and learning. The findings from these papers indicate implications for the teacher's role in the learning process as 'these studies offer a curriculum for the adults in the room. In matters of educational study, it is *our* instruction that may be the most neglected' (Macbeth, 2011, p. 450).

Research investigating teachers use of questions reveals such techniques as initiation-response-evaluation (IRE) (Mehan, 1979) and initiation–response–feedback (IRF) (Sinclair and Coulthard, 1975) techniques as well as with 'open-ended' questions in early childhood education (Siraj-Blatchford and Manni, 2008). Even though these studies did not use a CA approach in their investigations of teacher-child interactions, they acknowledged the orderly sequences of the turns of talk that were apparent in everyday exchanges around knowledge building. In research that has used a CA approach to the study of children's interaction, children have been observed using questions when initiating interactions with their peers through asking questions regarding an object, where the use of a question regarding an item provoked a reaction from the recipient child as they were required to provide an answer to the prior question about the selected object (Bateman and Church, in press 2015).

The social competencies of children in co-producing interactions with their peers in systematic ways have been explored (e.g. Bateman; 2011, 2012b, 2012c; Bjork-Willen, 2012; Butler, 2008; Butler and Weatherall, 2006; Church, 2009; Cobb-Moore, 2012; Cobb-Moore, Danby and Farell, 2008; Cromdal, 2001, 2004, 2009; Danby, 2002, 2005, 2009; Danby and Baker, 1998a, 1998b, 2000, 2001; Goodwin, 1990, 1998, 2002, 2006; Goodwin and Kyratzis, 2007; Kidwell, 2011; Kyratzis, 2004, 2007; Sidnell, 2011; Theobald, 2013; Theobald and Danby, 2012; Theobald and Kultti, 2012; Lerner and Zimmerman, 2003), as have their interactions with adults (e.g. Bateman, 2013; Bateman, Danby and Howard; 2013a; Burdelski, 2010; Danby and Baker, 1998a; Mashford-Scott and Church, 2011; Filipi, 2009; Cekaite, 2010; Pike, 2010). These insightful studies reveal the affordances of CA in understanding the social worlds of children through exploring what is important to the participants themselves. In doing so they acknowledge children as socially competent members of society who actively contribute to their lives, and the lives of others, in knowledgeable and orderly ways.

In terms of relationships shared understandings and knowledge asymmetries can be linked to morality and 'have critical consequences for our social relations, most directly through our moment-by-moment alignments and affiliations with others' (Stivers, Mondada and Steensig, 2011, p. 3). The distinction between social alignment and affiliation has been made in relation to storytelling where an alignment can be observable as a general agreement whereas an affiliation with someone is evident where there is a shared understanding and experience of an event and can be perceived as 'sociorelational' (Stivers, 2008, p. 53). Within storytelling the social situation often consists of storytellers and hearers where a telling can be prompted by the hearers' request for the story in the systematic progression of a storytelling activity (Goodwin, C., 2013). Likewise, research investigating conversations in child counselling sessions reveals that these episodes often involve counsellors prompting a telling from the child being counselled to encourage the child to tell about their emotional upset (Hutchby, 2005). In response to the child's telling of an emotional trouble, counsellors were found to produce a formulation of the child's utterance in their third position of talk (Peräkyla, 2005) in a similar way to teacher's in early childhood setting when children tell about a task problem (Bateman, 2013).

Relational talk involving past troubling experiences in educational settings have been investigated in Christchurch, New Zealand with children and teachers who were affected by the 2010 and 2011 earthquakes. The research revealed that teachers took every opportunity possible to discuss the earthquake and associated after-effects with the children during their everyday interactions at the preschool. This was reflected in the video footage collected by the researchers, which involved going on exploratory walks when events occurred, such as when diggers appeared to fix holes in the road and when the water mains were damaged. During these daily expeditions, talk that oriented to the broken environment prompted spontaneous tellings about the day of the earthquakes by the children (Bateman, Danby and Howard, 2013a). Likewise, the use of children's Learning Story books, intended for documenting children's learning episodes, as well as episodes of pretend play, also prompted emotional recall around the earthquake experience (Bateman and Danby, 2013; Bateman, Danby and Howard, 2013b). These episodes of talk provided an opportunity for spontaneous sharing of troubles talk in everyday interactions between teachers and children in relational ways, a vital process for coming to terms with traumatic events.

Teacher and Child Interactions – Institutional Talk

Atkinson and Drew (1979) suggest that talk is used in a certain way during institutional settings. A person's identification of the specific roles and identities of the members in an institution is demonstrated by their orientation to specific ways of talking which, for example, is reflected in the allocation of turn-taking and ways in which roles are invoked as observable in the co-production of the context (Drew and Heritage, 1992). In primary schools and early years settings, the social organisation within is specific to each individual institution as each context is co-constructed through the participants' talk and actions (Butler, 2008). Although this is apparent, there remain some similarities in each institution, such as the teacher instigating the allotment of turns between themselves and the children through question and answer sequences. In these institutional interactions there is a more formal pre-structure to the conversational turns than is evident in non-institutional environments (Francis and Hester, 2004) where the teacher presents actions that produce a formal, 'institutionalized order of action' (Butler, 2008, p. 27).

The allocation of turns of talk map the teacher and children as a standard relational pair (SRP), which enforces the rules of conduct that are tied to each role. An SRP consists of members who belong to the same group and have obligations bound to their membership (Benwell and Stokoe, 2006). However, these institutional rules of conduct do not remain in the classroom setting; children also construct social order through their institutional talk during their play. This has been demonstrated through the analysis of talk at school during break-time where there is evidence of the mapping of one 'person in charge' that is similar to the teacher/pupil pair in the classroom (Butler, 2008). This therefore suggests that 'institutional talk is an interactional practice rather than a feature of a setting' (Butler, 2008, p. 28).

In CA research context is viewed as being co-produced by each participant's unique interactions with one another; context is perceived *as* immediate social order. Unlike the concept of context being a physical environmental space, an ethnomethodological perspective offers the perception of context as being co-constructed by the participants through their immediate interactions (Goodwin and Duranti, 1992). The physical environment is then made relevant by a person's acknowledgement of it through their talk, rather than the environment imposing on, and influencing people's conversation and interactions (Housley and Fitzgerald, 2002). That is, children and teachers will attend to their surroundings through their own personal interpretation and social requirements. Through verbal orientation to specific features, the members make those features contextually relevant and the context is established through this orientation (Schegloff, 1992b).

It is therefore understood that in each individual social situation, the context will be co-constructed through the turn taking of the members within (Sacks, Schegloff and Jefferson, 1974). When people are brought together in a new environment they will categorise other members so to understand the situation better where their 'categorization reflects not the structure of the world but the order that humans impose on it' (Markman, 1989, p. 8–9). The categorisation of members sequentially establishes social organisation as 'what does matter about a category is its indexical use ... what is made of it there and then' (Antaki and Widdicombe, 1998, p. 80), thus further supporting the notion of context being 'intra-interactional' (Schegloff, 1992b, p. 195).

The co-construction of an institution is also produced by positioned categories (Sacks, 1992a) where high category positions are observable in contrast to lower category positions in everyday interactions. The concept of 'ratification' is also present in positioned categories as a member's behaviour will be assessed either positively or negatively by comparing them to a lower or higher category than they actually belong to depending on their behaviour (Sacks, 1992a). Goffman's concept of 'ratification' occurs when 'the identity assumed by one party is ratified, not by her own actions, but by the actions of another who assumes a complementary identity towards her' (Goodwin and Heritage, 1990, p. 292). Positioned categories involve two class sets where one set has a higher category level than the other (Sacks, 1992a). The person who holds the higher category position in the set, such as the mother in the family category set or teacher in the school category set, is legitimately entitled to assess and comment on the behaviour of the person in a lower position, such as the child/pupil; therefore organising the social environment. As the context is co-produced by each member's contribution, the positioning of categories will change for each member in different places. These positioned categories go some way to explaining how social order is co-constructed by the participants to form the immediate context or 'context in action' (McHoul, Rapley and Antaki, 2008, p. 831).

The perspective of the co-construction of social order actually *being* context is essential to understanding the orderly features of teacher-child interactions. This co-production of social worlds initiates a move away from the broader perspective of context to one that is co-produced between the interactions of the participants themselves (Dupret and Ferrie, 2008).

> Instead of viewing context as a set of variables that statically surround strips of talk, context and talk are now argued to stand in a mutually reflexive relationship to each other, with talk, and the interpretative work it generates, shaping context as much as context shapes talk. (Goodwin and Duranti, 1992, p. 31)

Social worlds are created within the multiple situations that a variety of people attend, where verbal and non-verbal actions work in systematic ways. Through the nature of conversation being context free and context sensitive, the analysis of it 'seeks to reveal how speakers draw upon universal procedural rules to create locally relevant shared understanding' (Lepper, 2000, p. 55).

The systematic employment of membership categories – Membership Categorisation Analysis

MCA is useful for investigating interactions between teachers and young children as direct observations of their orientation to categories in the co-construction of the interaction is afforded. Through observing the participant's explicit reference to categories during their turns at talk, an insight into their understanding of daily interactions in situ is afforded (Hester and Francis, 1997). An exploration of the systematic use of categories in everyday social interactions can offer an understanding of the social organisational practices that are evident between young children and teachers.

In order to investigate the use of membership categories in the systematic turn-taking of everyday conversations, it is important to acknowledge how MCA and CA are linked. Although CA has gained an increased amount of interest in the last 50 years since its conception, MCA has received comparatively less; so much so that MCA has been suggested as being the 'milk float' in relation to CA's 'juggernaut' (Stokoe, 2012a). This suggestion, as headline to a special issue, worked to stimulate the debate about the ways in which MCA could possibly move forward. Stokoe's response to the discussions by the commentators (Fitzgerald, 2012; Gardner, 2012; Rapley, 2012; Silverman, 2012; Whitehead, 2012) suggests that, like CA, studies using MCA 'should also begin to build a robust corpus of studies of "categorial systematics"' (Stokoe, 2012b, p. 345). In doing so, Stokoe's suggestion reafirms Sacks' (1972) aim to reveal just how membership categories are methodically used in systematic ways: 'Members' activities of categorization are not only describably methodical, but also ... quite essential to the ways that they are seen as graspable my Members' (Sacks, 1972, p. 37).

That the use of categories is a members matter that the participants of the talk use and respond to in the co-production of social organisation is of import, primarily to the participants (Schegloff, 1991; Stokoe, 2012b). During interaction categories are made relevant for the participants rather than the analysts where the analyst has to, '*show how the parties are embodying for one another the relevancies of the interaction*' (Schegloff, 1991, p. 51, original italics). Observing and analysing which categories people orient to offers an understanding about what is perceived as important to them, at that time and in that place with those people, making it also observable to the researcher.

Sacks (1972) defines a membership categorisation device (MCD) as 'a *collection* plus rules of application' (Sacks, 1972; p. 32, original italics). An MCD can be applied to people who form organised groups and also those who do not (Sacks, 1992a). Furthermore, an MCD is used when a person insinuates that they are a member of a certain group in society; inference-rich evaluations of that person can be made due to their membership to a particular group. This is relevant to the membership inference-rich representative (MIR) device where a person's name is replaced with a category. For example, rather than using the personal identification of an individual, the category to which they belong is used such as 'a soldier' or 'a Gypsy'. This is evident when a person is described as a woman, a mother or a teacher, the person can belong to either category, but it is why a particular category is used, by whom, and when that is of analytical interest.

Sacks notes that when an MCD is employed, there are 'not some exclusively appropriate or required choice of devices' (Sacks, 1992a, p. 206). There are alternative devices that can be employed when people are involved in social situations where the most appropriate category is used to accomplish an individual's social goals (Sacks, 1992a). An order of relevancy distinguishes which category is the most important at that time, as there are multiple categories that a person can belong to; this is termed as a hierarchy of relevance as the most obvious aspect of a person's identity is used to describe them (Sacks, 1992a).

People who are unfamiliar with each other ask questions regarding MCDs on meeting that might involve asking where a peer lives or works, or who their favourite TV character is so that inference can be made about that person (Maynard and Zimmerman, 1984; Sacks, 1992a). This sharing of personal information between people is acknowledged as 'doing description' (Schegloff, 2007b, p. 463), where MCDs hold the resources for a greater understanding of that person through the knowledge that we hold about a mentioned category (Sacks, 1992a). Through using these resources for the classification of a person, children demonstrate their social competency and ability to construct social networks in their own culture (Butler, 2008).

When a person is socially located using a MCD, then other categories from the same MCD can be applied to the other members using the consistency rule (Sacks, 1972). The consistency rule suggests that what can be said about one member of a group or culture can be said about all of the other members (Sacks, 1972). Asserting membership to a group makes 'stateable about yourself any of the things that are stateable about a member' (Sacks, 1992a, p. 47). In terms of the category 'teacher', there are certain activities that are bound to being a teacher, such as passing on and extending knowledge, giving professional care and support. Whereas a member of the category 'parent' infers a far more emotional and relational type of care and support towards a child.

Omni-relevant Devices

During the co-production of context an *omni-relevant device* may be evident where it has priority over all other things being done in that situation. Sacks' (1992a) identification of what an omni-relevant device is and what it achieves has also been noted in prior research investigating children's play and games in New Zealand (Butler, 2008) as follows:

> An 'omni-relevant device' is one that is relevant to a setting via the fact that there are some activities that are known to get done in that setting, that have no special slot in it, i.e., do not follow any given last occurrence, but when they are appropriate, they have priority. Where, further, it is the business of, say, some single person located via the 'omni-relevant device', to do that, and the business of others located via that device, to let it get done. (Sacks, 1992a, pp. 313–314)

An example of how an omni-relevant device is oriented to having first order relevance and priority in children's interactions can be observed in their games where each participating child's actions are deemed as legal or illegal. 'If an action in a game is attempted, and is done illegally, then the attempted action does not count at all' (Sacks, 1992a, p. 500). This co-production of moral order in children's play displays the 'omni-presence of right-wrong considerations for actions' (Sacks, 1992a, p. 500). In the context of children's interactions, an 'illegal' action is one which is shown to be problematic by the children through their orientation to it as unacceptable behaviour for a specific situation; legal actions are not usually oriented to by the members who accept the behaviour as conventional conduct. Children's use of the omni-relevant device 'rule-enforcer' and 'offender', and 'offender' and 'victim' have been observable in dispute situations (Hester and Hester, 2012). Within their analysis of the children invoking these omni-relevant devices, the authors considered the following criteria:

> There are, then, two tests for the omnirelevance of a social context. One is that the parties analyze each other as having produced category-bound activities bound to the categories comprising the collection parties to a particular context. The second test is that of anytime invocability. (Hester and Hester, 2012, p. 15)

Sacks also provides some guide regarding how to identify an omni-relevant device in everyday interaction:

> One way that we can see that a device (a set of categories and some ways of using it) is omni-relevant, turns on there being some insertable sequences ... The device is omni-relevant by virtue of the fact that the insertable sequences, while having various kinds of priorities, don't occur at any specified point, i.e., any point located by virtue of, for example, a last occurrence. (Sacks, 1992a, p. 315)

Within conversations during everyday activities, there is a systematic flow of turn-taking between people during their transfer of information to each other. However, there are also occasions where a turn at talk will not be sequentially related to the immediate prior turn of the interlocutor; these turns have been identified as having priority over the ongoing activity (Sacks, 1992a).

> It does appear that there are some 'priority items' and they're priority items whose character is not given by the last thing that occurred, in the sense that given a question an answer may be a priority item, given a first greeting the second may be. But these seem to have rights and obligations to be done, perhaps without regard to what it is that has been taking place. (p. 269)

In relation to the social organisation of giving and receiving help in a relational way, the suggestion that these priority items 'have rights and obligations' tied to them indicates that when these priority items are evident in ongoing interactions between SRPs they organise those people as members of the collection R category, as that category of people 'constitutes a locus for a set of rights and obligations concerning the activity of giving and receiving help' (Sacks, 1972, p. 37). As this is the case, an orientation to a relational activity shaped as a priority item, in whichever environment, requires priority over the ongoing situation through the members' rights and obligations to one another as members of a collection R category SRP.

Omni-relevant devices can also have cover devices 'Where a "cover" is an identification which is more palatable, which can hide the problematic one, and which nonetheless allows whatever it is that the problematic one can do, to get done' (Sacks, 1992a, p. 317). Sacks suggests that the omni-relevant device 'therapist/patient' may have such a covering device, as being a psychiatric patient could be deemed as problematic in the sense that the person might be ashamed of belonging to such a category. Sacks suggests that a male adult psychiatric patient could be seen out in public with a female nurse as the cover device could infer a more socially acceptable pair of 'male-female'.

Within these cover devices there needs to be '*partitioning constancy*' (Sacks, 1992a, p. 317, original italics) where the same members of one population can also belong to another population as a way of asserting 'cover' identities. Sacks' observation of patients and their therapist behind a one-way mirror, where the patients approach the mirror and announce the 'starting' of the session, suggests that such a partitioning constancy was apparent where 'all the persons who are patients by reference to the one MCD are performers under the other'

(Schegloff, 2007b, p. 468). Although the same people are members of these partitioned categories, it is their actions that assert which category they belong, so that talking about their emotional problems with the therapist would categorise them as belonging to the patient category, whereas tapping on the mirror and making announcements to others categorises them as performers; it is their actions that make the partitioning observable and demonstrable.

Category Bound Activities

Category bound activities (CBA) can be described as actions (verbal and non-verbal) that are observable as being tied to a particular category of people in society; a person can be identified as a member of a specific group through the CBA they engage in. When people display a CBA in their talk or through physical gesture, it makes their membership visible to other people. If a member of a category behaves in a way that is not recognisable as a CBA for that category, they are seen as deviant (Sacks, 1992a) and an exception rather than the common sense knowledge about that category being changed (Schegloff, 2007b). This is due to internal systems of control whereby the existing members enforce the rules of CBA that are acceptable for membership in their own group (Sacks, 1992a). The displayed CBA sequentially offers solidarity, as it is known that certain groups have members who act in a specific way (Sacks, 1992a). This is associated with Goffman's concept of *ratification* where the actions of each member are held accountable by the other members, as what can be said about one member of a category can be applied to subsequent members by the consistency rule (Sacks, 1992a, 1992b).

With regard to CBA, research using conversation analysis shows increasing acknowledgement of the importance of embodied actions and prosody situated within activity (Cekaite, 2014; Goodwin and Goodwin, 2000; Goodwin. C., 1981, 2000, 2014; Goodwin. M. H., 1998, 2006, 2014). Through acknowledging embodied actions, prosody and verbal action together in the co-production of interaction, a thoroughly detailed representation of interactional processes are presented, affording more insight into the activity at hand than through analysing the talk alone (Goodwin, C., 1981). For example, through engaging in the embodied action of a collaborative embrace accompanied with talk using a 'creaky voice', members of society make demonstrable their affiliative relational status to each other (Goodwin, M.H., 2014). Likewise, when the recipient of a storytelling nods their head they demonstrate their affective affiliation with the teller, rather than mere alignment (Stivers, 2008). CBAs have been important in identifying an omni-relevant device, along with the anytime availability of its invocation (Hester and Hester, 2012; Sacks, 1992a). In research investigating the social organisation processes of four-year-old children beginning primary school in Wales, children were excluded when not displaying the appropriate CBA displayed in the specific play activities of their peers (Bateman, 2010).

The consideration of these collective actions in the co-production of social interactions is particularly important with very young children where research has found that their embodied actions of eye gaze and pointing serve as a conversational turn as these actions are treated as such by adults, who then respond to their actions in their next turn at talk (Filipi, 2009; Kidwell, 2005). These non-verbal actions help to maximise a shared understanding between children during interactions as they affiliate and disaffiliate (Bateman, 2012a).

Sacks' Collection R and K Categories

Sacks referred to a standard relational pair (SRP), a pair of people who share an interaction together and have a set of rights and obligations to each other regarding the giving and receiving of help (Sacks, 1972). A bond of obligation between people means that each person in that bond has a responsibility to the other and that they can call on that person for help as that person is obliged to be of assistance. Sacks (1972) suggests that each SRP can be categorised as either relational or linked to knowledge:

> The two collections with which we shall be dealing may be called (1) R – a collection of paired relational categories, and (2) K – a collection constructed by reference to special distributions of knowledge existing about how to deal with some trouble. (Sacks, 1972, p. 37)

A SRP can be observable when two people are interacting as part of a coequal relational category, otherwise termed as collection category 'R', where they have an equal friend-friend relationship (Sacks, 1992a). Collection 'R' members have rights and obligations for giving help to one another in a specific place at a specific time (Silverman, 1998). This makes a relationship as part of the collection 'R' category indexical and occasioned as the members interact to make a specific situation with particular people in the co-production of the context. In a collection 'K' category the members who belong to this category of people are those who are knowledgeable about a specific item and can therefore offer help through a cognitive awareness of how to approach a trouble, rather than in the collection 'R' category of people who have emotional bonds of rights and obligations.

Sacks (1972) discusses ways in which each collection comprises members who are obliged to turn to each other in the search for help, whether the help that is needed requires knowledge (K) or is more relational (R). It is important to note that relational and knowledge categories are co-produced through verbal and non-verbal actions and are ever changing through the systematic turn taking of the interlocutors, not static roles discriminatively assigned to specific persons. For example, a husband and wife do not necessarily belong to the R category collection just because they are married; it is their co-production of talk and actions at specific times that reveals their membership to either an R or a K category collection.

Other work in the area of R and K categories have shown that, even when the interaction has initially co-produced a collection K category by the members, they can work through subsequent turns at talk to restructure the social organisation of the interaction as a collection R category (McHoul and Rapley, 2005). Butler and Weatherall (2006) also acknowledge Sacks' collection R and K categories in their work on children's categorisation in games where they demonstrate that 'for the games that were being played, the relevant category-set of players, the activities bound to those players, and the relevant game events were produced in situ' (p. 465). Butler (2008) also provides details about the relevance of collection R and K categories in children's social organisation processes, offering insight into how they are negotiated and applied during everyday interactions with each other.

People can be categorised as classes of 'insiders' and 'outsiders' where insiders can include family members or friends and outsiders can involve unfamiliar others (Sacks, 1992a). When requesting help from outsiders, a different format of asking for assistance is procured than if a person was asking for help from an insider. Sacks suggested that an outsider is only asked for help as a last resort; if an insider is approached for help but no offer is secured, an 'outsider' will be referred to. However, Schegloff (2007b) suggests that people occasionally view an outsider as more knowledgeable in the experienced area of trouble and therefore more proper to confide in. In this latter situation, the troubled person approaches a member from the more knowledgeable 'outsider' category of people before initiating contact with a member who belongs to the 'insider' category.

In an 'insider' SRP such as husband-wife or friend-friend for example, the paired friend or spouse would be the first person to turn to for help as that person is obliged to give help to the other member of the SRP through the collection R category (Sacks, 1972). SRPs such as spouse-spouse and friend-friend are known as first position R pairs, meaning that each member of the pair will turn to the other for help with an *emotional* problem, but not necessarily for help with a *knowledge* based problem. If someone has no collection R person to turn to for help they will systematically turn to someone who is a member of the 'Relationship improper' (Ri) category (Sacks, 1972). Someone who is improper to turn to for relational help may be a person who is classed as having a particular professional knowledge in the area of trouble, making him or her also 'Knowledge proper' (Kp). An example of this systematic way of dealing with trouble is acknowledged in Sacks' work on suicide helpline calls. 'The transformation of the call-taker from 'stranger' using collection R, to 'professional' using collection K, means that they are the proper and exclusively appropriate person to help for the suicidal person's troubles' (Butler, 2008, p. 35).

A person who is categorised as an 'outsider' tends to be one that is unfamiliar to the person with the trouble and so they do not hold the same rights and obligations for giving and receiving help as an 'insider' would. Instead, the interaction will be co-produced by way of seeking professional knowledge about a particular thing from particular people. As there is a knowledge proper collection, there is also a 'Knowledge improper' (Ki) collection of people to turn to; these people who may be Rp, such as a spouse or best friend, but may not have professional knowledge about the thing the trouble is associated with and so would not be the first person to turn to in this situation. Collection K categories tend to be made up of professional-layperson or teacher-pupil where, rather than being obliged to help each other as in Collection Rp, the members have rights and privileges to deal with trouble around knowledge (Sacks, 1972).

Sacks (1972) suggests that 'subset Rp is properly used in an orderly fashion – that there is a proper sequence in the use of the classes it contains' (p. 41). This suggests that there is pattern in the use of Rp and Kp applications, in the first instance you have an emotional problem (such as feeling suicidal) you turn to help from someone belonging to the Rp category, if there is nobody there to provide help (either unavailable or non-existent) then you turn to someone from the Ri category; although this second person may be improper in terms of the Relational category they are proper in terms of the Knowledge category (Kp). The orderly way in which this sequence occurs provides an insight into the systematic search for help.

When considering the use of relational categories in interaction, there can be an explicit reference to the categories employed, or not. Pomerantz and Mandlebaum (2005) provide details regarding these issues and explore examples where people explicitly employ relationship categories and also how, although not making explicit reference to close relationships, relational categories are enacted through the category bound activity of sharing of problems that would be deemed 'inappropriate for incumbents of the categories of acquaintances and strangers' (p. 162). The importance of the systematic turn-taking in the co-production of talk is then discussed in relation to the relevance of recipient uptake, where an empathic response to troubles telling was noted as securing moments of intimacy between the incumbents, thereby co-producing a collection R category.

Relationships and Knowledge in Early Childhood Education

The research explored in this chapter provides details of the growing academic awareness of the benefits of approaching teaching and learning in the early years from a sociological perspective. The systematic transition of knowledge exchange as a social process was also explored through research that has used an ethnomethodological approach, CA and MCA to reveal how a shared understanding is co-produced in everyday interaction. This book aims to build on the important work of the scholars included in this chapter in order to address limitations in understanding further the social and relational co-production of knowledge in early childhood education.

In order to do so, the following chapters explore how the social interactions between early childhood teachers and children aged two and half to five years during everyday activities involve knowledge exchange, and also relational activities that work to 'do' early childhood education. To begin this journey, the project that informed the findings presented in this book is introduced in the next chapter, Chapter 3. Chapter 3 will describe how the project was conducted and will include information about the research participants, ethical procedures, research design and data collection and how the data was analysed.

Chapter 3
The Research Project

Chapter 2 introduced research that investigates teaching and learning as a social and interactional process from an early childhood perspective where, within the literature, a significant focus was given to knowledge exchange *or* relational, emotional interactions between children and teachers. The study of interaction from an ethnomethodological approach and conversation analysis and membership categorisation analysis were then discussed and offered insights into the co-production of relational and knowledge category collections. The subsequent chapters aim to reveal how interactions between teachers and young children are co-produced through both knowledge exchange *and* relational activities in systematic and orderly ways.

In order to get to that point, this chapter sets out the current project from which these findings emanated. This chapter describes the research project in detail and includes accounts of the process, ethical procedures, the place of research and the participants. A discussion of how the emerging themes were identified for transcription from the everyday, mundane teaching and learning interactions is offered towards the end of the chapter.

The study discussed in this book was initiated in order to address the interest that teachers have about how to initiate and implement 'teachable' moments in their everyday interactions with the children in their care, as identified in prior national Teaching and Learning Research Initiative (TLRI) projects and the international Effective Provision of Preschool Education (EPPE) and Researching Effective Pedagogy in the Early Years (REPEY) studies. These prior studies highlighted the need to investigate current teaching practice in the early years and the study discussed in this book aimed to contribute to that ongoing investigation. The current project offers insight into everyday teaching and learning interactions between teachers and children in situ where verbal and non-verbal exchanges were investigated in detail. This data-driven approach of investigating interactions as they occur helps to create a clearer picture of everyday practice and the things that are attended to as important by the people at that time and in that place (Garfinkel, 1967).

The broad interests of this project aligned with the more specific questions raised in national New Zealand research posed by teachers themselves in prior TLRI studies that included:

- What types of actions should teachers respond to and how do we respond? (Davis and Peters, 2008)
- How do teachers respond to children's questions without hijacking their progressive working theories? (Davis and Peters, 2008)

- When is it more appropriate to respond through active listening? (Davis and Peters, 2008)
- How can teachers extend on children's interests to develop learning? (Carr, 2007)
- How can the use of 'identity references' (Carr, 2011) be offered as a teaching strategy?

On a larger international scale, the current research also addressed questions posed by the international EPPE and REPEY studies that include:

- Do questions really stimulate knowledge?
- If so, what types of questions extend children's possibility thinking and extend learning opportunities? (Siraj-Blatchford et al., 2002, 2003)
- What do open-ended questions look like in situ? (Siraj-Blatchford et al., 2002, 2003)
- What responses are stimulated through teachers' use of open-ended questions? (Siraj-Blatchford et al., 2002, 2003)

The current study aligned with these prior questions raised by teachers and researchers concerning how early childhood teachers and children can engage in ways that stimulate teaching and learning episodes in everyday practice. In doing so it aimed to assist in unveiling the elusiveness of how teachers implement the curriculum and the strategies that they used for initiating and maintaining teaching and learning moments. Importantly, by looking at teaching and learning episodes as a collaborative achievement between teachers and children, the study valued and carefully considered the contributions of children and the strategies that they also used in their interactions with teachers. This approach recognised the importance of children's, as well as teachers' interactions in the co-production of a teaching and learning episode. The development of a deeper understanding of children's interactions and how these can be noticed, recognised and responded to has been identified as significant by teachers themselves and so was of interest in the current study. The process of the research project is now discussed, beginning with how the research was initiated.

The Research: Place and Participants

When conducting research with young children there are strict sets of criteria that researchers must adhere to in order to ensure ethical practice, the process of which will be discussed later in this chapter. Prior to the stringent ethical procedure, possibilities about what the research could look like were conceptualised and discussed with early childhood teachers who shared with the researcher the same interests about everyday teaching and learning. As the researcher was a lecturer in early childhood education and visited students during their practical placements in early childhood centres, there was ample opportunity to engage with early childhood teachers in various settings. Regular interactions with teachers led to discussions that revealed a shared interest in investigating teaching and learning episodes through a broad, data-driven approach by analysing everyday verbal and non-verbal interactions in detail.

The teachers who were interested in collaborating in a project were three experienced teachers from a well-established early childhood centre that had been in operation for over 40 years. The centre where the teachers worked catered for a wide age range of children from three months to five years and employed approximately 30 early childhood teachers. Of the three teachers who were interested in collaborating on the project, one worked in the toddlers centre with children aged between two and a half and three and three quarters years, and two worked in the pre-school centre with older children aged between three and three quarters and five years. At the request of the early childhood teachers, this range of ages was incorporated into the research plan, as the teachers involved were particularly interested in their interactions with the children within this age range. These particular age groups also helped the project align with the prior discussed research projects; therefore extending the knowledge about teacher interactions with these particular age groups.

When considering the initiation of the project, it was imperative to have the teachers' expert personal knowledge of the children involved in the centre in order to capture the mundane activities that occurred during daily interactions between the participants on a regular basis. The three early childhood teachers brought with them the expertise of having the knowledge and experience of teaching the attending children in their early childhood centre over a period of years as well as having a clear interest in the aims of the study. Each teacher had years of experience of working in the centre and so had established close, reciprocal relationships with the children in their centre. These established teacher-child relationships were deemed as beneficial to the study in order for routine interactions to naturally emerge, as they would in the everyday exchanges between these people.

The expertise of the teachers was also thought to be imperative during the analysis stage where they identified the interactions that they felt were a good teaching and learning moment; this aspect of the research is discussed further towards the end of this chapter. As the teachers held the knowledge of what everyday teaching and learning between themselves and the children in the centre looked like, their opinions regarding what constituted 'a good teaching and learning moment' were fully respected and accepted as the first stage of data analysis when considering which interactions should be transcribed.

Each of the three teachers made their interest in the study explicit, adding strength to the usefulness of the project in practical terms for teachers. For example, the toddler teacher stated that she had a particular interest in improving the learning environment through investigating how she initiated and maintained interactions with these young children, and in what situations, echoing the dilemma documented in research regarding when to intervene in children's peer-peer interactions (for example Bateman, 2011; Davis and Peters, 2008). Furthermore, the toddler teacher and one of the pre-school teachers indicated that they were keen to promote learning through quality provision, and wanted to know what 'quality' interactions might look like in everyday conversations with young children. Both pre-school teachers expressed a particular interest in exploring one of the *Te Whāriki* strands 'communication' and how they implemented that strand effectively in their everyday use of verbal and non-verbal interactions with the pre-school children.

Ethical Procedure

Once preliminary discussions regarding the outline of the project were complete the researcher began writing a more detailed research plan, including the ethical procedures that were to be involved. A formal meeting between the early childhood centre director, teaching team and researcher was established at this point in order to discuss the role of the teachers and researcher in the implementation of the study.

To initiate the process of ethical consent, an application to conduct the research was written and submitted to the researcher's Research and Ethics Committee within the university. The application involved detailing how the recruitment of participants was to be achieved; in research involving young children a hierarchy of consent is usually applied to address this issue. In educational establishments the hierarchy involves a 'top down' approach whereby the principal is contacted first, followed by the teacher of the children that the researcher wants to do research with. Once consent has been achieved from these people the consent of the children's parents is requested and then, finally, the people who the researcher is ultimately interested in working with are consulted, the children. Due to the hierarchical way in which consent to research with children has to be achieved, the term 'gatekeepers' is often given to the top layers of people that the researcher has to gain permission from prior to discussing the proposed research project with the children. This process of consent is detailed in prior research using CA to investigate children's social interactions in a New Zealand playground (Butler, 2008).

Within the present study, cover letters informing about the research and accompanying consent forms were drawn up for the director of the early childhood centre, each of the interested teachers, and for the parents of each of the children who attended the centre. Once consent was achieved from the centre director and teachers, the parents of the children were given their cover letters and consent forms. The children who were given parental consent to participate were then approached by the researcher and participating teachers to ask if they would like to be involved.

The important task of providing informed consent about the practicalities of conducting the study were explained and discussed with each person in detail, particularly with regard to the use of video and audio data gathering. When talking with the children about contributing to the project, the teachers and researcher worked together to ensure that the children were aware of what was happening, particularly with regard to being filmed where the video camera and microphone were presented at the discussion. To ensure that the children understood the process of video and audio recording, it was explained to them that they would be filmed when they were talking to the teacher who was wearing the microphone with the bright blue light on it.

Research Design and Data-collection Methods

As the research was interested in collecting examples of everyday interactions between the participating children and teachers, audio and video recorders were used. The video camera had a pull out screen that enabled the researcher to observe the footage as it was being recorded without looking directly at the children. This enabled more detailed observation of the children and teachers as, although they were informed that they would be recorded, the researcher was able to avert her gaze from looking straight at the children to looking directly at the camcorder screen. This allowed the children and teachers to be less conscious about their interactions and provided a more inconspicuous form of observation (Pepler and Craig, 1995). The zoom lens on the camcorder also allowed the researcher to record footage at a distance so that there was less interference in the interaction, whilst also being able to zoom in to record the subtle and detailed interactions between the children and teachers. The use of the video recorder afforded the opportunity to revisit the captured footage of social interactions repeatedly, assisting in the subsequent analysis (Tapper and Boulton, 2002), highlighting the importance of the use of the video camera in this study.

Along with the video camera, a wireless microphone was used to capture the talk between the children and teachers. The device used in this project had one microphone and one microphone receiver unit. The microphone receiver was compatible with the video camera and clipped on to the top of the camera whilst the teacher wore the microphone. The microphone recorded the teachers' talk directly onto the video footage rather than picking up any sound around the location of the video recorder, even when the teacher was quite a distance away from the video recorder. This technology provided very clear audio footage of the teacher-child interactions that was immediately synchronised to the visual footage, an invaluable documentation of the interactions in situ that made the subsequent transcription process more accurate and manageable.

The first round of data collection began at the beginning of the year in February. During the first day of filming the teachers at the early childhood centre, the teachers chose which order they wanted to be recorded in and wore the wireless microphone with the researcher videoing them for a small period of time (approximately 15 minutes each). This preliminary exercise provided an opportunity to gain familiarity with the data collection process for the teachers and researcher in preparation for the subsequent weeks.

The subsequent three weeks in February involved the audio and visual recording of one teacher per week. The teachers took turns at having their interactions with the children audio and video recorded by the researcher for the three mornings of their chosen week. During their three mornings the teacher wore a wireless microphone and was videoed by the researcher in order to capture a reliable account of both verbal and non-verbal interactions for analysis.

As one teacher expressed an interest to be recorded outside of the early childhood environment, and in a natural, outdoor environment at a nearby New Zealand bush land (part of the teacher's usual routine) this situation was also included in that particular teacher's three-day observation. The teachers continued with their everyday teaching during their week and reflected on the moments where they felt significant teaching and learning had occurred at the end of each day; the researcher then made a note of these episodes to transcribe later. This process marked the beginning of the data analysis where common themes that emerged from the daily events began to be identified by the team.

The second stage of data collection involved the teachers being recorded a second time later in the year so that more interactions could be gathered. The audio and visual recordings were conducted over a shorter, single day during the month of August. As with the first stage, the teachers were invited to discuss the interactions that they felt were of significance at the end of their day so that the researcher knew which interactions to transcribe and analyse.

Once the recordings of the teacher-child interactions were collected and the teachers had identified the moments of significance, the footage was stored in a file on the researcher's laptop and subsequently transcribed using CA transcription symbols (see appendix 1), as developed by Gail Jefferson (Sacks, Schegloff and Jefferson, 1974). The transcription process revealed a more in-depth understanding of the footage collected where the systematic ways in which the teachers and children attended to some things and not others in their interaction became more visible.

Identification of Teaching and Learning Episodes

CA encourages unmotivated looking when approaching the analysis of talk-in-interaction, where repetitive themes emerge from data through the iterative process of investigation. The underpinning of unmotivated looking and data-driven analysis is imperative in the use of CA, where the risk of the researcher applying their own set of categories prior to the analysis is unacceptable (Schegloff, 1996a). The concept of unmotivated looking has been challenged where it is argued that the analysis of data emanates from the researcher's motivation for investigation; therefore declaring the 'looking' motivated (see Psathas, 1990 for a discussion). In CA research the topic under investigation must serve as the motivational aspect of the research process. The data analysis should then be approached with an open mind where no pre-theorised categories are used; therefore allowing the data to guide the emerging themes found within (ten Have, 2000). This perspective allows the data to inform the researcher, and in doing so provides an essential insight into the phenomena of interest. CA therefore offers an insight into how social conduct is co-produced by participating members in their everyday social meetings with one another.

The teacher-researcher partnership was imperative to this study in this respect as the teachers guided the researcher as to which interactions to start with to initiate the analysis process. The prior mentioned TLRI projects highlight the points of teaching practice which the teachers themselves indicate as worthy of further investigation, and this project was intended to follow that approach. This approach also builds on prior TLRI research findings concerning teacher–researcher partnerships which include the teachers being able to build on their practice through the experience of engaging with research findings, and the researcher learning more about teaching and learning through engagement with teachers' everyday experiences (Carr et al., 2008).

Data Analysis

An ethnomethodological framework (Garfinkel, 1967) was adopted for this research project in order to observe how children and teachers co-produce teaching and learning in their normal everyday interactions with each other. CA and MCA were used to examine the interactions in detail to reveal which types of verbal and non-verbal actions were apparent between teachers and children. This research approach encouraged data driven analysis of how children and teachers interpreted and responded to interactions as they happened, rather than reflective and third party reports where these aspects may become distorted over time (Benwell and Stokoe, 2006). In order to apply this method of data analysis, a detailed account of the transcription process is now offered.

CA and MCA are specifically useful for exploring early childhood pedagogy as they encourage unmotivated looking when approaching the analysis of talk-in-interaction so a reliable account of actions is presented without predefined ideas. Findings are revealed through repetitive themes that emerge from the data through the iterative process of investigation. This data-driven approach to the study of child-teacher interactions affords a close look at the everyday co-production of teaching and learning as it unfolds. Although the teachers had some idea about what a teaching and learning episode might feel like in their everyday practice, the details of how that interaction was co-produced in the details of conversational turn-taking remained unexplored. CA provided a useful approach to do this exploring.

Through their sequential turns at talk, the members make demonstrably relevant issues that are perceived as important to them through their verbal and non-verbal orientation. Therefore this affords a unique insight into how knowledge is co-constructed through the systematic turn-by-turn orientation to specific items by each participating member. Through the use of CA, the transcription of the moments identified as teaching and learning shed light on the turn-taking processes involved in the co-production of these interactions, revealing how each participant contributed.

To begin the data analysis, the footage selected by the teachers was watched through at the end of each data collection week. Due to the data-driven nature of the analysis, the data was approached with unmotivated looking to see what was happening in the interactions between the teacher and child without preconceived ideas (Sacks, 1984b). With this approach to the data analysis, the footage is watched and listened to repeatedly over a period of time, allowing consistent themes to emerge, affording a closer look at what is being oriented to by the people being observed as important to them.

The findings from data-driven research appear initially as 'noticings' that can include such phenomena as an extended length of pause time in a conversation between the teacher and child, for example, or a certain phrase or word being used frequently. The noticings trigger the start of the fine-grained analysis as the footage associated with the noticings is transcribed. This approach enables the researcher to focus on these specific noticings in the interactions rather than transcribing all of the data, which would be an unrealistic and time-consuming task where a large corpus of data has been collected. Through the transcription of specific episodes of interaction, further details begin to emerge which give a unique insight into the phenomena studied.

In the current study, the transcripts were written as the video footage was played and each specific detail of the interaction between the child and the teacher was transferred into writing. The continued relationship between the teachers and researcher was also needed at this point where the teachers' expert knowledge of the children was called on to discuss what a child was saying at particular times in the footage when their speech was inaudible to the researcher, in order to allow the researcher to make the transcription reliable.

This aspect of data-driven analysis is imperative in the use of CA as a method, where the risk of the researcher applying their own set of categories prior to the analysis is highlighted as unacceptable (Sacks, 1984b; Schegloff, 1996a). In CA research the topic under investigation must serve as the motivational aspect of the research process, which in this project is a broad interest in the everyday interactions between teachers and children aged two and a half to five years. This perspective allows the data to inform the researcher, and in doing so provides an essential insight into the phenomena that motivated the investigation, revealing issues that may have otherwise been missed.

The validity and reliability of using CA and MCA as a research methodology are discussed by Perakyla (2004), who argues that, to ensure the validity and reliability of the observed interactions, the combined use of video and audio footage help to provide detailed representations of events. The particular aspect of reliability has been an instrumental factor in the development of CA (Perakyla, 2004) as the direct and detailed accounts of interactions represented in CA provide a reliable representation of each episode as displayed by the members themselves

(Sacks, 1992a, 1992b). It is further argued that CA is more reliable than other methods of sociological data analysis as it offers the benefit of providing a detailed account of interactions between people rather than 'summarised representations' (ten Have, 2000, p. 9).

The repeated access to the audio and video footage of the collected data helps to provide a true representation of the footage (Leung, 2002; MacWhinney, 2007). The accuracy of the transcription is essential for conversation and membership categorisation analysis and so the symbols are used to inform the reader of how the speech was conducted, 'because they're "there" in the talk' (Jefferson, 2004, p. 23). During the transcription process, each person who is involved in the observed episode is identified at the beginning of the transcript so that the reader is aware of all the members involved. The audio and visual footage are then studied and the name of the person who is speaking is entered on a new line in the document, followed by their verbal utterance or a description of their non-verbal gesture. The convention symbols are inserted into the text during transcription to allow the reader to see where the person places emphasis on their speech, raises or lowers their tone, whispers or laughs.

The inclusion of both verbal and non-verbal actions is of particular benefit to the current study as people in everyday society interact both physically and verbally (Goodwin, 2000, 2006; Goodwin, Goodwin and Yaeger-Dror, 2002) and young children often use gaze and gesture to express themselves (Bateman, 2012b; Filipi, 2009; Kidwell, 2005). Through the iterative process of the transcription of data, reoccurring themes emerge which may not have been noticeable to the teachers or researcher from first impressions. Consequently, new information regarding teaching and learning moments that have been identified by teachers can be made available and hold important implications for practice and future research.

Whilst engaging with the transcription process, the emerging themes involved the participants' orientation to sequences of knowledge exchange and also how these interactions were abruptly suspended when there was an emotional upset or relational trouble present in the ongoing interaction. This orientation to knowledge exchange and relational activities were present during pretend play, in disputes, when talking about an environmental feature and when managing illness.

To explore these findings further, the following chapter, Chapter 4, will present the first of these empirical findings. During the observations of child-teacher interactions, pretend play episodes were very frequently engaged in, making the activity significant in the everyday organisation of the early childhood education day. The ways in which episodes of pretend play were managed are explored in Chapter 4 now by taking a close look at the turns of verbal and non-verbal action engaged in by teachers and young children during pretend play activity.

Chapter 4
Doing Pretend Play

The usefulness of a data-driven approach to the study of interactions between teachers and young children has been discussed in the prior chapters of this book. Through taking such an approach, the importance given to specific activities by the children and teachers at that time and in that place are observable. This chapter presents the analysis of teacher-child interactions during pretend play episodes, as this was one of the activities found to be engaged in every day at the early childhood centre.

Through observing the turn-taking features of verbal and non-verbal interactions between adults and children (Filipi, 2009), the social relationships of affiliation and alignment (Stivers, 2008) can be seen. In order to reveal how knowledge and relationship categories are co-constructed, this chapter will draw on the work of Sacks (1972), offering new knowledge regarding how pretend play is negotiated between adults and young children, and how adults and children map their roles in a pretend play activity. A particular interest in non-verbal actions is considered here, offering insight into how gesture works during the turn-taking sequences of teacher-child interactions in pretend play. This chapter will reveal how being an affiliated co-equal player in pretend play involving adults and children is connected to relational categories, whereas aligning with the pretend play activity could be closer linked to knowledge categories.

Children's Pretend Play Activities

Existing literature investigating pretend play in early childhood has often explored these types of playful interactions from a psychological perspective. Not surprisingly then there are definitions of what pretend play is thought to involve, including 'the kind of play in which children use one thing, such as an object or language ... to represent the meaning of another entity' (Göncü and Gaskins, 2011, p. 48). Children's pretend play, also termed fantasy, symbolic or socio-dramatic play to name but a few, has long been understood as providing benefits to children's psychological development (Piaget, 1976; Vygotsky, 1976) and, more recently, children's holistic health (Kitson, 2010). There has been a vast amount of research and discussion involving the phenomena of pretend play between children, but less attention has been given to exploring how adults engage with young children in pretend play (Kitson, 2010).

In one historical paper that discusses how adults play games with children, Bruner, Jolly and Sylva (1976) make explicit links between the 'make believe' game of 'peek-a-boo' (make believe in the sense that the mother simply hides and does not actually disappear away from the child never to return) and language:

> Our own studies at Oxford on language acquisition suggest that in exchange games, in 'peek-a-boo' ... young children learn to signal and to recognize signals and expectancies. They delight in primitive rule structures that come to govern their encounters. In these encounters they master the idea of 'privileges of occurrence' so central to grammar, as well as other constituents of language that must later be put together. (p. 19)

This insightful early work acknowledges a link between conversational turn-taking sequences in language and young children's turn-taking during make believe play with adults and, as such, has been of significance to early childhood teachers learning about language development through play. Bruner's emphasis on the social nature of play is also closely aligned with the underpinning of conversation analysis where order can be seen at all turns in social interaction through the detailed turn-taking positions of each participant. However, a further exploration of the systematic features in the co-production of social interactions between children and adults through pretend play is relatively underdeveloped.

Pretend play between children has been investigated through a conversation analysis approach where the benefits of investigating these types of interaction from a data-driven approach were identified by the authors (e.g., Butler, 2008; Bjork-Willen, 2012; Cobb-Moore, 2012; Sidnell, 2011). These prior studies demonstrate how conversation analysis can provide a detailed description and analysis of the activity of pretend play as locally produced through the joint attention of the participating children in their turns at talk (Bjork-Willen, 2012). Through providing an insightful investigation into children's pretend play using conversation analysis and membership categorisation analysis, researchers reveal how membership categories are used effectively by children to initiate and maintain the social order of the playground (Butler, 2008; Butler and Weatherall, 2006; Cobb-Moore, 2012) and how an assertion about the transformation of an object can reveal a child's knowledge about what he perceives the object to 'be' as opposed to a co-production of transformation between two children (Sidnell, 2011). The inclusion of ethnomethodological research that explores pretend play is important to the analysis of the current interactions as it provides an insightful background for revealing the conversational features that co-produce knowledge and relationships as a members matter (Baker, 2000).

This chapter aims to build on prior understandings of pretend play by demonstrating how affiliation and alignment (Stivers, 2008) during pretend play episodes are linked to the distribution of knowledge between young children and their teachers. Stivers (2008) suggests that the social stances of affiliation and alignment can be observable in storytelling interactions between teller and hearer; affiliation is an affective understanding of the storyteller's stance whereas alignment is shown through mere acknowledgement. In this chapter examples of how teachers either align or affiliate themselves with children's pretend play activities are presented where alignment is observed as teachers talk about the play with the children from an outsider role, or become a participating insider in the play activity, co-producing affiliation. As with the work of Stivers (2008) where nodding was identified as a key feature of affiliation, this chapter also acknowledges the importance of children's non-verbal actions in their pretend play activities with their adult teachers, extending the important findings already established in investigations into parent and toddler interactions (Filipi, 2009).

Through considering the co-production of pretend play interactions between toddlers and their teachers, and young children and their teachers, Sacks' (1972) collection R and collection K membership categories will be explored further in relation to the ongoing activity. The interactions that are analysed and discussed here will build on the work of Sidnell (2011) with reference to his 'stipulations' (p. 133), by demonstrating how, when teachers and children both co-produce the transformation of an object in their everyday pretend play together, they demonstrate being members of a co-equal relational category. The presentation and analyses of episodes of pretend play between early childhood teachers and young children are now examined in detail in order to reveal how the participants achieve the management of knowledge and relationships during the activity of pretend play.

Initiating Pretend Play

To reveal the systematic ways in which pretend play episodes are managed between teachers and young children it is logical to initially look at how these episodes are initiated. The following excerpts are just a couple of many examples of pretend play initiations that were collected during the study. They show how the children 'map out' roles for the players within a pretend play episode, so that each player has knowledge of the pretend play situation. Although these episodes of mapping here are co-produced between teachers and young children, they contain the similar conversational strategies of mapping during the initiation of a new pretend play activity between child-child peers in Sweden (Bjork-Willen, 2012), Australia (Cobb-Moore, 2012) and also in New Zealand (Butler, 2008; Butler and Weatherall, 2006).

Excerpt 1: Jamilla

In this first instance, the early childhood teacher Jamilla is engaging in pretend play with one of the older toddler children, who is aged approximately three years old. She is sitting inside the hut acting out the role of a lollipop seller and Jamilla is sitting outside of the hut looking in through the window and takes on the role of a customer buying the lollipops. The players use stones of varying sizes from the playground to represent the lollipops. One of the toddler children, Daniel (DAN) approaches Jamilla (JAM).

```
01  DAN:      ((walks up to Jamilla and stands next to her))
02  JAM:      ↑Hi Da:ni:el
03            (1.5)
04  JAM:      how are you:↓
05            (1.4) ((Daniel and Jamilla have eye contact))
06  JAM:      ↑good↓ do you want=to ↓play with us↑
07            (1.6)
08  JAM:      we're playing sh↑ops
09            ((Daniel walks away. Ashley (ASH) enters the hut))
10  JAM:      ↑hi Ashley:↓= ((looks at Ashley))
11  ASH:               =↑(what's those:)↓
12  JAM:      ↑we're ↓hav-=↑we're ↓selling lolly↑pops↓=(Ngawy)
13            is selling me some lolly↑pops↓ . would you like
14            some ↑too::↓
15  ASH:      °>↓yes↓<°
16            (1.0)
17  JAM:      maybe you could ask Ngawy what flavor you'd like
```

Jamilla initiates contact with the approaching child, Daniel, by using the conversational opening 'Hi' (lines 02), demonstrating her interest in interacting with that child at that time. In her conversational opening, Jamilla uses Daniel's name in tag-position as an appended address term or 'final position address term' (Wootton, 1981, p. 143). This positioning of the child's name in tag-position provokes a situation where, rather than using a name to initiate a sequence of turns which bring the conversation back to the initiator, the appended address term requires the recipient to analyse the prior talk and respond accordingly (Baker and Freebody, 1986; Wootton, 1981). Jamilla's interest in initiating an interaction with Daniel is observable in the first section of the interaction (lines 02–08) where, when the turn allocation space is repeatedly not taken up by Daniel, Jamilla continues her pursuit of an interaction with him in her next turns of talk.

Jamilla's initial 'Hi Daniel' is followed by her asking a question (line 04) that requires Daniel to provide an answer; this is not taken up verbally, but does secure a response from Daniel in the form of eye contact through mutual gaze. Daniel's non-verbal response to Jamilla is important to the interaction as mutual gaze between child and adult is perceived as, 'starting to do "interaction" ... the basic sequential organization of talk involving adjacency pairs' (Filipi, 2009, p. 3). Jamilla's receipt of Daniel's mutual gaze is responded to by a positive assessment of the situation in her next utterance 'good' (line 06) and extended with an offer of affiliation through an invitation to play.

Jamilla asserts her offer of affiliation to engage in the play activity with reference to the collective proterm 'us', indicating an already established group of players who are involved in the collaborative CBA of the play. However, Daniel does not respond and, instead, walks away in a disaffiliative turn. Although this initial offer of affiliation is not secured, the systematic way in which Jamilla shows her interest in gaining an interaction with Daniel through inviting him to engage with the ongoing pretend play as co-player is observable.

Ashley, another toddler, enters the hut and Jamilla addresses her in the same way that she greeted Daniel, by using the greeting 'Hi' followed by her name in tag-position. By orienting to Ashley in such a way, Jamilla makes Ashley's arrival to the hut a noticeable event to the other members present and to Ashley. Ashley responds with a possible question about the ongoing activity that Jamilla is involved in as she quickly latches on to Jamilla's opening utterance to attend to the identification of the stones (line 11). Jamilla responds to Ashley's question about the stones by engaging in the mapping of the ongoing pretend play, with some self-repair, as she shares her knowledge about the activity. Telling her 'we're selling lollipops', makes the activity around the 'lollipops' explicit as intonation is placed on the word 'sell'.

Jamilla also uses a collective proterm 'we' here to mark the activity of selling as a joint one (Bateman, 2012c; Butler, 2008) and attending further to the affiliation between herself and Ngawy, the child already involved in the play with her. Jamilla then quickly offers further information about the roles allocated in the current pretend play as she tells Ashley that Ngawy is selling her some lollipops, making noticeable the adjacency pair of 'seller – buyer' within the play. Jamilla's display of knowledge about the ongoing pretend play activity is presented as an assertion as she informs Ashley of the imaginative transformation of the stones into lollipops, and in doing so maps out her epistemic primacy (Sidnell, 2011), or first-hand knowledge, regarding the ongoing pretend play.

Once the mapping of the pretend play activity and roles are managed, Ashley is invited to become a co-player in the game by Jamilla (lines 13–14). Interestingly, Ashley's invitation is not given as a direct offer, but is accomplished in a way that attends to the activity of the play; if Ashley accepts the offer of having a lollipop then she is also agreeing on the stipulation of the stones becoming the lollipop and so becomes an affiliated member of the group. Through engaging in the category bound activity (CBA) of 'buying a lollipop', Ashley becomes a member associated with the category-set of players who are also involved in the activity through the consistency rule (Butler and Weatherall, 2006; Sacks, 1972) and, as such, becomes an affiliated member of the pretend play activity.

Ashley quickly and quietly accepts Jamilla's offer of a lollipop and Jamilla responds by attending to the pretend play activity as she suggests that Ashley ask Ngawy about available flavours, reiterating the appropriate CBA of the game where the seller is the member allocated to the role of lollipop distribution. By doing this Jamilla further supports the transition of the affiliation of the new play member into the already established pretend play, encouraging the two children to interact together under these new titles. This type of commitment to the ongoing activities and roles involved in pretend play affiliate the members as they engage in the CBA of buying and selling lollipops where they agree on the stipulation (Sidnell, 2011) of the stones transforming into lollipops.

Although Jamilla's initial invitation to Daniel to engage in the pretend play is not taken up, her subsequent offer to Ashley is. Through attending to the mapping of the ongoing pretend play activities and roles with Ashley, the members become affiliated in a lollipop 'buyer – seller' adjacency pair as they share the stipulated activity of imaginative transformations and the social rules tied to such an activity (Sidnell, 2011) in a locally occasioned way. In her turns at talk, Jamilla shares her knowledge about the ongoing activity with the children in a way that maps out the play (lines 08 and 12–13), as well as offering invitations to the children to become affiliated through their CBA of joining in with the play (lines 06 and 13–14).

Excerpt 2: Sam

This second episode shows another teacher, Sam, approaching a group of four-year-old preschool children who have positioned themselves around an outdoor table under a tree. Two of the girls present, Gracey (GRY) and Amber, (ABR) talk to Sam about their ongoing pretend play.

```
01 SAM:        what are y↑ou girls doing↓ ((moves towards the
02             table))
03 GRY:        we're making a p↑arty::↓=
04 ABR:                                 =for ↑me::↓
05 SAM:        ↓cool↑ ((sits down on one of the chairs))
06 GRY:        we're making a p[↑arty::↓=
07 ABR:                        [you're ↑invi↓ted
08 GRY:        would you like-=
09 ABR:                       =do you wanna come
10 GRY:        your seat is over ↓there:

Later in the observation

11 SAM:        you're M↑argret's sister↓
12 GRY:        ↓yes↓
13             (0.6)
14 SAM:        so I'm your Dad too↓
15             (1.2)
16 GRY:        but I'm ()
17 ABR:        you the- and you the um-·and you the um- and you
18             the daddy up here ↓okay↑
19 SAM:        okay↓ hell↑o:: ((a girl approaches and sits on
20             Sam's knee))
21 GRY:        the baby's name is ↓Polly okay↑
22 SAM:        okay so Polly is over there- Margaret is Po↓lly
23 GRY:        ↓yes↓
24 SAM:        ↓okay↓ ( ) and ↑is it her birthday ↓today
```

Sam initiates this interaction with the children as he approaches them and asks them a question, not selecting any specific child through reference to their name. Gracey immediately answers Sam, suggesting that they are currently engaged in the collective action of 'making a party', achieved through her use of the collective proterm 'we're' (line 03) as she identifies herself and Amber as incumbents of a specific category set of people. Amber quickly latches on to Gracey's utterance and offers further information about the situation to Sam as she informs him that it is 'for me'. In doing so Amber can be seen to complete Gracey's utterance to give a full account of the situation to Sam. This type of conversational feature has been observed in Sacks' (1992b, pp. 437–443) 'spouse talk', where the members finish each other's sentences and co-tell about shared experiences to others who are not members of the spouse partnership. Through sharing their collective knowledge about the situation in such a way, Amber and Gracey can be seen as being together in a co-equal relational category of people where their collective CBA makes them observable as an affiliated, unified entity.

Sam shows approval of the girls' joint activity through his assessment 'cool' (line 05) and moves to physically include himself in the group of children by sitting down at the table with them. Gracey subsequently retells Sam about the activity in the same way as she did initially (line 03) and Amber slightly overlaps this as she eagerly invites Sam to join them in the game. The subsequent utterances from Gracey and Amber formulate the invitation (lines 07–09) and finally Gracey informs Sam of where he has to sit, involving him more fully into the party play and his place within it. Through his close physical proximity, Sam displays his willingness to engage with the ongoing play and play-partners (Goodwin, 1981).

The initial openings of this interaction work to co-produce an understanding about the activity that is currently being done through a question-answer knowledge exchange sequence, where the questioner, Sam, presents himself in a less knowledgeable position to the 'girls' who have more knowledge about the ongoing play. This initial knowledge exchange then progresses, as Gracey and Amber show their shared willingness for Sam to be engaged in their party with them as co-player through several invitations and a direction of where he has to sit, encouraging him to participate in the CBA of joining the party.

Once Sam is sitting in the place nominated by Gracey as 'correct', showing his willingness to be involved in the party by engaging in the appropriate actions required of a party member, more mapping of the pretend play begins. This is achieved over several turns where Sam asks which children are allocated which roles (lines 11–24), demonstrating that the children are the more knowledgeable about the mapping of the social roles than Sam. The importance of gathering such background knowledge is essential to avoid provoking moral outrage during interactions and to ensure the avoidance of social faux pas as the interaction progresses (Heritage, 1984).

The mapping of members to the membership categorisation device (MCD) *family* is attended to as significant by the children here, where Sam is mapped into the role of a family member in the same way as each of the children present. Even though Sam is a teacher in his official capacity in the early childhood centre, here he is treated as another co-player in the game of pretend play where such titles are suspended and replaced to compliment the imagined situation. However, opportunities for subordination and assertions of authority over other 'family' members have also been tied to a parental role in such 'family' pretend play (Cobb-Moore, 2012). Through transitioning from the world of the early childhood centre to a family party, the members make relevant relationships between the players that are of immediate importance, those being within the relational category R collection of sister, Dad, baby etc. Those members who belong to the collection R category have rights and responsibilities to give and receive help through their bond of obligation, whereas members of the collection K category turn to each other for help with 'special distributions of knowledge' (Sacks, 1972, p. 37). However, although the members make their participation in the relational category collection clearly observable, the mapping of such roles are executed within the K collection where Sam seeks knowledge to clarify the mapping and the children competently demonstrate their knowledge.

Knowledge and Alignment in Pretend Play; Adult as Teacher

Excerpt 3: Sam

The preschool teacher Sam is sitting in the sandpit with four preschool boys aged approximately four years old. The boys stand in a circle around a hosepipe that is running water into an area of the sand. One of the boys (Max) begins this episode:

```
01: MAX:     ↓what's that↑ (0.5) ↓looks like cof↑fee::↓ ((leans
02:          over the sand for a closer look))
03: SAM:     ↓That's wha:t ((looks at the sand))
04: MAX:     That looks like coffee↓= ((points to sand))
05: SAM:                           =↑it looks like↓ co↑ffee::↓
06:          ((makes eye contact with Max))
07: MAX:     ye↑ah↓
08: SAM:     why do you think it looks like co↑ffee↓
09: MAX:     °coz it ↑does↓°
10:          (2.2)
11: MAX:     °coz=it's° bu↑bbly↓
12: SAM:     oh=it's bu↑bbly↓ (0.8) and bro:wn↓
13: MAX:     yeah (1.2) because it's co↑ffee::↓
```

Max initiates this interaction by attending to a particular feature of the sandpit where he suggests that the sand and water mixture 'looks like coffee' (line 01). This utterance indicates that Max has prior knowledge (Hayano, 2011) and previous access to what coffee 'looks like' in order to make the correlation between the appearance of actual coffee and how it is similar to the water and sand mix available to him in situ. Max's knowledge enables him to make this assessment as, with an assessment 'a speaker claims knowledge of that which he or she is assessing' (Pomerantz, 1984, p. 57). An opportunity for affiliation or disaffiliation between Max and the teacher is mobilised here through Max's assessment, which could be responded to as a subsequent agreement or disagreement about whether the sand and water mix does, or does not, look like coffee.

Although Max's likening the sand mix to coffee could be accepted by Sam as a representation of symbolic play, as he transforms one entity for another (Göncü and Gaskins, 2011) in his opening assessment, Sam does not immediately accept this representation as legitimate. Instead Sam marks a failure of a shared understanding as he initiates an 'other repair' sequence by asking for more information from Max (line 3). Sam's dispreferred response here disrupts the flow of conversation so that, rather than progress the interaction, Max repeats his utterance in a bid to establish a collective understanding about the situation based on shared knowledge between himself and Sam. Whilst making his repeat, Max supports his verbal utterance with a physical gesture as he points to the area in the sand that he is referring to, maximising the potential for knowledge transference that will regain a shared understanding (Bateman, 2012b).

As with other findings presented in this book (Chapters 5, 6 and 7), here the teacher responds to the child's utterance with a formulation of the child's words (line 05) as Sam changes the first word from 'that' to 'it', whilst making eye contact with Max. A teacher's repeat or formulation of a child's utterance has been found to demonstrate that the teacher is acknowledging the child's conversational turn, showing that they are listening to the child's contribution without giving a premature evaluative response (Bateman, 2013).

These features of talk represent an adjacency pair that embodies a patient-counsellor relationship (Peräkylä, 2005; Hutchby, 2001) rather than that of teacher-pupil where the teacher is traditionally the more knowledgeable and evaluates the pupil's answer as either correct or incorrect (Cazden, 2001; Mehan, 1979; Wells and Arauz, 2006). Here, the teacher's formulation of Max's utterance is followed by an agreement from Max, indicating that Sam has understood what Max has told him and marking the other initiated repair as successful. The knowledge transfer between Max and Sam is marked as successful and a shared understanding has been jointly accomplished so that the interaction can once again progress.

However, in the next turns at talk, Sam questions Max's assessment and in doing so questions his knowledge (Hayano, 2012). Sam's insertion of a 'why' question is a dispreferred response to Max's assessment about the sand looking like coffee, as it offers no alignment or affiliation with Max in the form of an agreement (Stivers, 2008). The 'why' type question is also problematic as this type of question has been found to 'display a challenging stance' (Bolden and Robinson, 2011, p. 94) to the recipient speaker; an important point that needs to be considered with regard to research that encourages questioning in early childhood education with the aim to promote best practice through stimulating enquiry. This challenging stance is noticeable in the next turn of conversation as the recipient systematically orients to it as such.

Max's subsequent utterance demonstrates that Sam's 'why' question was problematic for him as he responds with 'coz it does' (line 09), offering no further explanation or display of additional knowledge. This type of utterance has been found to mark a child's reluctance to answer a teacher's question (Bateman, Danby and Howard, 2013a), much the same as patients use the utterance 'I don't know' in therapy situations (Hutchby, 2001). Max's reluctance to engage in an interaction with Sam here is therefore similar to a patient's avoidance to engage with a therapist to co-produce a relational SRP through talk about emotions.

The interaction is further demonstrated as problematic through the significant pause (line 10), followed by Max offering a justification for his assessment (line 11) as he specifically makes reference to the appearance of the sand to provide an account of 'why' he said it looks like coffee. Sam responds with a change of state marker (Heritage, 1984) and another formulation of Max's utterance here, although this time he supports Max's description regarding the appearance of the sand and water mix by providing another adjective that extends the description of the mix as also being 'brown' (line 12). Sam's extension on the likeness of the sand mix to coffee offers an agreement with Max's assessment as he adds his own knowledge about coffee and how it could possibly be represented in a credible way by the sand mix. Following this alignment, Max provides a 'bald assertion' (Sidnell, 2011, p. 133) about the transformation of the area from a sand and water mix to coffee as he explicitly states 'because it's coffee' (line 13).

In this episode Max demonstrates that he has prior knowledge of what coffee looks like by likening its appearance with that of the appearance of the sand-water mixture. Max's assertion of this 'stipulation' (Sidnell, 2011, p. 133) could have initiated the interaction as problematic from the beginning, as it offered no affordance for discussion about the possible stipulation between the teacher and himself. In other words it asserted Max's knowledge rather than providing an opportunity for co-equal participation. As Max asserted an independent stipulation, the next turn at talk could have either worked to align with Max's stance through simple recognition, affiliate with him through agreement in a joint affective stance regarding the stipulation (Stivers, 2008), or disaffiliate through disagreement or ignoring him (Bateman, 2010).

In this instance, Sam initially marks a failure of mutual understanding and then responds to Max's repeat by questioning Max's knowledge; both of these actions are acknowledged as being problematic to the progression of the talk (Sacks, Schegloff and Jefferson, 1974) as they are 'dispreferred turn shapes' (Pomerantz, 1984, p. 57). This prompts Max to offer a response that marks his reluctance to affiliate or align with Sam as he states 'coz it does'. However, following a significant pause, Max further demonstrates his knowledge by offering information on what coffee looks like and in doing so legitimises his earlier assessment for Sam, and re-establishes a shared understanding.

Max closes the interaction through a further stipulation, which indicates that he is engaging in symbolic play where he explicitly identifies and shows the sand *as* being coffee. Sam does not touch off on this final utterance and subsequently disaffiliates himself from Max as he engages with another child briefly and then moves on to another part of the outdoor area. This response from Sam mirrors the findings from Sidnell (2011), suggesting that such stipulations 'make relevant a restricted set of responses in second position' (p. 141).

Throughout this interaction Max appears to be the more knowledgeable other as he initially makes a comparison between two liquids with an account of why he made the comparison. He then continues demonstrating his knowledge when he asserts his 'stipulation' (Sidnell, 2011, p. 133) by representing one object for another and, in doing so, demonstrates he has unique knowledgeable access to the object (Sidnell, 2011). Sam demonstrates that he is the less knowledgeable in this episode as he asks questions (lines 03 and 08) which relate to achieving epistemic access to Max's assertions.

In relation to Sacks' (1972) work on collection K categories, Sam's questions identify Max as the appropriate person to receive help regarding knowledge about the situation, and Max provides the information as he explicitly asserts his knowledge and offers relevant answers for Sam's questions. As this is noticeable in the interaction Sam and Max co-produce a K category collection through knowledge exchanges, and in doing so can be seen as belonging to the K category collection of people.

Excerpt 4: Jamilla

Here, the toddler teacher Jamilla (JAM) approaches two 2 ½ year old toddler girls who are sitting in the sandpit, Judah (Juda) and Tia (Tia). The children are engaged in a game where the activity involves spooning sand into bowls and then pretending to eat the sand out of the bowls.

```
01 JAM:      are you helping Juda ↑cook ((leans over the
02           children and makes eye contact with Tia))
03           (1.3)
04 TIA:      ((looks at Jamilla))
05 JAM:      ↑yes
06 TIA:      mahi in the↑re ((looks down and points to a bowl))
07 JAM:      oh you making some food in the↑re ↓ok↓ I'm gonna
08           put this down so I don't get a wet bottom↑((picks
09           up a tray and sits on it))
10           >Oopsy< (kicks a bowl. Puts bowl straight))
11           There we go:↑
12 TIA:      [un I dat] ((looks at Jamilla and pats bowl))
```

```
13  JAM:        [what are we] gonna put in here ((looks at Tia's
14              bowl and then looks away from the children))
15  TIA:        ((looks at Jamilla and puts handfuls of sand
16              into the bowl))
17  JAM:        what we gonna put in here Juda (0.3) what are we
18              cooking ((looks at Juda))
19  JUDA:       ↑We:lla:↓ ((Juda makes eye contact with Jamilla
20              then looks away))
21              (1.2)
22  JAM:        what is ↓wella↓
23  JUDA:       in the ↓wella↑ ((looks at Jamilla and points to a
24              bowl in front of her))
25  JAM:        ↓ok what are we going to put in there
26  JUDA:       ↓wella↓ ((looks away and starts digging the sand
27              and giggles quietly))
```

Jamilla initiates an interaction with the two toddler girls in this episode by physically approaching them and immediately asking a question about their ongoing play. The use of questions in everyday conversations between people have been studied in the area of CA where the asking of a question in a first pair part (FPP) is known to require an answer by the recipient in a second pair part (SPP) where the lack of an answer is noticeably problematic; therefore securing an interaction between the two speakers (Sacks, Schegloff and Jefferson, 1974). In the area of early childhood education, teachers are advised to use 'open ended questions' with children to stimulate their possibility thinking and develop their theories about how the world works (Carr, 2011; Peters and Davies, 2011; Hargraves, 2013; Hedges, 2011). Not only do questions seek knowledge from the desired recipient, but they also manage the social organisation between the people, in this case the child and the teacher.

Through her questioning Jamilla makes an assertion of knowledge about what she perceives to be happening between the two toddlers as she specifically asks Tia if she is helping Judah cook (lines 01–02). In this instance, although Tia makes eye contact with Jamilla, there is a significant pause that is ended by Jamilla's prompt for a response (line 05). Jamilla's prompt works to stimulate a further interaction with Tia as she subsequently indicates that she is doing something 'in there' and supports this with her non-verbal gestures as she looks at the bowl and points to it (line 6). In doing so Tia asserts her knowledge about the situation and demonstrates her agency in her play. Jamilla demonstrates that she understands Tia's intentions through her next turn as she indicates her change of cognitive state with 'oh' (Heritage, 1984) and follows this by telling about her knowledge of the situation, repeating Tia's use of the words 'in there' (line 7). Through these initial turns at talk, Jamilla and Tia each make their understanding of the ongoing activity known to each other where a shared understanding is gained through both verbal and non-verbal actions.

Doing Pretend Play 53

Tia further progresses the interaction with Jamilla by offering more information about the activity she is engaged in, again supporting her verbal action with a non-verbal gesture as her gaze is fixed on Jamilla and she pats the bowl (line 12). Toddlers' use of non-verbal gesture to express their willingness to be involved with an adult is acknowledged in CA research (Kidwell, 2005) where it is believed that 'gaze and gesture are the early means through which the child can take part in conversation and maintain participation across sequences of talk' (Filipi, 2009, p. 2). However, Tia's utterance here is overlapped by Jamilla as she asks another question about the play, this time using the collective proterm 'we' to indicate that the action will be a collective one involving herself (line 13). Although the first part of Jamilla's utterance was overlapped with Tia's, Tia demonstrates her understanding of Jamilla's question through her non-verbal next action that involves putting sand in the bowl, showing Jamilla exactly what she is 'going to put in' the bowl (lines 15–16).

Up until this point Jamilla has asked Tia questions about the pretend play that is already occurring and possibilities of what will happen next in the play, and Tia has offered a preferred response in each instance as she has shared her own knowledge both verbally and non-verbally. These turns at talk work to align Jamilla and Tia in an interaction through knowledge exchange where the requesting and giving of knowledge co-produces a category collection K.

The subsequent lines of interaction (17–27) demonstrate a break down in a shared understanding where Jamilla repeats her previous question about what they will put in the bowl, even though Tia has shown her intentions in her prior non-verbal turn by physically putting handfuls of sand in the bowl (lines 15–16), and therefore already answering this question. There is a slight pause followed by Jamilla asking Judah what they are cooking, seeking further knowledge from the more knowledgeable others and allowing the toddler to take the lead in the play. During this utterance Jamilla uses the collective word 'we' again to imply a joint activity between herself and the children, indicating a preference for affiliation, but as with the prior use of the word 'we' by Jamilla in this interaction (line 13), this is not followed by a *collaborative action* between Jamilla and the toddlers.

Judah demonstrates her understanding that Jamilla has asked her a question and that she needs to answer this in her next turn at talk as she replies with 'wella' (line 19). However, there is a long pause before Jamilla indicates that there is a break down in a shared understanding and knowledge transfer as she asks for further clarification about what 'wella' is (line 22), marking other initiated repair (Schegloff, Jefferson and Sacks, 1977). Other initiated repair, or the repair of an utterance initiated by another person, is found to be the non-preferred strategy for correction due to it being less effective compared to self-correction, as it involves a more complicated arrangement of turns at talk (Schegloff, Jefferson and Sacks, 1977). Judah responds to Jamilla's request for further information, as she offers more knowledge about the situation through extending her utterance to 'in the wella' and pointing to the bowl in front of her (lines 23–24).

Through these actions Judah communicates about her play activity and tells about her plan for her next action to Jamilla whilst maintaining her gaze with Jamilla as she talks. Jamilla responds by marking a close of the prior interaction and signalling a move towards another topic with 'OK' (ten Have, 2000) before asking another question about what they will collectively put 'in there' (line 25). Jamilla has designed her turn to align with Judah's orientation to the bowl, but there is an indication of a lack of understanding of the knowledge being transferred between herself and Judah. This is demonstrated as Judah repeats the word 'wella' for a third time and then turns away from Jamilla and giggles to herself quietly (line 26–27). Through turning away from an ongoing interaction with someone, children can demonstrate their desire to disaffiliate away from that person and interaction (Bateman, 2010).

Throughout this interaction although Tia and Judah have a limited vocabulary they do respond to Jamilla with verbal utterances and work to maximise a shared understanding by supporting their verbal talk with non-verbal gesture (Bateman, 2012b; Filipi, 2008). Although Jamilla responds to these combinations of verbal and non-verbal actions, the lack of a shared understanding often present means that Jamilla is repeatedly in the less knowledgeable position and giving a dispreferred response (Pomerantz, 1984) to the children, disrupting the progression of the pretend play. Although the collaborative term 'we' is used by Jamilla, as is apparent in establishing a cohort (Butler, 2008) and in securing affiliation (Bateman, 2012c), there is a lack of affiliation present where both members are affectively engaged with each other (Stivers, 2008) in the shared actions of CBA (Francis and Hester, 2004; Hester and Hester, 2012; Sacks, 1992a).

The frequent use of 'OK' works to close the current actions and start new topics, and the repeated questions also work to disrupt the flow of the pretend play where there are pauses where the children do not answer, or Jamilla does not respond to their non-verbal gestures. As with the prior excerpt, the children demonstrate their knowledge in this interaction as they respond in the correct turn allocated space and provide answers to the teacher's questions (Cazden, 2001; Mehan, 1979; Wells and Arauz, 2006). The features of these conversational turns at talk work to co-produce a category K collection through knowledge exchange and talk that is positioned *about* the pretend play rather than engagement *in* it.

Knowledge and Affiliation in Pretend Play; Adult as Co-player

The following two excerpts reveal conversational features during pretend play that are different to the prior two excerpts, as here the teachers take on the role of co-players *with* the children, rather than talking *about* the pretend play activity. The participants fully engage in the make believe play through CBAs that assert co-membership to the play and the displayed CBA offers solidarity and affiliation where the members act in complementary and supportive ways to their co-players (Sacks, 1992a).

Excerpt 5: Jamilla

Jamilla (JAM) has returned to the sandpit and is sitting with Tia (Tia), who is still there from the prior observation (Excerpt 4). Tia has a container and Jamilla begins talking to her about it.

```
01  JAM:      what are you going to put ↑in there↓ ((points to
02            the container))
03  TIA:      ((shrugs her shoulders))
04  JAM:      what would you ↓like↓ to put in there↓
05            (3.4)
06  TIA:      ((lifts up a spoon full of sand and holds it out to
07            Jamilla, they have eye contact))
08  JAM:      should I:: make something too↓=should I make a big-
09            should I <ma::ke so::me >↑chicken<
10  TIA:      ((nods and maintains eye contact))
11  JAM:      do you like chicken
12  TIA:      ((nods and maintains eye contact))
13  JAM:      ↓well we'll put some↓ ↑chicken↑ (0.5) what shall I
14            put ↓in↓ ↑the chicken↓ ((digs sand and puts it into
15            a bowl))
16  TIA:      ((shrugs shoulders))
17  JAM:      ↓put so::me↓- ↑gonna chop some onion like this
18            °↓chop=chop=chop=chop↓° ((makes chopping action with
19            spoon in sand))
20            (1.1) put some onion in there (0.9) cut so::me
21            ↑carrots do you like carrot
22  TIA:      °↓no↓°
23  JAM:      put some carrot in there then <we::'ll::>=
24  TIA:                                                =tamamati
25            ((spoons sand into a container next to Jamilla's))
26  JAM:      what are you: making
27            (4.2)
28  JAM:      got some ↑celery to put it in there and I'll put
29            some spi:ce sprinkle some spice in there and do you
30            like ↑curry powder↓ ((sprinkles sand into bowl))
31  TIA:      °↓yeah↓°
32            ((a girl approaches and Jamilla talks to her
33            briefly before returning to her 'cooking'))
34  JAM:      put some curry powder in here and then I'm gonna
35            tip some stock from here ((adds more sand to bowl))
36            ((a group of children come and talk to Jamilla for
37            a few seconds and then move on))
38  JAM:      put some ↑stock in here ((holds small saucepan and
```

```
39                     pretends to transfer liquid into her bowl))
40                     ok and then I'm gonna put my (1.3) ↑chicken to
41                     cook on the::- (1.2) ↓oh=pretend this is our stove
42                     and I'll cook it on there (1.3) and then we gotta-
43                     ((rests the bowl on top of a saucepan))
44   TIA:              ((lifts up the bowl that she has been adding the
45                     sand to and places it on top of Jamilla's bowl))
46   JAM:              you wanna add some of your food in there too
47   TIA:              ((nods her head))
48   JAM:              °↓ok↓° (0.8) we gotta make sure its mixed all nicely
49                     in there ((stirs the bowl of sand with her spoon))
50   TIA:              ((joins in the stirring))
51   JAM:              ↓stir ↑it nice:ly: (1.0) give it a **big** stir (1.2)
52                     tha::t's it↓
```

This extended sequence of interaction between the toddler teacher Jamilla and the toddler Tia starts with Jamilla talking to Tia about the object she is currently playing with, in this instance a plastic container. Asking a question about an object that someone has is found to be a useful way to start an interaction with them as it provides a reason for one person to approach another person (Bateman and Church, in press, 2015; Cromdal, 2001; Sacks, 1992b). In research with young children, Cromdal (2001) found that boys between the ages of six and a half and eight years attended to a basketball as a way to access an interaction with their peers in Sweden; Bateman and Church (2015) found similar instances of reference to objects to initiate play with peers with younger children aged four years old in the UK. Here, Jamilla makes reference to an object that the two-and-a-half-year-old child has as a way of initiating an interaction with her, prompting a response from the child.

Jamilla's question about the object in a first pair part provokes an answer from Tia in a second pair part in the form of a non-verbal shrugging of her shoulders (line 3). Jamilla responds to Tia's non-verbal 'don't know' response by formulating her prior question and changing the word 'going' to 'like', placing intonation on the word 'like', making it stand out in a 'contrast stress' (Sacks, 1992b, p. 558) within the utterance. The use of the word 'like' (line 04), a relational term with a focus on preference based on feelings and emotions, is significant here through Jamilla's inclusion of it in her formulation and the stress she places on it. This is followed by a significant pause that provides a next turn space for Tia to respond; Tia eventually offers a second non-verbal reply by lifting up her spoon that is full of sand and looking at Jamilla (lines 06–07). Jamilla's formulation of her question into a relational approach to Tia's play activity stimulates a preferred response by Tia. This is evident as Tia answers Jamilla in a non-verbal action that demonstrates Tia's willingness to engage as her response contributes to the activity of using the sand in the play.

Jamilla responds to Tia's action by subsequently engaging in the activity of pretend play with Tia as she asks Tia 'should I make something too' (line 08) and then more specifically asks if she should make some 'chicken' (line 09). Jamilla's verbal action indicates that she is seeking acceptance to join in with an already established activity, and this is met with approval from Tia as she nods her head, giving Jamilla the go-ahead to engage in the pretend play. This acceptance into play is co-produced through Jamilla's initial opening as she asks questions about the ongoing play, initially met with an 'I don't know' action from Tia, but then responded to positively as Tia physically shows Jamilla what she would like to add to the container.

Jamilla's action of asking Tia if she should 'make some chicken' (line 09) suggests that she is making the transformation of the sand into 'chicken' as a collaborative action where 'the activity is treated as a matter to be negotiated by the participants' (Sidnell, 2011, p. 141). Here, the activity is co-produced through shared knowledge about the ongoing actions and works towards eliminating the failure of a shared understanding that was present in the prior interaction between Jamilla and Tia (Excerpt 4). Further affiliation with Tia is prompted as Jamilla asks her if she likes chicken (line 11), again using the relational term to enquire about Tia's preference. Jamilla accepts Tia's preferred response of a nod as the interaction then progresses the pretend play where both participants use the sand to engage in the CBA of 'cooking' (line 13).

Jamilla's subsequent turns at talk see her giving an ongoing dialogue of her imaginative actions and the ingredients she is using (lines 14–20) to the point where she asks Tia if she likes carrots (line 21) and when Tia replies 'no' (line 22), Jamilla does not attend to Tia's response as dispreferred and she goes on to 'add' the ingredients anyway. Jamilla's full engagement in the pretend play activity provokes an affiliative response from Tia, again non-verbally, as she joins in the CBA of using the sand as food as she spoons sand into a container that is located next to Jamilla (lines 24–25). Through engaging in the CBA associated with the pretend play activity, both members display complimentary behavior to each other and the displayed CBA offers solidarity (Sacks, 1992a). This affiliation between members through their shared activity is associated with Goffman's concept of 'ratification' where 'the identity assumed by one party is ratified, not by her own actions, but by the actions of another who assumes a complementary identity towards her' (Goodwin and Heritage, 1990, p. 292).

Throughout the subsequent turns at talk in this episode, Jamilla tells about her imaginative actions and Tia offers preferred responses to her in her non-verbal agreements. This joint attention to the activity of pretend play is co-produced through CBA where a shared understanding is gained through collaborative actions (Bjork-Willen, 2012; Cobb-Moore, 2012; Schegloff, 1991). Jamilla treats Tia's verbal and non-verbal utterances as turns at talk as though they are indistinguishable (Filipi, 2009). Tia's turns at communicating with Jamilla demonstrate how toddlers communicate their playful actions non-verbally, showing the part that very young children can play in the co-production of affiliation with other members of the play through their contributions to the turn-taking process.

This interaction demonstrates the importance of early childhood teachers being actively involved in the story of the pretend play through displays of CBA in order to support the suspended reality engaged in by the child. Although this interaction involves Jamilla and one of the children (Tia) from the prior observation (Excerpt 4), it contrasts in that Jamilla engages in the activity of pretend play *with* the child in this excerpt, co-producing an affiliative interaction where each member is involved in the 'co-experience' (Lindstrom and Sorjonen, 2013). This interaction demonstrates how the members are co-equal players in the suspended animation of the pretence where each member, adult and child, engages with the shared transformation of the objects used (Sidnell, 2011) as they both engage with the CBA of cooking. This co-player interaction then progresses over a sustained period of time, an aspect of child–teacher interaction that is valued in early childhood education (Siraj-Blatchford and Sylva, 2004).

Excerpt 6 – Sarah

The preschool teacher Sarah (SAR) has been sitting at a picnic table in the sandpit with Toia (TOI) for a couple of minutes when another preschool child approaches her and asks her to push him on the swings. Sarah leaves the sandpit to push other children on the swings while Toia continues to play with the sand. Toia then calls Sarah back and the following interaction occurs.

```
01  TOI:        Sar↑::::ah I made some toast↓
02              (0.7)
03  SAR:        ↑Oh: ((looks at Toia))
04              (0.8)
05  SAR:        >m=toast< is ready↓ ((pushes TOD on the swing))
06              (1.9)
07  TOD:        $I can do this myse::lf$ ((kicks legs out))
08  SAR:        ↑WOOHOO::↓
09              (10.2) Sarah walks towards Toia
10  TOI:        H↑ere these↓ are °()°
11  SAR:        which one's mine ((there are 2 silver bowls filled
12              with sand on the table))
13  TOI:        ((taps the silver bowl nearest to Sarah))
14  SAR:        this one↑ ((touches the bowl that Toia tapped))
15  TOI:        yeah↓ ((taps the second bowl))
16  SAR:        ↑two of them↓
17  TOI:        yea↑h:↓
18              (1.5)
19  SAR:        woh↓ ((almost falls off the seat when she sits down
20              at the picnic table))
21              (1.7)
22  SAR:        is it ready
```

```
23 TOI:      >yep< ((puts more sand into the second bowl))
24 SAR:      tnum=tnum=tnum=tnum ((picks up the first bowl with
25           both hands and holds it up to her face making
26           loud eating sounds))
27 TOI:      you just have to eat one eh↓
28 SAR:      hhh. ↓Just one ((places bowl back on the table))
29 TOI:      ((swaps Sarah's bowl for the second bowl))
30 SAR:      ↑oh (0.5) is that my seconds↓
31 TOI:      >yep<
32           ((Some nearby children start giggling and Sarah
33           talks to them briefly))
34 SAR:      tnum=tnum=tnum=tnum hhh. De::licious↓ ((picks up
35           second bowl with both hands and holds it up to her
36           face making loud eating sounds then puts the bowl
37           back on the table))
38 TOI:      [a:-]((pulls the second bowl towards her))
39 SAR:      [you] are s::↑uch a ↓good cook↓
```

As with the prior observation where the early childhood teacher Jamilla and child Tia co-produce affiliation through engaging in the pretend play activity, here Sarah and Toia are also engaging in the shared CBA of being co-players in a pretend play activity. Prior to this observation Toia had initiated an interaction with Sarah by suggesting the game of make believe where sand was used as a replacement for food. Sarah was subsequently called away from the play by another child who needed her help; these brief interactions between children and teachers are frequently observed in the area of early childhood where teachers are required to attend to the needs of all of the children in their care where, although brief (usually just over one minute in duration), they are also recognised as involving rich teaching and learning features (Bateman, 2013; Carr, 2011; Carr, Lee and Jones, 2004).

Toia now returns to the game of cooking and eating with the sand by calling Sarah and telling her that she has made some toast, marking a stipulation about the pretend play. Sarah demonstrates her uptake of this new information with a change of state token 'oh' (Heritage, 1984) and then relays the new information to the boy that she is pushing on the swing, Todd. Sarah's telling of news to Todd works as a pre-closing to their ongoing interaction and the boy attends to this closing also as he informs Sarah that he can do the activity of pushing the swing himself and demonstrates the truth of his utterance in a physical gesture as he kicks his legs out (line 07). Both teacher and child co-produce the closing of their interaction (Schegloff and Sacks, 1973) and Sarah moves away.

Toia attends to the bowls filled with sand that she places on the table at Sarah's arrival (line 09) and Sarah responds by also attending to them (line 10), making these the main conversational items through talking them into being significant at that time, in that place, to those people (Heritage, 1978). The mapping of the items follows as Toia is placed in the more knowledgeable position of knowing which bowl belongs to whom (lines 10–16). Sarah displays a lack of knowledge by asking for further information about the bowls from Toia, enquiring whether they are ready (line 21). Once the attention has been drawn to the bowls and the roles around the bowls organised, Sarah begins engaging in the pretend play as she lifts one of the bowls up to her face and makes loud eating noises (lines 23–25 and 33–36). During this time Toia plays her part of managing the food provision for Sarah as she swaps over the 'empty' bowl for a full bowl of 'toast' and offering rules on the quantity of food Sarah is allowed to eat (line 26). Sarah offers further reinforcement of Toia's role in a relational way as she tells her that she is 'such a good cook' (line 38). Through these actions one of the participants of the pretend play activity, Toia in this situation, is positioned in a role of authority as a collaborative achievement by both players (Cobb-Moore, 2012).

The use of both verbal and non-verbal CBAs here allows the members to practically demonstrate that they belong to the pretend play that involves providing and receiving food. Through engaging in such shared CBA their actions make their joint membership and affiliation visible to each other and those people who are observing them. Although knowledge exchange was observable here as important for the co-production of the interaction, a relational SRP was also apparent as the teacher and child engaged in shared CBAs that complemented and worked to secure affiliation by sharing the play activity.

Moments of Reality in Pretend Play

Two further observations are now presented to demonstrate how, when engaging in the pretence together, the teachers and children co-produce an affiliative and relational stance, breaking their collaborative play only when a possible trouble is oriented to. The following examples demonstrate how the reality of actually eating an object during pretend play is attended to by teachers and children as not an expectable thing to do. In both excerpts these moments of reality are attended to as having priority in the ongoing play where the pretence is suspended for the duration of the brief exchange. Clarifying that you do not *actually* eat stones (Excerpt 7) and sand (Excerpt 8) demonstrates how the participants attend to the importance of the issues of safety and well-being as having priority over the ongoing pretend play involvement.

Excerpt 7: Jamilla

In a continuation of Excerpt 1, one of the toddler teachers, Jamilla (JAM), is sitting outside one of the playground huts engaging in pretend play that involves using stones as lollipops with one of the two-and-a-half-year-old toddler children, Ngawy (NWY). Daniel (DAN), one of the three-year-old toddler boys approaches Jamilla and she invites him to join in the play; the following observation occurs:

```
01 JAM:        They're selling lolly[pops
02 DAN:                        [all s:↑and on the ↓lollypops
03 JAM:        you want what lolly↑pops
04             (0.6)
05 DAN:        sand on the lollypops ((some of the stones
06             have sand on them))
07 JAM:        sa:nd lollypops↓
08 DAN:        ↓yeah↓=
09 JAM:        =I can- ↑maybe Ngawy'll give you a sand
10             lollypop=↑but you have to give ↓her two ↑do:llars:↓
11 DAN:        ↑two ↓dollars ((hands over an invisible $2))
12 NWY:        ((pretends to take the money and gives him a
13             large sandy stone in exchange))
14 DAN:        ((holds the stone up in the air and looks at it
15             inquisitively))
16 JAM:        ((smiles at Daniel and laughs))
17→DAN:        ↑this one's a ↓r:o:ck
18 JAM:        I know↓ but it's a <pre↑tend> lollypop↓
19             (0.8)
20 JAM:        you could pretend it's a lollypop and eat it
21             (0.5) >well<=you don't <↓rea:l↑ly> eat it . because
22             it's a ↓rock↓
```

Daniel initiates the interaction by approaching Jamilla and the group of toddler children who are engaging in the pretend play activity of selling lollipops. Jamilla responds to Daniel's presence by sharing her knowledge with him about the play activity that is currently occurring and mapping out the play scenario by informing him that the children are selling lollipops (line 01). Daniel responds by joining in with the play activity through displaying the CBA of labelling the stones 'lollipops' (line 02). There is a brief lack of a shared understanding, as Jamilla orients to what lollipop Daniel has said that he wants (line 03), initiating other-initiated-repair (Schegloff, Jefferson and Sacks, 1977) followed by a brief silence, indicating Jamilla's problematic, dispreferred turn (Pomerantz, 1984), or a waiting time for Daniel to respond (Bateman, 2013). Daniel then repeats his prior knowledge about there being sand on the 'lollipops' (line 05). Jamilla repeats Daniel's utterance by formulating the two main words from his utterance 'sand' and lollipops', to which Daniel gives a preferred turn shape response in an agreement 'yeah' (line 08). As with Excerpts 3 and 4 in this chapter, there is evidence of talk about the play episode rather than engagement in it.

Jamilla's next utterance demonstrates her willingness to advance the pretend play as she tells Daniel that he needs to give the lollipop seller, Ngawy, two dollars and then she might give him a sand lollipop (lines 09–10). Daniel's next action asserts him as a co-player in the game as he engages with the CBA that ties him to the role of lollipop buyer as he pretends to give Ngawy money. This action is responded to in a preferred turn as Ngawy hands Daniel a stone in exchange (line 12).

These actions, facilitated by the teacher Jamilla, demonstrate Daniel and Ngawy as being affiliated in their actions of co-producing the pretence. This is evident by their demonstration of shared understanding of their new roles: lollipop buyer and lollipop seller, through their CBA as the buyer gives money to the seller and the seller hands over the merchandise.

Although the children demonstrate their affiliated interaction through their CBAs during the co-production of the pretend play, the next sequence of actions shows a suspension in the ongoing pretence to orient to a possible trouble. Once Daniel (the lollipop buyer) has received the stone 'lollipop' he holds it up in the air and looks at it inquisitively, prompting Jamilla to smile at him and laugh (line 16). Daniel then announces that the lollipop he was given is in fact 'a rock' (line 17). In doing so he disengages with the prior stipulation and declares his independent perspective around the object.

When considering how utterances work to secure social relationships, Sacks (1992b) discussed how turns at talk are shaped to be specifically designed for the recipient. One aspect of recipient design is that people should not tell others something that they already know (Sacks, 1992b). In this situation Daniel's announcement that the 'lollipop' is in fact a rock is not newsworthy, as the other members of the play had prior knowledge of this situation before Daniel announced it. As this is the case, Jamilla responds with an explicit statement about her own knowledge state: 'I know' (line 18), and then clarifies the situation by passing on her knowledge to Daniel and telling him that 'it's a pretend lollipop'. This is followed by a pause, which is ended by Jamilla adding further information to Daniel suggesting that he 'could pretend' (line 20) and that 'you don't really eat it' (line 21). Although all members engage in the pretend play of buying and selling lollipops, the pretence is immediately suspended once a trouble is elicited and the teacher responds by ensuring that the safety and well-being of the children is attended to as a priority over the ongoing play. A similar situation where pretend play is suspended in relation to a possible trouble is also evident during a pretend play episode between children in Sweden where one of the children in the game of 'Doggy' checks that 'it is just pretending isn't it' to her co-player the 'doggy' before reprimanding her (Bjork-Willen, 2012).

Excerpt 8: Sarah

As an ongoing activity from Excerpt 6, one of the preschool girls Gemma (GMA) is playing in the sandpit area. She is filling up containers with varying amounts of sand and placing them in an outdoor cupboard that is also located in the sandpit area. Gemma shouts out to one of the preschool teachers, Sarah (SAR), across the playground to invite her to eat some pretend 'food' with her, which is in fact made of sand. Sarah approaches Gemma.

```
01 SAR:      ↑oo:: (0.3) ↓that looks interesting
02 GMA:      yeah ↓would you l↑ike to ↓eat it
03           (4.1) ((Gemma holds a bowl of sand. Sarah sweeps
```

```
04                  sand off a bench with her hand then sits down))
05    SAR:          .hhh
06    GMA:          it's your fa::vori[te↓ ((carries one of the sand-
07                  filled bowls over to Sarah))
08    SAR:                             [well↓
09                  (1.3)
10    GMA:          [ it's yu:m-  ]
11    SAR:          [°it's=my° fa:vorite↓]
12                  (0.4)
13    SAR:          what ↑is it°↓
14    GMA:          it's yum p↑i::e↓:::
15    SAR:          yummy p↑i.e. oh I do like p↑i.e.↓:
16    GMA:          ((hands Sarah a plastic fork))
17    SAR:          ↑tha:nks::
18                  (1.9)
19    SAR:          ((pretends to eat the 'pie' by lifting forkfuls of
20                  wet sand up to her mouth and making 'eating'
21                  noises))
22    GMA:          Is it yummy
23                  (0.9) ((Sarah continues to 'eat' while Gemma
24                  stands next to her and watches))
25 →  GMA:          yu-yu you jus- you just ↓can't put it in your
26                  mou↑th aye↓=
27    SAR:                              =↓no not for re:als coz I don't think
28                  that would f↑eel very nice↓=
29    GRL:                                     =↓no because- because we
30                  just only pretend ↑to eat it↓
31    SAR:          ↓that's right
```

Sarah initiates this interaction by showing her willingness to be involved in the play with Gemma as she makes a positive assessment of the situation in an agreeable turn at talk, again using an available object with which to initiate an interaction (line 01). This is followed by Gemma responding in a preferred way and using the pretend play activity to offer Sarah the opportunity to 'eat' the sand (line 02). Gemma's invitation to Sarah in the form of a question requires an answer, and the preferable answer would be one where Sarah accepts the invitation, as this would mark her affiliation (Lindström and Sorjonen, 2013) with Gemma.

There is a brief silence whilst Sarah prepares her seat, indicating the possibility of a dispreferred response to Gemma's question, as no immediate agreement is given (Schegloff, 2000a). The silence is then brought to a close by Gemma as she self-selects to pursue a response (Pomerantz, 1984) from Sarah by making an epistemic claim to Sarah's food preferences through an assessment as she tells Sarah that 'it's your favourite' (line 06). Gemma's utterance works to indicate that she has prior knowledge of what Sarah likes to eat, indicating a close affiliation in an already established relationship. Through indicating that the sand meal is Sarah's favourite, Gemma's utterance also restricts the response that Sarah can give and encourages her to offer a preferred response and participate in the 'eating', and therefore the pretend play activity with Gemma.

There is an overlap (lines 06 and 08) followed by a second silence that is again ended by Gemma as she goes on to further encourage Sarah to join in the playful activity of 'eating' as she begins to tell her that 'it's yum' (line 10), but this is also overlapped by Sarah (line 11). These overlapped utterances are both followed by silences (lines 09 and 12) indicating a momentary disruption to the ongoing talk as only one person can speak at a time (Sacks, Schegloff and Jefferson, 1974). Following this Sarah asks Gemma a question about the bowl of sand, attending to the ongoing pretend play, affording Gemma the opportunity to transform the bowl of sand into an imaginary object (Göncü and Gaskins, 2011). Gemma's response is to take that opportunity as she does transform the bowl of sand into 'yum pie' (line 14), making a bald assertion and passing on her knowledge to Sarah about what the object now 'is'. Gemma's use of an assertion of the sand transforming to 'yum pie' suggests that she has 'epistemic primacy' (Sidnell, 2011) over the activity at hand, but here there is ambiguity of what exactly the 'yum' is and so making the pie appealing to the recipient whatever their food preferences. As this is the case, Sarah affiliates herself with Gemma's stipulation in a preferred response as she takes on the role of a person enjoying her favourite meal of yummy pie (lines 15–24).

In the beginning of this interaction, Gemma makes a bald assertion about the sand representing food, restricting the possibility for collaboration about the stipulation (Sidnell, 2011) but also cleverly ensuring that her recipient will like the food through calling it 'yum pie'. Sarah responds by showing her willingness to participate in the pretend play activity with Gemma as she physically approaches her and presents her interest in the activity that Gemma is engaged in with the sand (line 01), showing an affiliative response and display of engagement (Goodwin, 1981). This affiliation is further progressed in the sequential turns at talk where Gemma invites Sarah to eat the sand and, after a brief break down in a shared understanding, Sarah offers a preferred, agreeable stance towards the pretend play activity. The affiliation between the members is evident as they both engage in the activity of the pretend play (Sidnell, 2011).

After working together on presenting the bowl of sand as a favourite type of food, 'yummy pie', where both members attended to the eating as paramount to the play activity, the situation changes from play to serious through an orientation to reality. Here, as with the prior excerpt, the joint engagement in the pretence is subsequently abandoned as Gemma watches Sarah 'eat' the yummy pie for a moment and then makes explicit reference to the reality of the situation as she checks with Sarah that 'you just can't put it in your mouth' and adds a tag 'aye' (lines 25–26). The tag 'aye' here is important as it presents an opportunity for Sarah to provide a response that could either agree or disagree with Gemma's statement as 'the availability of the 'tag question' as affiliable to a turn's talk is of special importance' (Sacks, Schegloff and Jefferson, 1974, p. 718).

Sarah responds with a preferred reply as she supports Gemma's assertion by making explicit reference to reality 'not for reals' (line 27), also suspending her engagement in the play. Sarah offers an affective stance about the possible experience of eating sand, suggesting that it would not 'feel very nice' (line 28) and Gemma follows this by making 'an explicit claim to pretend' (Butler, 2008, p. 88), which is agreed by Sarah, continuing their affiliated stance towards each other.

Throughout the interaction Sarah and Gemma engage with each other in a world of pretence until a matter of importance arises that may compromise the safety and well-being of a play partner, and when it does it is treated as a matter of priority as the ongoing activity is suspended to attend to it.

Knowledge and Relationships in Pretend Play

This chapter demonstrates how knowledge and relationships are co-produced by teachers and young children and teachers and toddler age children, initially in the initiation of an interaction around the topic of a pretend play activity, and then when the teachers and children either discuss or are actively involved in the pretend play. The final observations demonstrate the importance of safety and well-being when involved in pretend play where the ongoing play activity is suspended by the players as they attend to the rules of reality to check that you don't really eat sand and rocks.

The first two excerpts show how the mapping of pretend play is co-produced through knowledge exchange between teachers and children when initiating and negotiating entry into a pretend play episode. A lack of a shared understanding between the teachers and children around the transformations of the objects involved leads to an unclear 'stipulation' regarding the object in excerpts three and four. In both observations where this occurs the children present themselves as having epistemic primacy over the transformation of the objects (Max with the 'coffee' in Excerpt 3 and Juda with the 'wella' in Excerpt 4). The lack of a shared understanding was demonstrated in these excerpts where dispreferred answers and other initiated repair were evident, leading to the child's assertion of the stipulation as not being accepted by the recipient teachers as 'conditionally relevant' (Schegloff, 1968; Sidnell, 2011).

A demonstration of how teachers and children can be affiliated through their joint membership to the roles of pretend play together through their collaborative engagement in the pretence was observable in Excerpts five and six. This was achieved through displaying the specific CBA that was required to become an active member of the pretend play episode where the systematic turn taking determined their affiliation by fully engaging in the activity of the pretence as reality.

Finally, Excerpts 7 and 8 demonstrated how the teachers and children worked together to co-produce affiliation through pretence, but suspended the ongoing play when issues of safety and well-being were jeopardised. The abrupt shift out of the turns at talk that co-produced pretence demonstrated the importance of attending to physical welfare as a priority. This issue of priority items during everyday interactions is explored further in the next chapter, Chapter 5, which looks at how knowledge and relational activities are managed between children and teachers during disputes.

Chapter 5
Relationships and Knowledge in Disputes

The study of disputes among children has long been investigated from a psychological, developmental perspective, whereas a sociological approach that considers the wider social context of such situations is relatively new (Bateman, 2010). The use of conversation analysis (CA) to investigate the social process of disputes is becoming more prevalent due to the insight it offers in revealing the systematic ways in which disputes are co-produced by each participating interlocutor. Within the CA literature, attention has been given to how disputes are initiated (e.g., Danby and Baker, 2000, 2001; Maynard, 1985) and resolved (e.g., Danby, 2005; Danby and Baker, 1998a; Church, 2009; Cromdal, 2004) between children in various situations and with a range of interlocutors (see Danby and Theobald, 2012 collected volume).

Research using a CA approach for investigating children's disputes in educational settings reveals how the disputing interlocutors attend to the possession of an object (Church, 2009; Cobb-Moore, Danby and Farrell, 2008; Theobald, 2013) and ownership of space (Danby and Baker, 2000; Cromdal, 2001). The significance of a teacher's presence during these disputes is important when considering how children manage their disputes in an educational setting, as teachers have been found to negotiate reconciliation between children (Cekaite, 2012; Church, 2009; Corsaro, 1985; Danby and Baker, 1998a). The link between disputes and emotions is also considered in CA literature where disagreements between young children are acknowledged as being emotionally charged exchanges that prompt teachers to intervene in a way that mediates conflict resolution (Cekaite, 2012). However, the dilemma still stands for teachers of when to intervene in children's disputes and when to allow the children time to resolve their dispute independently, often provoking debate amongst teachers (Bateman, 2011; Danby and Baker, 1998a).

This chapter will explore examples of children's emotional displays within disputes in an everyday early childhood education setting and the ways in which the teachers attend to them. The examples provided in this chapter demonstrate how teachers attend to children's crying and loud arguing and go about trying to resolve these disputes. In doing so the analysis will reveal how the interactions orient to knowledge and relational activities during the co-production of disputes and dispute resolution. Although the disputes ordinarily consist of relational interactions where emotions run high and there is often upset involving personal feelings, these observations also demonstrate how knowledge exchange is imperative in order for the teacher to manage the dispute once sufficient knowledge about the incident has been gathered.

These observations begin with the presentation and analysis of disputes that are initiated with a child marking a sign of their emotional upset through crying or arguing loudly with their peers, and the teacher responding to the crying or argument as an interactional *next action* (Danby and Baker, 1998a; Harris, 2006). The teacher's initial relational response to a child's cry is sequentially attended to as a co-production of knowledge exchange throughout the unfolding of the interaction. The second section of this chapter includes observations of children approaching a teacher with an emotional problem and an analysis of how that problem is also unpacked through the co-production of knowledge exchange by the interlocutors. Finally, the third section will include disputes that arise from each child explicating their own knowledge in their 'side of the story' (Pomerantz, 1980) to the intervening teachers and explores how the teachers promote the relational activity of compromise between the children to resolve the dispute.

Through examining the co-production of disputes from the initial turn-taking that starts the dispute through to the dispute resolutions between children and teachers, this chapter will demonstrate how collection R and collection K categories are co-produced in systematic, orderly ways through each interlocutor's turn at talk during dispute interactions. In doing so the analysis aims to build on and extend Sacks' (1972) work in this area and provide new knowledge in relation to early childhood education through offering a better understanding of how young children's disputes are managed in everyday practice. As with the final excerpts in Chapter 4, the following interactions demonstrate how relational troubles are attended to as a matter of priority over other ongoing activities during the everyday events in the early childhood centre.

Teachers Approaching an Emotional Upset and Eliciting Knowledge

Excerpt 1: Sam

Sam (SAM), a preschool teacher, is standing in the outdoor area of the preschool setting talking to a preschool child when one of the four-year-old children, Aata (ATA), starts crying loudly. Aata is standing next to another preschool child, Matthew (MTW). Even though Sam is in an interaction with another child, he leaves that interaction to approach Aata and seeks knowledge about what had happened.

```
01 ATA:      ((sitting down crying loudly))
02 SAM:      what's ↑wrong A↓ata ((walks towards Aata))
03 ATA:      Ma↑tthew ↓hurt me:::=
04 MTW:                         =no: ↑I >di↓dn't< (0.3) it was my-
05           ↑I- I had th↓at=
06 SAM:                    =↑can you come here pl↑ease
07           (1.6)
08 MTW:      ↓no↓ [I ( )]
```

Relationships and Knowledge in Disputes 69

```
09  SAM:            [↓Matthew] I need you to come ↓here pl↑ease
10                  (4.9)
11  MTW:            ((stands up and twirls a hosepipe around in front
12                  of his face))
13  SAM:            ↓Matthew↑ (1.2) ↓come here↓
14                  (4.3) ((Matthew approaches Sam. Sam reaches towards
15                  Matthew, holds his hand and gently pulls him
16                  towards him. Aata continues crying))
17  SAM:            what hap↑pened to Aa↓ta
18  MTW:            (2.1) we what- we were h↑aving tha↓:t (1.0)
19                  ((points to the scooter that Aata is sitting
20                  on))[with the-
21  SAM:               [you were having what↓
22                  (0.8)
23  MTW:            ↓that↓ ((points to the scooter)) [(      )]
24  SAM:                                              [the scooter]
25  MTW:            [↓yeah::↓]
26  SAM:            [but Aa↑ta's] on the s↓cooter at the mo↑ment
27  MTW:            ↓but but but↓ (    ) >I=was< pretending to be a
28                  ↑fi:re en↓gine
29  SAM:            but ↓Aata's on the s↑cooter at the ↓moment↓ (1.5)
30                  that means it's Aata's turn not your turn↓
```

The interaction begins with Aata crying loudly, a social signal that is acknowledged as demonstrating emotional upset to others (Danby and Baker, 1998a; Harris, 2006). Crying as an observable action of being upset is demonstrated in this episode as Sam immediately suspends his current interaction with another child to approach Aata (line 02).

When Sam reaches Aata he orients to Aata's crying as a problem, as he asks Aata 'what's wrong' (line 02). This mobilising of a problem is acknowledged in prior early childhood research where a teacher orients to a situation as problematic in order to gain knowledge about the incident with a child (Bateman, 2013; Bateman, Danby and Howard, 2013a; Danby and Baker, 1998a). Through asserting this question, the teacher makes observable his availability to listen, offering help with the problem. Prior CA research in the area of child counselling reveals that adult enquiry into a child's problem is essential in identifying the issues that the children themselves perceive as problematic in order to provide essential insight through *feelings talk* (Hutchby, 2005). Aata's crying here demonstrates his emotional upset as observable, which is subsequently attended to as such by Sam as he provides an opportunity for Aata to express his *feelings talk* about the situation. Through approaching Aata and positioning himself as a person that Aata can talk to about his emotional problem, it is possible that Sam initiates a collection R SRP 'that constitutes a locus for a set of rights and obligations concerning the activity of giving help' (Sacks, 1972, p. 37).

Aata responds by making a complaint about one of the children that he is currently playing with, as he tells Sam that Matthew has hurt him (line 03). Harris (2006) discusses how the production of crying can be tied to enforcing blame on an interlocutor for being responsible for the cause of the emotional upset. By making a complaint about this emotional upset to an 'outsider' of the group of players (in this instance, the teacher Sam), Aata asserts himself as not aligning with the CBA available with those particular friends at that time. This is achieved through his cry for help to an outsider and the supportive response given by Sam as a willing party who provides the help for him.

These first turns of the interaction detail how Aata sets aside his membership to the present group of friends through making a complaint about one of them as he turns to Sam for help. With regard to category collections, incumbents of category R are describable as members of a collection of people who have rights and obligations to provide and give help to each other (Sacks, 1972). Where one member of the collection R category SRP is no longer available, the remaining member can search for help from a person who is not a member of the collection R without violating that rule. Sacks further suggests that children learn about categorising members of the population through category collections of which 'combinatorial problems are between classes of modifiers, of which (good and bad) are prototypes' (p. 35). In the current episode Aata being hurt by one of his friends demonstrates a problem with the collection 'friend' as the CBA tied to membership of the 'friend' category conflicts with the actual activity he has just experienced; being hurt by a friend is observable as being a trouble with which to turn to someone for help.

This is explainable through reference to collection R where there are people who are proper to turn to for relational help – 'Rp' – and those who are improper to turn to for relational help – 'Ri' (Sacks, 1972). Aata demonstrates that Sam is the correct person to turn to for help in this situation with this trouble through his actions, as he tells him about this emotional problem. As Sam approaches Aata's cry for help, he makes himself available as the appropriate person to turn to about the trouble (Sacks, 1972). Aata has been involved in a friend-friend relational R collection with Matthew until this point; as Matthew is now the cause of the trouble Aata cannot call on this R member for help with his emotional trouble. Therefore Aata now turns to the teacher for relational help, as his co-membership collection R with Matthew is no longer available.

Following these initial turns (lines 01–02) the interaction progresses through knowledge exchange where each child offers their side of the story (Pomerantz, 1980) and Sam requests further information about the event:

```
03  ATA:        Ma↑tthew ↓hurt me:::=
04  MTW:                         =no: ↑I >di↓dn't<(0.3) it was my-
05              ↑I- I had th↓at=
06  SAM:                       =↑can you come here pl↑ease
07              (1.6) ((Sam and Matthew have eye contact))
08  MTW:        ↓no↓ [I (     )]
```

```
09   SAM:               [↓Matthew] I need you to come ↓here pl↑ease
10                 (4.9)
11   MTW:          ((stands up and twirls a hosepipe around in front
12                 of his face))
13   SAM:          ↓Matthew (1.2) ↓come here↓
14                 (4.3) ((Matthew approaches Sam. Sam reaches towards
15                 Matthew, holds his hand and gently pulls him
16                 towards him))
17   SAM:          what happ↑ened to Aa↓ta
18   MTW:          (2.1) we what- we were h↑aving tha↓:t (1.0)
19                 ((points to the scooter that Aata is sitting
20                 on))[with the-
21   SAM:               [you were having what↓
22                 (0.8)
23   MTW:          ↓that↓ ((points to the scooter)) [(        )]
24   SAM:                                            [the scooter]
25   MTW:          [↓yeah::↓]
```

In this section of the unfolding interaction, Aata offers information to Sam in a preferred response to his question (line 02), offering his knowledge about the event, that Matthew hurt him. Matthew quickly latches on to the end of Aata's utterance to offer his own knowledge about the event, which is in contrast to Aata's perspective. Matthew attends to the issue of ownership over a specific object, a scooter (lines 04–05), making this of importance in the current dispute situation. Sam responds quickly to this new knowledge about the dispute he now has with 'come here' whilst making eye contact with Matthew, indicating that his requirement to have a close physical proximity to Matthew at that time during the dispute is important.

The importance of being physically close is further demonstrated as Sam reiterates his request three more times; initially with a mitigating and modelling of politeness (Burdelski, 2010; Labov and Fanshel, 1977): 'please' as he makes reference to the child's availability to do the action in his first request 'can you come here please' (line 06). This way of requesting Matthew's presence gives Matthew the opportunity to answer in a dispreferred way, which he does with 'no' (line 08). Sam then rephrases his question with a name calling to ensure he has Matthew's attention (Wootton, 1981) and the preface 'I need you to' (line 09). Rather than giving an option of a yes or no answer, Sam's second question shows his need for Matthew to be near him, giving Sam's utterance more urgency. This is responded to in a more preferred way by Matthew as he stands up and starts to approach Sam, albeit very slowly. As Matthew stands for some time without approaching Sam, Sam formulates his request a third time. This time he is much more direct as he calls Matthew's name once again to secure his attention and gives him a direct instruction as he tells him to 'come here' (line 13), restricting the possible response that Matthew can give. This third request for Matthew to approach Sam is met with a preferred response as Matthew makes his way, slowly, towards Sam.

The knowledge exchange evident in this section of the interaction (lines 06–15) co-produces a category K collection between Aata, Matthew and Sam. This is initially apparent when Aata and Matthew both provide their knowledge about the situation to Sam, and subsequently when Sam demonstrates his teacher authority when he asks Matthew to approach him as 'the teacher can initiate activity, reprimand, self-select at any time and so on while the students have to request speaking rights and do what they are instructed to do' (Butler, 2008, p. 157).

Once Matthew is standing next to Sam, the interaction progresses, made observable as Sam asks Matthew for further details about what happened to Aata (line 17-25). This progression of knowledge exchange between Aata, Matthew and Sam is organised around Sam asking more questions about the event, demonstrating Sam's K- position and situating him as the less knowledgeable, whereas Matthew provides the information needed, demonstrating his more knowledgeable K+ position (Heritage, 2012a). The knowledge that Matthew asserts shows his side of the story (Pomerantz, 1980) where he uses physical gesture to support his verbal expression in an embodied action to communicate his intentions as he points to the scooter when there is a momentary breakdown of a shared understanding (lines 21–25). The final section of the interaction then unfolds:

```
26  SAM:     [but Aa↑ta's] on the s↓cooter at the mo↑ment
27  MTW:     ↓but but but↓ (    ) >I=was< pretending to be a
28           ↑fi:re en↓gine
29  SAM:     but ↓Aata's on the s↑cooter at the ↓moment↓ (1.5)
30           that means it's Aata's turn not your turn
```

It is not until Sam has received the information he has requested to gain sufficient knowledge about the situation that he can make a response that is affiliated with one of the children. Through asserting his knowledge about Aata being on the scooter, Sam positions his moral stance as being affiliated with Aata, as he presents an argument for why Aata can use the scooter (because he is physically 'on' it) rather than offer the scooter to Matthew. This affiliation between the two members shows the orderly progression from Sam and Aata's prior initial co-production of a collection R SRP where rights and obligations to give and receive help were played out (lines 01–03), which is now returned to in their shared moral stance over who should have the scooter.

Matthew responds to Sam and Aata's affiliation by offering more information about the situation, referring to how he was using the object being fought over in his pretend play activity. This strategy of using pretend play to manage social organisation through employing pretend play characters is evident in prior research demonstrating children's social competencies (Bateman, Hohepa and Bennett, forthcoming 2016; Bjork-Willen, 2012; Butler and Weatherall, 2006; Butler, 2008; Cobb-Moore, 2012; Kyratzis, 2007). Here, Matthew makes reference to his pretend play when giving his side of the story as a legitimate reason for taking the scooter off Aata. However, this is met with Sam's reiteration of his prior knowledge assertion as he repeats his utterance about Aata having the scooter. There is a slight pause followed by Sam offering further explanation of his utterance, 'that means' as a way of marking his prior knowledge distribution that was not accepted by Matthew. Sam then goes on to offer further information to Matthew that clearly states the social order surrounding the dispute 'it's Aata's turn not your turn' (line 30).

Aata's initiation of the interaction by displaying his emotional upset through his cry for help is responded to by Sam who initially provides an opportunity for feelings talk through approaching Aata and enquiring about his trouble, co-producing a possible collection R SRP with Aata. Sam's affiliation with Aata is observable throughout this interaction where a 'them and us' type of social situation between himself and Aata, and Matthew is established. Through a detailed look at the systematic way that the interaction was managed by the members, it is observable that Sam and Aata's co-production of a collection R SRP at the beginning of the interaction is returned to at the end of the interaction, as affiliation between Sam and Aata was evident through their shared moral stance.

Collection K was also evident through the co-production of professional and laymen memberships (Sacks, 1972) as Sam initiated activity and requested further information from Matthew, and Matthew (reluctantly) did as he was instructed to do by Sam. Sam's actions during this episode demonstrate that, in order to resolve the emotional trouble, Sam had to find out as much information as needed about the event. He achieves this by initially asking Aata why he is crying and then responds to Aata's complaint by questioning Matthew, ensuring that he has heard both sides of the story before taking a moral stance. The knowledge exchanges evident in this interaction work to explain the reason for the emotional upset, and the teacher subsequently uses this knowledge to assert his moral stance in the resolution of the dispute. By gaining this knowledge through a category K collection, Sam is able to provide emotional support for Aata as he affiliates himself with Aata through the collection R SRP.

This dispute over the ownership of the scooter is settled here as Aata continues using the scooter, but the interaction between Matthew and Sam continues on to a subsequent dispute about using another piece of playground equipment (Excerpt 2), this time a small, thin rubber tube:

Excerpt 2: Sam

Sam walks with Callum (CLM) and Matthew to the playground shed so that the preschool children can choose a piece of play equipment, as Aata is now using the scooter (see Excerpt 1). Callum and Matthew interact together next to Sam and then both boys run away and Matthew quickly disappears out of sight. The following interaction occurs:

```
01  CLM:     ~↑A::Rrrr↑~
02  SAM:     Cal:lum↑ (4.9)((walks towards Callum)) >hey< (0.3)
03           ↓Matthew↓
04  CLM:     ↑no:↑ ((jumps up and down))
```

```
05            (3.0) ((Sam continues quickly towards Callum))
06 SAM:       ↓here↑((gently holds Callum's arm))
07            (1.3)
08 CLM:       °>↑hu↑<°
09 SAM:       ↓come aw↑ay from ↓Matthew:↓
10 CLM:       no he (    ) on me::=
11 SAM:                          =I know he did that to you but
12            that's because you were annoying him=you [were
13 CLM:                                              [°urgh:
14 SAM:       [trying to ↑take awa::y (0.9) what he was playing
15 CLM:       [°ur:::hhh::: get off::: me::::°
16 SAM:       [with you need to ↑come and calm down↓
17 CLM:       [↓°mmmmm::::°↓ ((sits on the floor))
18 SAM:       st↑and up↓
19            (0.6)
20 CLM:       ~↑no:↑~
21            (0.8)
22 SAM:       ↑come and calm down↓ please ((gently lifts Callum))
23 CLM:       [~n↑o:::::↓~]
24 SAM:       [co↑me=on↓]
25            ((Sam and Callum start walking slowly together))
26 CLM:       ↓n:::↑o: ((sits on the floor again))
27            (2.0)
28 SAM:       can you stay away from Matthew
29 CLM:       ↑>mm<↑
30 SAM:       I can go and get you ↑another hose if you↓ want
31            one↑
32            (0.7)
33 CLM:       ↑>mm<↑
34 SAM:       but you need to stay away from him↓
35 CLM:       ↑>mm<↑
36 SAM:       come on
37            (3.3)
38 SAM:       tsk .hhh okay↓ you c↑ome and sit here then↓ ((lifts
39            Callum up gently and places him on a step))
40 CLM:       n::↑o:::::↓ ((folds his arms and drops his head
41            down))
42            (2.1)
43 SAM:       c↑alm down↓
44            (0.6)
45 CLM:       °↑hu↓° (0.4) °↑hu↓° ((shuffles along the step))
46 SAM:       ↓are you al↑righ:t::
47 CLM:       °↑hu↓° ((still shuffling))
48            (2.0)
```

```
49  SAM:        ↓are you happy to go and play no:w↑((crouches down
50              to Callum's eye level in front of him))
51              (10.7) ((Callum continues shuffling along the step
52              while Sam remains crouched down close to him))
```

At the start of the interaction Callum shouts loudly and with a wobbly voice, indicating that he is experiencing an emotional upset (Goodwin, Goodwin and Yaeger-Dror, 2002). As with Excerpt 1, Sam attends to the child's crying as a matter of priority as he abandons the activity he is engaged in (finding equipment in the shed) to approach the crying child.

In lines 01–09 Sam responds to Callum by shouting his name loudly, approaching him and then shouting Matthew's name (lines 02–03) to secure their attention (Wootton, 1981). However, both children offer a dispreferred response as Callum shouts 'no' very loudly and jumps up and down, demonstrating his disagreement both verbally and with gesture (Birdwhistell, 1970; Goodwin, 1981) and Matthew disaffiliates himself from the possible interaction with Sam as he runs away (Bateman, 2010). These initial signs of an emotional upset are quickly attended to by Sam, shown by his immediate response and physical actions as he quickly approaches Callum.

Sam then goes on to provide help through holding Callum's arm gently and instructing him to 'come away from Matthew', indicating that Callum is the one who needs to be moved away from the space he shares with Matthew, as there is a problem when he is near Matthew. Rather than asking for information regarding the emotional trouble, as was evident in Excerpt 1, these actions show how Sam readily takes a moral stance on the situation without requiring further knowledge. Callum demonstrates that he is aware that he is being blamed for the trouble in his response to Sam's actions in the next sequence of the interaction (lines 10–17):

```
10  CLM:       no he (   ) on me::=
11  SAM:                            =I know he did that to you but
12              that's because you were annoying him=you [were
13  CLM:                                                  [°urgh:
14  SAM:       [trying to ↑take awa::y (0.9) what he was playing
15  CLM:       [°ur:::hhh::: get off::: me::::°
16  SAM:       [with you need to ↑come and calm down↓
17  CLM:       [↓°mmmmm::::°↓ ((sits on the floor))
```

Sam's actions are met with Callum's partly inaudible reply, which does offer further knowledge about the situation from Callum's perspective and takes the stance that Matthew did something to him, indicating that Matthew is the one to blame (line 10). In doing so Callum demonstrates a K+ position in his interaction with Sam, suggesting that Sam has a lack of knowledge about the event, as he needs to be given the relevant information. Although Callum initiated the sequence of events through his cry and the teacher responded to this emotional upset by approaching him, as was evident in Excerpt 1, the child's contributions to the interaction are not responded to in the same way by Sam where he requested further knowledge. Here, rather than asking the approached child questions about what initiated the emotional upset, Sam asserts his knowledge of the situation as he responds to Callum by saying, 'I know he did that to you' (line 11). Through this action Sam reveals that he already has knowledge about the event and so is in a K+ position to take a moral stance without the need to engage in the co-production of knowledge exchange with Callum.

Sam subsequently asserts his moral stance on the dispute, and his affiliation with Matthew as he shares his own knowledge about what happened (lines 11–16). As Sam begins offering a rationale for Matthew's actions, Callum begins to make loud noises in overlap, giving a 'talking' rather than 'listening' position in the conversation (lines 10–15). Through both members offering their K+ position of what they believe to have happened in the dispute interaction, further conflict arises, this time between Sam and Callum. These turns at talk demonstrate how collection K membership is co-produced between Sam and Callum in their opposing accounts about what happened in the dispute between Matthew and Callum.

In the next turns of interaction, Sam and Callum further invoke collection K membership as Sam asserts his position as a professional (teacher) as he instructs Callum to stand up and tries to guide him to another place (lines 16–36):

```
16  SAM:      [with you need to ↑come and calm down↓
17  CLM:      [↓°mmmmm::::°↓ ((sits on the floor))
18  SAM:      st↑and up↓
19            (0.6)
20  CLM:      ~↑no:↑~
21            (0.8)
22  SAM:      ↑come and calm down↓ please ((gently lifts Callum))
23  CLM:      [~n↑o:::::↓~]
24  SAM:      [co↑me=on↓]
25            ((Sam and Callum start walking slowly together))
26  CLM:      ↓n:::↑o: ((sits on the floor again))
27            (2.0)
28  SAM:      can you stay away from Matthew
29  CLM:      ↑>mm<↑
30  SAM:      I can go and get you ↑another hose if you↓ **want**
31            one
32            (0.7)
33  CLM:      ↑>mm<↑
34  SAM:      but you need to stay away from him↓
35  CLM:      ↑>mm<↑
36  SAM:      come on
```

Callum initially responds to Sam's instructions with a dispreferred response as he refuses to comply and remains seated on the floor. There are several interactional turns where Sam tries to move Callum away from his current location and each of these times Callum gives a dispreferred response with 'no'. Following this Sam returns to his prior stance about Callum staying away from Matthew, but this time he uses a question format to ask Callum if he is able to do this rather than instructing him to do so. Callum maintains his minimal response to Sam and so Sam continues to ask another question, placing himself in the K- position as both questions seek Callum's knowledge, initially about whether or not he can stay away from Matthew, and then asking if he would like Sam to get him another hose. As Callum's minimal responses do not answer Sam's questions, Sam gently lifts Callum up off the floor and sits him on a nearby step, once again telling him to calm down (lines 38–43). This action demonstrates how Sam asserts collection K membership as he affirms his 'exclusive rights for dealing with some trouble' (Sacks, 1972, p. 39), that being the right to assert that an action he has requested from the layperson be done.

Within this sequence Sam also makes reference to relational aspects of the trouble where he suggests that the way that this conflict can be resolved is by Callum altering his emotional state, as he needs to 'calm down' (lines 16 and 22). This relational talk about emotional feelings is progressed further in the end of the sequence:

```
44                  (0.6)
45   CLM:           °~↑hu↓~° (0.4) °~↑hu↓~° ((shuffles along the step))
46   SAM:           ↓are you al↑righ:t::
47   CLM:           °~↑hu↓~° ((still shuffling))
48                  (2.0)
49   SAM:           ↓are you happy to go and play no:w↑ ((crouches down
50                  to Callum's eye level in front of him))
51                  (10.7) ((Callum continues shuffling along the step
52                  while Sam remains crouched down close to him))
```

Callum is now sitting on the step, making little sounds with a tremble in his voice, once again indicating that he is experiencing an emotional upset (Goodwin, Goodwin and Yaeger-Dror, 2002). Sam responds to Callum's utterances in a more sensitive way in these closing turns of this episode, as he asks Callum if he is all right (line 46). As Sam's question attends to Callum's emotional state, he prompts the possibility of feelings talk (Danby and Baker, 1998a; Hutchby, 2005), making Sam's interest in Callum's emotional well-being observable. Through asking Callum if he is all right, Sam places himself in the position as a person that Callum can talk to about emotional troubles, and demonstrates his willingness to give help, as observed in the beginning of this interaction when he initially approached Callum about his trouble.

In relation to Sacks' work on collection R category collections, he discusses the *programmatic relevance* of such a collection where 'if R is relevant, then the non-incumbency of any of its pair positions is an observable' (Sacks, 1972, p. 39). In this instance, as with Excerpt 2, the absence of an adult to comfort an emotionally upset child would be observable in an early childhood centre. In such a situation, the teacher attends to the non-incumbency of a collection R SRP member and provides for this position in his next action as he approaches the child and asks if he is 'all right', demonstrating his obligation to provide help for the upset child.

Callum responds quietly with a repeat of his prior utterance, indicating that he is still experiencing the same emotional upset. There is a slight pause followed by Sam offering a second relational utterance as he enquires about whether Callum is happy, placing emphasis on the word 'happy', drawing attention to its use. Whilst doing this Sam crouches down so that he is physically positioned at Callum's eye level during this utterance, a technique promoted for establishing positive relationships with young children, and making his affiliation and engagement with Callum observable (Goodwin, 1981). These actions demonstrate the incumbents as positioned as a collection R SRP through their giving and receiving of help about an emotional upset, making the programmatic relevance of collection R membership observable (Sacks, 1972).

This series of actions between Callum and Sam demonstrate the systematic processes involved in managing a dispute in everyday practice. Initially, Sam approached the emotional trouble, showing his willingness to give help to the children as a priority over his ongoing interaction with another child. This was followed by an assertion of a collection K SRP where each person declared their own knowledge of the situation demonstrating K+ & K+ positions. At the end of the interaction, Callum demonstrated his emotional upset and this was attended to in a more relational way, demonstrating the child and teacher's collection R SRP as Sam attended to Callum's emotional well-being. In this instance the interaction reveals how a K+ & K+ interaction can lead to a dispute and how this is systematically resolved when a K- & K+ situation is co-produced, leading to a relational SRP collection.

Excerpt 3: Jamilla

A three-year-old toddler girl, Kate (KAT), is sitting in a small tree in the outdoor area shouting that she 'got up first' in a distressed voice a few metres away from the early childhood teacher, Jamilla (JAM). Jamilla leaves the interaction she is currently engaged in to approach Kate and the young toddler boy.

```
01 KAT:      ↑I: got up fi:rst↓ (3.9) ((shouts something
02           inaudible)) ↑I: GOT UP FI::RST↓ (1.7) ↑I: got up
03           fi:rst↓ (0.9) ↑I: got up fi:rst↓ (2.0) ~↑I::
04           go↓::t~ up first (3.8) ~I↑↑ got up first↓~
05 JAM:      (4.3) ((looks towards the shouting and approaches
06           the tree))
```

```
07    KAT:        ↑I got up fi:::rst↓=
08    JAM:                             =↑it's okay you can get up on
09                 th↑at si↓de (1.0) you can go on th↑at si↓de
10    KAT:        no::↑ (1.6) I'm try::ing to find a la:d↑ybug↓ (0.7)
11                 but- (1.8)
12    JAM:        I saw: a ↑few ladybugs on the ↓other tree::↑ (2.8)
13                 there might be a few on that tree↓ (0.4) did
14                 [you have a look on that one
15    KAT:        [↑I: ↓ca::n't ↑get ↓do::wn because he's in the
16                 wa:y↓
17                 (3.1)
18    JAM:        do you want me to ↑he:lp you ↓do::wn
19                 (1.3)
20    KAT:        °↓yeah↓°
21                 ((puts her arms around Jamilla's neck and
22                 Jamilla gently lowers her out of the tree to the
23                 ground))
24    JAM:        ↑careful↓ °↓yeah↓°
25                 ((Jamilla and Kate walk around the garden looking
26                 for 'ladybugs'))
```

This interaction is initiated with Kate shouting very loudly, repeating the same utterance several times with varying levels of prosody. Kate's verbal actions prompt the nearby teacher Jamilla to abandon the interaction she is currently involved in with other toddler children to physically move closer to Kate as a matter of priority. This action mirrors the systematic process of attending to a trouble in such an immediate way, as is evident in Excerpts 1 and 2.

Kate's repeat of the utterance 'I got up first' is of analytical significance, as demonstrated by the following three points. First, Kate identifies the importance of being 'first' in her utterances, marking this as something of importance to her at that time and in that place. Young children's identification of *first possession* of objects in their everyday play with each other is documented in children aged four and five years where disputes were co-produced over ownership of an item (Cobb-Moore, Danby and Farrell, 2008). The children in the research were found to justify their ownership over an item through a first possession rule where members were legitimately allowed to play with an item if they were the first to procure it. This 'ownership' of an item worked to organise the social order between the young children. Children's ownership over specific play spaces have also been found where they produce disputes over defending a particular space (Church, 2009). In the current research Kate's declaration of first possession over the tree demonstrates that the rule of first possession is also used in younger three-year-old children. However, Kate's assertion of first possession is not accepted as legitimate here, and so she repeats her utterance several times to reiterate her argumentative stance and becomes increasingly upset when the recipient shows no sign of listening to her.

The second analytical point concerning the start of this dispute lies within Kate's repeat of her utterance. Repeats of utterances have been found to indicate a lack of understanding between interlocutors during the flow of everyday conversation (Schegloff, 1968). A direct repeat of the utterance, or a formulation of it, is used as an attempt to regain a shared understanding so that the conversation can continue with as little disruption as possible. Here, Kate repeats her knowledge regarding the situation as she informs that she was in that place first. Repeats have also been explained as 'try marked' attempts at establishing an interaction with a person where the same utterance can be used until there is some recognition provided by the recipient (Sacks and Schegloff, 1979). In both instances the wider interactional significance of the repeat is acknowledged as problematic and detrimental to the ongoing progression of the interaction. When an answer is given, it can be done through a preferred or dispreferred response whereby the recipient aligns as either agreeing or disagreeing with the first person (Goodwin and Goodwin, 1992). This response action works to co-produce the establishment of social order as the participants display their congruity or incongruity with one another (Goodwin and Goodwin, 1992). The spaces between Kate's utterances are turn allocation spaces that are not taken by the toddler boy who is sitting in the tree with her.

What is evident here though is that Kate's repeated utterance becomes progressively problematic, as is evident in Kate's voice as it becomes unstable and starts to wobble and tremble as she begins crying during the last two repeats of her utterance (lines 3–4). The varying levels of prosody mark the third analytical point as Kate's movement between speaking at an average tone and an elevated shouting pitch indicates a progressive arguable event between children where emotional stance taking is observable (Goodwin, Goodwin and Yaeger-Dror, 2002). These latter repeats mark Kate's emotional upset through her argumentative stance (Goodwin, Cekaite and Goodwin, 2012) that is not being accepted by the intended recipient.

Kate's use of the first possession rule coupled with her repeat of the utterance and the marked raising and lowering of pitch and volume demonstrates Kate's assertion of her emotional stance in the social order of the playground. Kate's knowledge sharing about being the first person who 'got up' the tree is not accepted as a justification for rights of Kate's ownership by the recipient in this interaction and so Kate repeats her utterance to mark her argumentative stance. As Kate becomes increasingly upset, her stance becomes an emotional one and responded to as such by the toddler teacher Jamilla as she approaches Kate with 'it's okay' (line 08). Kate's loud display of emotions is observable as being of interactional significance here through Jamilla's empathic response (Harris, 2006).

Jamilla's response to Kate's emotional upset with 'it's okay' reassures Kate that the situation is manageable. This approach to an emotional upset is mirrored in research where the same response utterance was also used by counsellors, medical clinicians and friends who were recipients of crying others (Harris, 2006). Danby (1996) also demonstrates how a teacher encourages a child to resolve a peer's crying and agrees with the child's suggestion to 'give him a cuddle' with the utterance 'Okay' (p. 9). It is suggested that the utterance 'it's okay' in response to a person crying gives permission for that person to cry, as well as offering a moral stance with that person's position. Harris (2006) suggests that, 'through their categorisation of the crying as being 'okay' or 'alright', they [health professionals] are assisting their patients to feeling comfortable with the demonstration of their emotions' (p. 232). Kate's emotional display and Jamilla's supportive response through approaching and comforting her verbally and with gesture, work to co-produce a collection R SRP where an emotional trouble is presented and attended to through the giving and receiving of help between the participants.

Jamilla's 'it's okay' response is a preface to a solution to the perceived problem as she goes on to offer Kate knowledge about a possible way that she can get up the tree (line 08–09), but Kate responds to this suggestion as an incorrect perception of what she is trying to do. Kate makes her intentions clear to Jamilla as she replies with a dispreferred response 'no' (line 10) followed by a brief pause and an explanation that she is 'trying to find ladybugs' (lines 10–11), before breaking off from her turn at talk as she starts to identify a possible problem with this action with 'but'. This offers Jamilla some knowledge about the situation and she responds by making reference to Kate's 'ladybugs', offering further information about where to find the insects (lines 12–14), a possible distraction and diplomatic way of diffusing the current dispute. However, this is also met with a dispreferred response from Kate as she gives further information about the difficulties of her situation to Jamilla as she tells her that she 'can't get down because he's in the way' with emphasis on the word 'he'. There is a slight pause before Jamilla offers Kate help in an explicit way that requires more knowledge from Kate about her situation.

Up until this point Kate's conversational turns have expressed some knowledge about her situation, telling about being in the tree first, looking for ladybugs and not being able to get down out of the tree. Jamilla has subsequently responded to Kate's conversational turns with more knowledge, demonstrating the conversational turn-taking evident in the co-construction of knowledge between teacher and child (Waters and Bateman, 2013a). This knowledge exchange is co-produced here in the systematic process of addressing a problem that has caused a child emotional upset. Both Jamilla and Kate offer their knowledge about the situation in a category K collection: 'a collection constructed by reference to special distributions of knowledge existing about how to deal with some trouble' (Sacks, 1972, p. 37). Following the knowledge exchange, Kate indicates that she does want Jamilla to help her out of the tree with her preferred response 'yeah' (line 20) and puts her arms around Jamilla's neck as Jamilla gently lowers her down. Jamilla accompanies this action with her utterance 'careful', indicating a caring stance towards Kate as she provides help for her in a relational way.

During this interaction Kate begins the episode through her dispute with one of the other toddler children as she shares her knowledge about being up the tree first and becomes increasingly upset, marking an emotional problem that attracts the attention of the toddler teacher Jamilla, establishing a collection R SRP.

The subsequent interaction between Kate and Jamilla involves them both telling about their knowledge, Kate in relation to her current problematic situation and Jamilla through ways of trying to solve Kate's problematic situation; therefore provoking a collection K centred on knowledge exchange. Once Jamilla is more knowledgeable about Kate's problem, she is in the position to offer help to Kate using the knowledge she now has regarding Kate's situation. The help is subsequently given in a relational way through close bodily contact between the two interlocutors (Goodwin, Cekaite and Goodwin, 2012) and Jamilla's use of the word 'careful', returning back to a collection R SRP as Jamilla exercises her right to provide relational help for Kate, and Kate her right to receive it.

Excerpt 4: Jamilla

Jamilla is joining in the play with a group of toddlers who are using the climbing frame. Jamilla is standing at the top of the slide behind several children, one of which is two-and-a-half-year-old Helen (HLN). Three children go down the slide together, two boys and one girl, Courtney (CNY). Courtney starts crying very loudly at the bottom of the slide.

```
01  CNY:       ↑A::::R:::G:::H:::↓ .HHH *ah*ha*ha=
02  JAM:                                     =↓what's
03              ha:↑ppe:ned↓((leans over top of the slide))
04              ((the boys move away))
05  CNY:       ↓↓u::r:::::::↓↓
06  JAM:       [Courtney]
07  CNY:       [↓Ee:::::]
08  JAM:       ↓what's ha↑ppened↓
09  CNY:       ↑Stephen ((stands up and steps off the bottom of
10              the slide, approaches Jamilla))↑A::::R:::G:::H:::↓
11              ((holds hand up towards Jamilla))
12  JAM:       [↓did your fi↑nger get squa:shed↓
13  CNY:       [Stephen ↑push::ed me::[:::↓ ((points to slide))
14  JAM:                              [who ↑pushed you::↓
15  CNY:       Stephen pushed me in then he (went [over) .hhh ()
16  JAM:                                          [I think it was
17              an accident (0.8) I think it was an accident
18              you=were=all=playing=Helen:: ((looks at a toddler,
19              Helen, who is standing at the bottom of the slide))
20  CNY:       ↓↓u::r:::::::↓↓
21  JAM:       ↑this way↓ (1.3) ↓this way↓ ↑come up ↓this way
22              (1.7) come up ↓that way Hel↑en on that side ↑do:wn
23              ((makes hand signal to Helen to come up the steps))
24  HLN:       ((slowly moves off the slide, looking at Jamilla))
25  CNY:       ((continues crying loudly whilst Jamilla talks to
```

```
26                  Helen))
27      JAM:        show me your ↑finger↓ ((moves towards Courtney.
28                  Bends down and reaches her hand out towards
29                  Courtney)
30      CNY:        ↑a::::r:::g:::h:::↓ ((holds hand up towards
31                  Jamilla))
32      JAM:        [*shall we give it a >nice=little< ru:b*] ((rubs
33                  Courtney's fingers between her hands))
34      CNY:        [↓↓u::r:::::::↓↓]
```

This interaction begins as Jamilla is alerted to a problem by Courtney's very loud crying, which she attends to immediately by asking Courtney 'what's happened' (lines 3–4), talking the problem into significance and demonstrating to Courtney that she has noticed that she is upset. As with the prior excerpts in this section, Courtney's crying makes her emotional upset observable as one that requires an immediate response (Danby and Baker, 1998a; Harris, 2006) and the teacher responds as a matter of priority.

As Courtney continues crying, Jamilla uses name calling to try to secure her attention (Wootton, 1981) and prompt an answer, but this is overlapped with Courtney's crying (lines 06–07). Courtney continues crying at first and so Jamilla repeats her question again (line 08), highlighting the importance of finding out what the problem is. As with prior findings concerning teachers use of 'what's happened' where it initiates a problem enquiry sequence with children who are experiencing an emotional problem or telling of traumatic events (Bateman, 2013; Bateman, Danby and Howard, 2013; Danby and Baker 1998a; Kidwell 2011), it also works this way here as is demonstrated in the subsequent turn taking sequences between the interlocutors as Courtney begins telling her trouble to the teacher. Through asking this question, Jamilla also positions herself as being the less knowledgeable in the situation (K-) and recognises that Courtney is more knowledgeable (K+) as she knows 'what happened'.

This time Courtney does answer and gives her side of the story (Pomerantz, 1980) as she tells Jamilla 'Stephen', and walks towards her holding her hand up (lines 09–11). Within this telling Courtney communicates both verbally and with a gesture to support her verbal action, allowing her to communicate the problem in multiple ways (Bateman, 2012b). The use of gesture in toddler's communication with their parents reveal the social implications of children's non-verbal actions, such as pointing and showing, where these actions are responded to as successful ways of communicating their intentions by the recipient adults (Filipi, 2009). Here, Courtney's 'showing' of her injury through lifting her hand towards Jamilla provides information about her emotional problem to Jamilla. Coupled together Courtney's verbal utterance 'Stephen' and the showing of her hand indicate that Stephen could possibly have been involved and that the problem may be linked to her hand. This shift in physical positioning frames the participants of the interaction as being *engaged* with each other where 'by displaying engagement towards another, one treats that other as available for such observation and coparticipation and not as someone then occupied with private activities that are not to be observed' (Goodwin, 1981, p. 97).

Through this engagement Jamilla demonstrates that she has some new understanding of the situation in her response to Courtney's actions, as she says 'did your finger get squashed' (line 12). Jamilla's utterance attends to the action that happened to Courtney's finger disassociated with blame and the name of a wrongdoing of one of the other children. In response to this, Courtney does mention a child's name in relation to the action as she goes on to offer further knowledge from her side of the story (Pomerantz, 1980) where she tells a more comprehensive story that Stephen pushed her, and points to the slide (line 13). There is a slight break down in shared understanding where Jamilla clarifies who it was that pushed Courtney before Jamilla takes a moral stance towards the situation as she suggests that the occurrence was 'an accident' (line 16–17), again disassociating any blame with the action. In doing so Jamilla formulates her response to Courtney's claim through the utterance 'I think' twice, making an awareness of her cognitive state explicit in the process of asserting her moral stance.

The sequences of actions here reveal how, when a toddler is upset, they still manage to inform adults of their problem through the use of a combination of verbal and non-verbal actions and how the adult, in this case a teacher, prompts the knowledge exchange so as to make an informed decision and take a moral stance in a dispute. The knowledge exchanges here, as with the prior observations so far in this chapter, reveal the teacher's less knowledgeable 'K-' position and the child's more knowledgeable 'K+' position (Heritage, 2012a). The co-production of the knowledge exchange here where Courtney offers information about her problem to a less knowledgeable teacher positions these members in collection K category where Courtney distributes her experienced knowledge about her problem to a person who can provide help (Jamilla).

Once Jamilla has declared her moral stance on the situation she immediately attends to the situation of a very young toddler, Helen, who is standing on the bottom of the slide; this is a potentially dangerous position as, if another child used the slide whilst Helen was standing there, she would be knocked over. Even though Courtney continues crying (lines 20 and 24–25) Jamilla talks to Helen to try to coax her off the slide (lines 21–23), marking a shift in engagement between participants. The potentially dangerous situation that Helen is in takes priority over the current interaction between Courtney and Jamilla and, as such, is observable as an insertion sequence (Sacks, 1992a) where Helen's safety is attended to as a separate issue to the ongoing conversation.

This priority of a child's well-being is evident here, as with the prior excerpts in this chapter and also mirrors the findings in the latter two excerpts in Chapter 4 regarding their pretend play episodes. Treating a possible threat to a child's safety and well-being in such a way marks its priority and demonstrates the importance of teachers' relational care for the children during everyday teaching practice.

Once Helen is safely off the slide, Jamilla returns to the interaction she was having with Courtney as she asks Courtney to show her fingers to Jamilla (line 27). Courtney continues crying and holds her hand up towards Jamilla and Jamilla offers further relational help as she suggests that she will give her fingers a 'nice little rub' and gently rubs Courtney's fingers (lines 32). This interaction is observable as one that provides relational care for the child through an empathic physical gesture. It is further noticeable as relational as the physical gesture is coupled with Jamilla's use of 'creaky voice' during her suggestion of 'shall we give it a nice little rub', presenting affiliation through affective interchange (M. H. Goodwin, 2014).

This part of the interaction is relational as Jamilla caresses Courtney's fingers in a response to her emotional upset and uses creaky voice to signal a heightened emotional stance while doing so, and Courtney fully engages in the interaction. This joint accomplishment of the interaction marks the relational category 'with one party engaging in practices that are understood as appropriate for incumbents of a relationship category and the other ratifying the practices of the first party' (Pomerantz and Maundlebaum, 2005, p. 150).

Throughout these excerpts we see that a child's upset is responded to immediately by a teacher, even when the teacher has not been previously engaged in an interaction with that child. This marks the attending to an upset child as being of omni-relevance (Sacks, 1992a) where it can be attended to without prior warning and as a matter of immediate importance in the everyday interactions of the teachers and children. A second priority then occurs, when Helen is in a potentially dangerous situation standing at the bottom of the slide, and so Jamilla momentarily abandons her interaction with Courtney to attend to the matter of Helen's safety as priority. Once Helen is in a safe place, Jamilla returns to comforting Courtney and heightens the relational interaction. As the interaction unfolds it is observable that the teacher's responses to the children's troubles are treated as acceptable by the recipient children and the observers, making observable the children's rights to receive help from Jamilla and Jamilla's obligation to provide help in the co-production of a collection R SRP.

Children's Emotional Offering of Knowledge to Teachers

As with the prior excerpts in this chapter, when a child experiences an emotional upset it is attended to by a teacher as a matter of priority over an ongoing interaction. In the following excerpts, the children are observed approaching a teacher to talk the episode into importance and the teacher responds to the child's upset in a supportive way.

Excerpt 5: Sam

Sam is sitting on the edge of the sandpit in the outdoor play area when one of the preschool boys, Mike, approaches and tells him that some children are calling him a name.

```
01  MIK:      (      )  ((approaches Sam and taps him on the
02            shoulder))
03  SAM:      pard↑on:
04  MIK:      °they s↑aid (I'm a ↓poop↑ybum↓°)  ((lifts his arm up
05            to cover his face))
06  SAM:      they sai::d (1.8) you're a wh↑a::t
07            (1.6)
08  MIK:      °~they said I'm a poopybum↓~°=  ((wipes his eyes))
09  SAM:                                     =well y↑ou're ↓not a
10            poopybum ↑are you↓  ((stands up))
11            (3.1)
12  SAM:      °excuse=me°  ((walks through a group of nearby
13            children and reaches to hold Mike's hand))
14            (7.5)  ((Sam and Mike hold hands and walk over to a
15            group of children))
16  SAM:      are you boys callin:::g my friend Mike
17            na↓:mes↑  ((stands in front of a boy on a swing))
18            (1.8)
19  IAN:      no
20            (1.3)
21  SAM:      he told me that you called him a ↓not very nice
22            ↑na↓:me↑
23  ATA:      we::↑ [won't do it agai:n↓
24  IAN:            [(      ) did
25  SAM:      well if you do: I will need you to come and hold my
26            hand because you're ↑**hurt**ing↓ (0.8) his
27            emo:tion:s↓=you're ↑hurting his >**fee**lings<↓
28            ((gently pushes Mike towards the swings))
```

This interaction is initiated by Mike as he approaches Sam to turn to him for help with an emotional trouble, although the specifics of the problem are difficult to hear in this first instance. Sam initiates repair, showing an interest in Mike's emotional state and Mike subsequently tells Sam about his trouble as he identifies his problem being about the children calling him a 'poopybum' (lines 4–5). Whilst doing this telling, Mike lifts his arm up to his face and wipes away tears, making the latter part of his sentence difficult to determine and so Sam asks for a second repair (line 06). Sam does this by repeating the first words used by Mike, indicating that he had heard this part of his utterance and then leaving a space for Mike to insert the rest of his utterance, but this is not taken and so Sam directly asks Mike what it was that the children called him (line 06). Sam then leaves another pause for Mike to talk and this time it is taken as Mike retells his trouble to Sam in the form of a complaint in a very quiet, wobbly voice coupled with the non-verbal action of wiping his face with his arm (line 08). By asserting this complaint about his fellow peers, Mike asserts his identity as being a member of an alternative category to the members being complained about (Sacks, 1992a) as,

> The one who uses a complaint can be heard as making an identification of himself. And that is obviously an enormous control on making complaints. It may be extremely difficult to be able to formulate a complaint about certain matters without having a perfectly standardized identification asserted (e.g., 'traitor'). (p. 362)

Sam responds to Mike's emotional telling through producing an affiliative stance with the complainant or troubles telling as he tells Mike that he is not a 'poopybum' and follows this with a tag question 'are you', which provides an opportunity for Mike to agree.

In early childhood education, teachers are often found to take the side of a child who has been at the receiving end of name calling, as is evident here. These types of insults are observable as part of the everyday social oganisation processes in the playground for both older (Goodwin, 2006) and younger children (Church, 2009, also see Danby and Theobald, 2012 collected volume). Furthermore, affiliation with members' complaints is found to be avoided in other institutions (Lindström and Sorjonen, 2013), making early childhood education a unique institution where this is an acceptable practice during everyday interactions.

Sam's affiliation with Mike's stance in the name calling dispute is further marked in his next action as he physically moves to approach the identified perpetrators responsible (lines 12–13). This joint moral stance on the wrong doing of the name calling affiliates Mike and Sam as belonging to a collection R SRP where relational help is provided for Mike's emotional problem, as they engage in the joint action of walking to confront the children together. This affiliation between Sam and Mike is further invoked in Sam's next utterance when he approaches the children (lines 16–17) as he refers to Mike as 'my friend Mike', using a possessive pronoun to assert his affiliation (Bateman, 2011; Butler, 2008). Through his assertion of 'you boys' in contrast to 'my friend', Sam's utterance here marks a 'them and us' situation. The collection R SRP is further oriented to at the closing of this interaction where Sam makes explicit reference to the name calling of Mike as 'hurting his emotions – his feelings' (lines 26–27).

This interaction demonstrates how a four-year-old child can be in the more knowledgeable position to the adult teacher about their emotional upset as he tells Sam news about the event he has just been involved in. In this instance Sam is the less knowledgeable (K-) and Mike is the more knowledgeable (K+) (Heritage, 2013). Sam reacts to this complaint by making his moral stance known in his subsequent response as he affiliates with Mike, marking a close empathic connection to him. In doing so Sam's affiliation with Mike is made hearable and this affiliation is progressed in the next series of actions as Sam holds Mike's hand and walks with him towards the identified children (lines 13–15) and he reprimands the boys for hurting Mike's feelings and emotions (lines 26–27). Interestingly, Sam suggests that the punishment for any subsequent name-calling would result in the perpetrator having to hold his hand (lines 25–26); a close physical action that would usually be associated with affiliation rather than a punishment but also an action that would require close physical contact with specific children and so allow close monitoring. Although Mike turned to Sam for help with a relational trouble, knowledge exchange about the event had to be co-produced in order for the details of the trouble to be understood between the participants.

Excerpt 6: Sam

Sam and a group of preschool children are on a routine excursion to the local bush area. Sam is walking on the bush trail with the children in front of him. Some of the children have a momentary dispute, which Sam settles. One of boys, Dane (DNE), is now walking in front of Sam; they continue to walk on the path whilst talking about the incident.

```
01  DNE:    John just- (0.4) Jo::hn just ↓bumped into her then-
02          then she::- then ↑he ↓bumped into ↑me::
03  SAM:    yes but I sa:w you ↓bumping on purpose
04          1.5
05  DNE:    but ↑he: ↓bumped me b↑a:ck↓
06  SAM:    ↑who bumped you back↓
07  DNE:    Ry↑:an↓
08  SAM:    yes he ↑did bump you back↓
09          1.9
10  DNE:    be↑cause (0.5) he wanted to=
11  SAM:                               =↓mmm=
12  DNE:    bump me back↓
13  SAM:    .hhh but it's not very safe: to be bumping each
14          other on slippery ground because somebody might
15          fall over: (0.3) .hhh and hurt themselves on a
16          ↓root
17          (1.8) ((Dane climbs over the first of a series of
18          large steps))
19  SAM:    you alright↑
20          (4.7) ((Dane continues climbing and Sam stands
21          behind him))
22  DNE:    >↑ah<
23  SAM:    they're big steps aren't they↓ .hhh (1.0) a bit
24          tricky when you've got little le↑gs
```

Relationships and Knowledge in Disputes 89

This interaction is initiated by one of the children (Dane) as he approaches the teacher (Sam) to tell him about his trouble. As with the prior excerpt, this action marks Dane's competence in asserting his right to seek and give help regarding his emotional trouble (Sacks, 1972). Dane's initial lines of talk show him offering his 'side of the story' (Pomerantz, 1980) to pass on the information he has about events to Sam. However, rather than accepting Dane's utterance as news, Sam gives his side of the story in response, indicating that he also has first-hand knowledge about the event. Sam does this by making explicit reference to what he 'saw' happen as he stresses and places emphasis on the word (line 03). This disagreeable stance towards Dane's troubles telling is met with a significant pause, followed by Dane making an account for his actions and offering further first-hand knowledge to Sam. The subsequent lines of talk involve a continued knowledge exchange between Dane and Sam regarding the situation, where both parties make observable their disagreement over the sequential pushing that produced the dispute, placing Dane and Sam as not morally aligned in their perspectives.

However, the moral stance of the exchange is then resolved as Sam provides a multi-unit turn at talk where he offers an account of why the children should not be pushing each other, placing emphasis on the words safe and hurt (lines 13-16), indicating that these are the significant aspects of the utterance. In doing so Sam demonstrates his role in educating about how to behave responsibly with his peers, with emphasis on the protection from being hurt or the 'care' with regard to the situation. Through this verbal action Sam highlights the relational aspects of his interaction with Dane where being safe and avoiding being hurt are significant aspects of their current situation. This relational aspect of care is accepted by Dane who does not offer any further argumentative stance to Sam and, instead, continues with his exploration of the natural terrain. This subsequently leads to Sam offering further concern for Dane's safety as he acknowledges the difficult terrain for Dane's personal situation with an emphasis on caring for Dane as he asks him if he is 'all right' (line 19). Sam offers further relational support for Dane as he offers empathy around what it must be like to be Dane and have 'little legs' in such terrain.

In a similar way to the other excerpts in this chapter where the teachers respond to a child's upset in an omni-relevant way, the excerpts in this section reveal how children also treat an emotional upset as a matter of priority in the everyday goings on of the early childhood centre. When a child approaches a teacher with an emotional upset, the teacher immediately responds to them. Even though they may be engaged in an interaction with another member of the early childhood centre at the time, the ongoing interaction is abandoned in favour of attending to an upset child; therefore making the collection R relational exchange associated with an emotional upset omni-relevant and a priority.

Relational Activities Following Knowledge about a Dispute

Literature that uses conversation analysis and ethnomethodology to investigate disputes between young children and the role of the adult in such disputes reveals how adults intervene and to what end. In the case of a mother intervening in an argument between her two sibling children, Busch (2012) identifies how the verbal and physical actions of the mother work to resolve the dispute. This systematic conflict resolution encouraged by adults is also present in literature involving a kindergarten in Sweden where the teachers questioned the children about how their disputes started, initiating discussions with the children about moral behaviour and accountability, and re-establishing moral order (Danby and Baker, 1998a; Danby and Baker, 1998b; Cekaite, 2012).

Although disputes offer the affordance for children to try out rules and test themselves against opposing others, it is often the case that adults will intervene in this aspect of children's cultural practices, although not always effectively (Danby and Baker, 1998a). One example of adult enforcement of rules on children's independent social organisation is evidenced in early childhood literature *You Can't Say You Can't Play*, where Paley (1993) famously banned children from excluding each other in their play activities. Likewise, Corsaro (1985) discusses the importance of the presence of the teacher and how teachers often want to disrupt conflict situations between children in order to get the child back to educational work.

The following excerpts demonstrate how the teachers in the current study manage children's disputes in such a way as to return to moral order through the co-production of knowledge and relationships.

Excerpt 7: Sam

The preschool teacher Sam is in the outdoor play area with two children, Matthew (MTW) and Callum (CLM), who are fighting over the use of the hosepipe. Callum has the hosepipe in his mouth and Matthew is not happy with this.

```
01  MTW:        no::: it's not for (cho↑mping) with (0.5) ↓anymore
02  CLM:        (2.5) ((dances around with the hosepipe in his
03              mouth looking at Matthew))
04  MTW:        it's not for cho↑mping insi:de::↓ ((pulls the
05              hosepipe sharply))
06  CLM:        ↑ye::↓s:: ((pulls the hosepipe back))
07  MTW:        ↑no it's ↓not
08  CLM:        ↑yes it [↓is it's pretending]
09  SAM:                [↑gu::↓ys:: stop ↓fighting↑] stop
10              ↓fighting ((holds onto the hosepipe))
11              (1.2) ((everyone is still))
12  SAM:        ↑stop figh↓ting
```

```
13 CLM:        it's pretending ((pulling at hosepipe))
14             (0.9)
15 MTW:        ↓no:::↑ ((pulling at hosepipe))
16 SAM:        ↓Matthew wh↑at's the ↓problem
17             (1.3)
18 MTW:        um he's (chomping) inside it
19 SAM:        ↓oh you don't like him bl↑owing inside it↓
20 MTW:        ↓no::↓
21 CLM:        I do:↑
22 MTW:        n- no tha↑::nk you (0.8) ↓I wanna put it in↑side
23             there↓
24             (2.2)
25 SAM:        you need to l↑isten to each other↓ (0.6)
26             <compromise::>
```

The beginning of this interaction shows two boys (Matthew and Callum) having a dispute over the use of a thin piece of hosepipe. Matthew asserts his knowledge about what the hosepipe is *not* supposed to be used for (line 01). Matthew's 'anymore' in tag position indicates that Matthew has prior knowledge that there was a time when this action was acceptable, but this is no longer the case. Callum's actions indicate his challenge to Matthew's asserted knowledge as he continues to use the object in the same way as he holds it in his mouth whilst maintaining eye contact with Matthew. This leads to Matthew repeating his knowledge about the incorrect use of the object again as it was not accepted by Callum in his subsequent turn, evidenced by his continued actions.

Following some 'yes' 'no' exchanges coupled with the physical actions of pulling the hosepipe towards themselves, Callum offers an account for using the hosepipe in such a way, saying that he is 'pretending' (line 08). Callum's verbal action here indicates that he shares the same knowledge as Matthew, that the object is not to be used in that way and that he is only 'pretending' to do the action that has been identified by Matthew as unacceptable.

In these first lines (01–08) both children verbally state their access to some knowledge about the uses of the hosepipe, but each point of view is in conflict and so their 'reported description gives only a perspective' (Pomerantz, 1980, p. 190). In relation to knowledge positions, each child here demonstrates their knowledge regarding the uses of the hosepipe, placing them both in the K+ position where 'the knowledge claims that interactants assert, contest and defend in and through turns at talk and sequences of interaction' (Heritage, 2013, p. 370). Although Enfield (2011) suggests that there is never complete symmetry in knowledge between interlocutors, there does appear to be symmetry in the presentation of knowledge regarding the uses of the hosepipe in this interaction. Likewise, whereas Heritage suggests that if both participants are in K+ & K+ positions the conversation would close, here it is observed that, when a K+, K+ position is present it causes a dispute, as the recipient does not accept the interlocutor's utterance. Similar

K+ & K+ positions over the use of an object have been found to co-produce dispute situations in other CA research involving young children (Rendle-Short, 2014).

This friction between the different knowledge stances with regard to the use of the hosepipe causes Sam to attend to the dispute by intervening and labelling the boys' actions as 'fighting' and in doing so makes the dispute recognisable as such an activity to all involved. Sam explicitly tells them to 'stop fighting' and takes hold of the hosepipe, immediately demonstrating his intention to bring an end to the dispute. This action works to calm the situation as the children and teacher become still before Sam reiterates his stance by repeating his utterance to 'stop fighting' (line 12).

There are two further opposing turns at talk by the children, followed by Sam mobilising the problem with the open question 'what's the problem' (line 16) and selects next speaker by addressing the question explicitly to Matthew. This action demonstrates Sam's interest in gaining information about the trouble from a specific person, listening to one side of the story (Pomerantz, 1980) at a time. There is a slight pause before Matthew responds by providing an assessment of the situation, and Sam responds by offering his new understanding, primed with his 'oh' (Heritage, 1984). This sequence of eliciting information is productive in the development of the interaction as Sam asks for information from the children, placing them in a K+ position, and demonstrating his receipt of new knowledge, co-producing a K category interaction.

Once Sam identifies this knowledge regarding the situation, Matthew indicates that Sam's summary is correct and Callum shows his preference for doing the action. However, Matthew responds to Callum politely this time with 'no thank you' (line 22) and calmly clarifies why he wants Callum to stop putting it in his mouth, because he wants to put the hosepipe somewhere else. In doing so Matthew shows a more amicable turn shape than his prior utterances where he displayed louder prosody in his disagreement and physically pulled at the hosepipe.

This episode is brought to a close as, once Sam summarises the knowledge exchanges that have occurred during the turns of talk in the dispute episode, he identifies that the episode was problematic because the children didn't *listen* to each other; each child gave their own knowledge regarding the appropriate use of the hosepipe, but neither accepted each other's knowledge as a legitimate action. Sam subsequently encourages a resolution as he tells the children not only to listen to each other but to compromise also. Through gaining enough knowledge to ascertain the trouble, Sam then uses that knowledge to prompt the children towards reconciliation and, in this case, attends to the importance of the turn-taking action of listening in resolving the dispute.

Excerpt 8: Sarah

Sarah (SAR), a preschool teacher, is standing in the outdoor area of the preschool setting next to the swings. A dispute begins when one of the preschool girls, Toia, (TOI) wants a turn of the swing that another girl, Abby (ABY), is using.

```
01  SAR:       Abby's on [(it:↑)]=
02  ABY:                [(I-)] ↑I just ↓got ↑on he:re↓
03  SAR:       ↓mmm
04  TOI:       but I want- but ↑I counted to her
05  SAR:       did you run to the chicken coop
06  TOI:       yeah
07             (1.4)
08  TOI:       [(yes I di::d↑)]
09  ABY:       [(I run to=the)] chicken coop too but >Toia< wasn't
10             getting ↓off
11  SAR:       Toia wasn't getting off↑
12  TOI:       ye:ah: and I wanted to go:: but I went just
13             to the chicken coop and touched it and run back and
14             <counted> to <twenty::>=
15  SAR:                             =ok↓ well I think you should
16             do it again just so that Ab has a decent swi:ng:↓
17             (1.4)
18  SAR:       because if you hop on the swing and then Abby
19             >runs=to=the=chiken=coop< runs back and counts to
20             twenty then it means that you only get to have
21             about ten swings and then your turn's finished↓
22             (1.9)
23  SAR:       aye↓
24             (2.1)
25  TOI:       °okay°= ((runs off towards the chicken coop))
26  SAR:              =okay↑ ((walks away))
```

The dispute starts with Toia telling Sarah that she wants a turn on the swing and Sarah responding by offering her knowledge of the situation: that Abby is currently occupying the swing (line 01). Abby adds to this knowledge by downgrading Sarah's observation as she says that she has 'just' got on the swing, indicating that time is an issue within the current interaction. Toia responds to this issue of time by attending to the rules around managing the time factor associated with using the swing, offering further information to the situation by telling that she engaged in the counting rule (line 04). The rule of counting to a specific number is employed when one child is waiting for another child to use a particular item, by the time the last number is counted, the child using the desired item must finish using it and hand it over to the child who is waiting. Sarah responds to this new information by requesting more knowledge about whether Toia also ran 'to the chicken coop', an additional action that is tied to the counting rule, and Toia confirms that she did (lines 06 and 07). Through talking these actions into importance, Sarah and Toia exchange their knowledge regarding the rules of turn-taking regarding the preschool equipment and equity of their use.

Abby next gives her side of the story and her knowledge about what has happened prior to this immediate exchange when Toia was on the swing prior to this and would not get off it. Sarah repeats Toia's utterance so as to acknowledge the new information without offering an assessment or premature judgment (Bateman, Danby and Howard, 2013a, 2013b). This is followed by Toia offering further knowledge to the situation regarding her enacting the correct CBA required by a 'waiter' (lines 12–14). The interaction then shifts as Sarah acknowledges that she has gained all the information that she needs to make an assessment about what she thinks should happen next. In this next move to resolve the dispute, Sarah suggests that Toia repeat the sequence of CBA tied to waiting for the swing and offers a rationale for this, so that Abby can have a 'decent swing' (line 16) indicating that this has not yet happened. There is a brief pause where Sarah's suggestion is not taken up immediately as no one supports or contests this suggested next action. This subsequently prompts Sarah to fill this next turn allocation space with an extended explanation that justifies her suggestion and offers the children knowledge about her decision (lines 18–21). As there is a further silence after this explanation, Sarah uses a further prompt in the form of a tag question 'aye', giving an opportunity for the children to agree or disagree with her stance. There is another significant pause before Toia finally agrees to do this (line 25).

This interaction is co-produced, initially with the preschool girls being in K+ position about their first-hand experiences of the event. As with the prior excerpts, this K+ & K+ position between interlocutors caused an argument as both tell their side of the story but neither side is accepted. Sarah then intervenes in the dispute and demonstrates her K- position as she asks for more information about how the dispute started. Once Sarah has gained all the information she needs to make a decision, she presents herself in a K+ position and suggests an amicable outcome. Sarah takes time to listen to the children and explains why she has come to her decision, to provide a fair turn-taking episode for both children, offering help to co-produce a collection R category.

Within this interaction the teacher attends to the centre's rules around using apparatus to try to negotiate a solution to the disputes, an issue also present in the next excerpt. This attention to environmental features in the co-production of knowledge and relationships is then further explored in the next chapter, Chapter 6.

Excerpt 9: Jamilla

Jamilla is sitting in the playroom with a group of toddlers talking about the pictures of ducks she has on her t-shirt; she is sitting opposite two toddler girls, Emma (EMA) and Rebecca (RBA). Prior to this interaction Emma and Rebecca were sitting on chairs opposite each other but left their chairs to join in the conversation about ducks. Now that they have returned Rebecca is sitting on the chair that Emma previously had, prompting Emma to orient to it as problematic to Jamilla.

```
01  EMA:        ~my::↑ chai::r↓~ (0.8) ~my::↑ chai::r↓~ ((sits on
02                    the small part of the chair that is accessible and
03                    looks at Jamilla))
04              (1.2)
05  JAM:        ↓well ↑how b↓out you get an↑other ch↓air and sit on
06                    th↑at ch↓air ((moves towards them on her knees))
07  EMA:        wanted th↑at ch↓air: ((points to the chair that
08                    Rebecca is sitting on))
09              (0.4)
10  JAM:        do you like th↑is ch↓air=
11  EMA:                              =~>↓yeah↓<~=
12  JAM:                                          =that ch↓air's
13                    pretty cool too do you ↓wanna get th↓at and sit by
14                    Rebecca ((leans on the back of Rebecca's chair and
15                    points to an empty chair))
16  EMA:        ((stops crying. walks over to the empty chair and
17                    pushes it towards Rebecca))
```

At the beginning of the interaction (lines 01–03) Emma solicits Jamilla's attention with her claim of ownership of an environmental feature; the prosody of her voice indicates emotional upset as it is quite shaky (Goodwin, Cekaite and Goodwin, 2012). This verbal claim and upset prosody is further elaborated physically as Emma sits on the small part of the chair that is available and her gaze is directed towards Jamilla. These actions together indicate a trouble that is communicated to the teacher as, although she speaks to the child who is now sitting on 'her' chair she looks at Jamilla, giving knowledge about her problem to the teacher through her gaze (Filipi, 2009). Emma's actions here work to give her side of the story, that the chair is hers, giving knowledge about why she is emotionally upset and placing her in a more knowledgeable position regarding the immediate situation (K+).

Following a brief pause, Jamilla responds by suggesting an alternative approach to Emma about the way she could go about resolving the problem of having lost her chair, priming her utterance with 'well', indicating that a possible problematic utterance will follow (Heritage, 2014). Jamilla's response (lines 05–06) demonstrates that she has enough knowledge about the problem to offer an opinion of a possible solution, as she attends to the item causing the problem (the chair) and the possibility of using a different chair. Even though, to the casual observer, the chair that Emma has lost is an exact replica of all the other available chairs in the room, Emma does not accept Jamilla's suggestion as she offers further knowledge about her feelings, that she wanted a *particular* chair (lines 07–08). In doing so Emma produces an opposition response to Jamilla's suggestion, and Jamilla's initial attempt at conflict resolution through her suggestion of using a different chair to solve the problem is abandoned.

Once again there is a marked pause (line 09) before Jamilla responds by demonstrating that she has heard Emma's preference and acknowledges this through using a relational term 'like' linked to the item (line 10). Although this is achieved through seeking knowledge in the form of a question, the utterance takes a relational turn shape, which seeks information about feelings related to the item. When Emma offers a preferred response to this (line 11), Jamilla quickly continues, keeping the momentum of the agreeable interaction going, as her prior utterance was not accepted by Emma (line 07–08). Jamilla continues to work at a conflict resolution in her next turn where she identifies a different chair as 'pretty cool', suggesting that this may be a feature that may make the chair more desirable to Emma. Jamilla also makes reference to sitting next to Rebecca, the girl that Emma has been playing with and is currently having a dispute with, showing that she has knowledge of the social implications in the dispute and that Emma might still want to sit next to Rebecca despite the dispute. This observation shows how knowledge exchange is important in this dispute situation where Jamilla seeks knowledge about the event before she is able to encourage a relational conflict resolution, and provide help for a child who is in need of it.

Knowledge and Relationships in Disputes

This chapter demonstrates how the teachers approach an emotional trouble by making observable their willingness to give help (Excerpts 1–4) and how children search for help with their emotional trouble as they approach a teacher (Excerpts 5–9). The rights and obligations for the giving and receiving of help are therefore demonstrable by the members in situ. 'Collection R and the rights and obligations organised by reference to its categories provide the propriety of engaging in a search for help … It provides for the permissibility of the search and also the procedure for doing that search' (Sacks, 1972, p. 41).

The observations included in this chapter also demonstrate how a collection K category is co-produced in a systematic way during disputes, as the child-teacher relationships juxtapose between that which involves knowledge sharing to that of a more relational and emotional interaction. In the four observations presented in the first section of this chapter, the systematic ways that these category collections were achieved were through the initial 'call for help' through the child's display of emotional upset through crying. The teacher responded to these cries in a relational way to co-produce a collection R category where obligations to ask for and provide help were evident through the interlocutors turns at talk. This was subsequently built on with knowledge exchange between the teacher and child where the teacher demonstrated their lack of knowledge about the situation in a K- position (Heritage, 2013) and the child provided the knowledge for the teachers through giving their side of the story (Pomerantz, 1980) in the more knowledgeable K+ position. Once the knowledge positioning of both members was more even, the interaction returned to a relational one where explicit caring for the child was demonstrated by the teacher's verbal and physical gestures, and the children took up these relational offerings in a preferred way.

The second section of four observations demonstrated the systematic ways that the children reported an emotional upset to a teacher and the teacher responded in ways that provided the relational support that the children needed as a priority in their everyday teaching. A commonality between these observations is that of the teachers being the less knowledgeable about the situation as the more knowledgeable children inform them. The observations all have an element of emotional upset displayed by the children through crying, lowered tone prosody and not accepting their peers' knowledge sharing as a legitimate action. These emotional cues are attended to and touched off by the teachers where knowledge exchange is initiated as a process of understanding the causes of the emotional upset and solutions are offered with regard to promoting harmony and co-operation between peers by the teachers.

These links between emotion and knowledge in institutional settings are recognised by Hepburn and Potter (2007) where they discuss how assertions of emotional upset of child callers into an NSPCC call line are responded to by the Child Protection Officers with response tokens such as 'Take your time' (TYT) along with other emotional receipts (ER). It is also suggested that 'a parent quizzing a crying child about something that had upset them might be a base environment for a TYT. These intuitions would need a broader collection of crying materials to test properly' (p. 98). This chapter has provided a collection of examples of such 'crying materials' in situ with transcriptions of children showing their emotional upset in everyday activity.

However, the incidents causing the upset in this chapter are co-produced in the immediate context, which is different to the calls in the Hepburn and Potter data where the children may have prepared for their retell of an upsetting episode. It is also important to note that the crying episodes here occur within the institution of an early childhood education setting where the interlocutors are children and teachers. In relation to this, Ruusuvuori (2013) suggests that the way in which emotions are attended to are institutionally bound 'as a way of attending to the institutional task at hand' (p. 340). In relation to the early childhood centre as an educational institution, the programmatic relevance of the interactions helped in understanding how teachers prioritised relational troubles over ongoing interactions. In relation to programmatic relevance, when a child displays that they are upset, the absence of an adult to provide comfort and care for that upset child would be noticeably absent. In an early childhood centre the teachers tend to be the only adults present and so are obliged to provide emotional care for upset children through their rights and obligations as members of a collection R category.

Within the New Zealand early childhood curriculum, *Te Whāriki*, such holistic aspects as 'well-being' and 'relationships' are on the agenda and so it is understandable then that attending to such emotional disputes in a way that enhances social solidarity would be expected. This finding aligns with Ruusuvuori

(2013) where 'another way to examine the management of emotion in institutions is to regard emotion displays not as a force to be controlled but as an affordance – an asset in performing professional tasks' (p. 348). In early childhood education, it would seem that the professional duty of attending to an emotional upset is a priority over other ongoing tasks in order to ensure the well-being and holistic care of all attending children.

Through providing response tokens that focus on the children's first-hand knowledge about the dispute episode, the teacher acknowledges the problem as belonging to the child and affords them the opportunity to discuss their understanding and feelings about the experience. This emotional disclosure between adult and child demonstrates how emotional, relational problems are attended to in compassionate ways, both verbally and with gesture, in the initiation of the interaction by the interlocutors. Subsequently, the interaction unfolds through the use of knowledge assertion and receipts where the teacher is often the less knowledgeable (K-) and the child is the more knowledgeable (K+), leading to a scaffolding of information (Waters and Bateman, 2013b) that co-produces a joint understanding about the occurrence of the episode between all members present.

Knowledge in disputes therefore appears as having systematic importance to the members in the process of addressing an emotional problem. However, the priority of a relational focus of affiliation is prominent in the interactions presented in this chapter where affiliation between teacher and child can be observed. These affiliations can be observed to be co-produced as a response to a troubles-telling and complaining action (Lindstrōm and Sorjonen, 2013) during disputes. Although working to produce an affiliation with a complainant or troubles telling is found to be avoided in institutions (Lindstrōm and Sorjonen, 2013), here in the institution of early childhood education, affiliation is found to be present between the interlocutors. This need for relational, affiliative interactions in the co-production of a collection R SRP is prevalent in the institution of early childhood education, even though it is an institution primarily concerned with teaching and knowledge. This important finding highlights early childhood education as an exceptional 'institution', the findings of which are attributed to the thorough and rigorous attention to talk available in CA.

Of particular significance to this chapter, and more broadly to the entirety of the book, is the work investigating children's disputes using MCA as complementary to CA, as this approach demonstrates how children attend to 'asymmetrical standard relational pairs (SRPs) of categories' (Hester and Hester, 2012) as a members' problem in the co-production of a dispute; the broader context of the analysis further reveals the 'omnirelevant category collection, namely, "parties to an oppositional relationship"' (p. 2). Through identifying the systematic ways in which the participants make relevant the category collections through their CBA and talk-in-interaction, the presence of omni-relevant devices becomes observable.

The next chapter, Chapter 6, will discuss how environmental features are talked into importance during everyday teaching and learning episodes between young children and their teachers. Through the detailed analysis of the talk-in-interaction in outdoor environments, the co-production of K and R category collections can be further explored in these situations. Observations of how safety and well-being are attended to as a matter of priority in these outdoor environments is also revealed.

Chapter 6

Learning Outside

The prior chapters have provided details of how social relationships between teachers and young children are co-produced through turns at talk and non-verbal gesture during pretend play episodes (Chapter 4) and in dispute situations (Chapter 5). This chapter will build on these prior findings in its exploration of how the environment is oriented to and utilised in the co-production of talk-in-interaction. More specifically, a focus on the way in which knowledge exchange and relational issues are managed around environmental features will be revealed, also building on the findings of the prior chapters. The observations in this chapter were taken in the outdoor areas of the early childhood education environment as well as from the regular weekly trip to the natural New Zealand bush. An analysis of the systematic organisation of turn-taking reveals the participant distribution of knowledge around environmental features as well as orientation to the emotional and physical care of the members present being of paramount importance during these interactions.

The Environment as a Pedagogical Tool

There has been an increased interest in academia regarding children's use of the natural outdoor environment due to a reduction in the amount of space that affords 'outdoor' types of play and limitations on the time that children spend playing outdoors without adult supervision (Maynard and Waters, 2007). As such, pedagogical practice in the outdoors has been a particularly significant area of interest with young children from early childhood through to primary schools. This interest is evident in the move to include outdoor education as an aspect of early childhood curricula (for example, in England and Wales). An increased interest in the environment as a pedagogical tool is also evident in Australasia where the benefits of risky play in the outdoor environment were explored in Australia (Little, Wyver and Gibson, 2011) and the bush environment was identified as a place that afforded unique opportunities for knowledge exchange between teachers and young children in New Zealand (Bateman and Waters, 2013; Bateman, Hohepa and Bennett, in press 2016).

A special issue of the Education 3–13 journal (see Maynard, 2007) highlights the importance of a natural outdoor environment for facilitating teaching and learning in early childhood, but also highlights some of the concerns facing teachers. Although the benefits of the outdoor environment in early childhood education are widely discussed (e.g., Bilton, 2010; Fjørtoft, 2004; Maynard,

Waters and Clement, 2013; Ouvry, 2003; Tovey, 2007; Waters and Maynard, 2010; Waters and Bateman, 2013a) the danger of the development of an over prescriptive use of the natural environment is also acknowledged (Waller, 2007). These issues call for further investigation into how natural outdoor environments are being used as part of everyday pedagogical teaching practice in relation to supporting educational curricula.

Environmental Noticings

When exploring interactions in the outdoor environment using a CA approach, an interest in how people engage with the environment by talking specific features into being is of significance (Heritage, 1984). By taking this perspective, what is important to those people at that time and for what purpose is revealed, as it becomes observable that whatever social action people are doing, they are doing it via that thing (Sacks, 1992a; 1992b).

Schegloff (2007a) discusses how orientation to a specific feature within an environmental surrounding is produced by members as a way of making something in the immediate environment 'noticeable' to others. This way of orienting to an environmental feature is described as being 'recipient-designed' to stimulate a response about that noticed thing from the recipient or interlocutor. In this situation, if the interlocutor does not respond to the noticing by also orienting to that thing, then it is a dispreferred response (Schegloff, 2007a). In this respect the preferred response to a noticing in a first pair part (FPP) would be to also orient to the thing being noticed in a second pair part (SPP) response. By both parties engaging in an interaction about a specific environmental feature, the interlocutors co-produce an affiliated interaction (Waters and Bateman, 2013) where an affective interest (Stivers, 2008) is shared between both members.

This can be achieved either by each member adding their knowledge about the specific environmental feature in a co-equal way, or by one member offering more information about the feature in a scaffolded 'teaching and learning' episode where there are asymmetries of knowledge present (Bateman and Waters, 2013). Schegloff (2007a) suggests that there must always be effort put in to the production of a noticing with regard to how the noticing of a specific feature has been carefully designed for a particular recipient. The rules of recipient-design suggest that the FPP utterance must always account for the recipients' prior knowledge concerning the thing that is being talked about to avoid telling others things that they already know. Therefore the prior knowledge of the recipient must always be taken into account.

Sacks (1992b) also discusses noticings and suggests that, by making a noticing about a physical attribution of the current speaker (in Sacks' example, a hole in the speaker's shoe), the attention is directed at the person who has the floor in an organised and obliged way. In this sense the speaker is the person who all the members are directing their attention to, producing the speaker as the main environmental interest, at that time in that place. This use of an orientation to an environmental feature can be broadly used to assert a speaker's immediate interests aimed towards a main subject of attention, where subsequent noticings from present others are not only expected, but are obligated. This is further supported by Sacks, who suggests that, 'the local resources are what people make conversations out of' (1992b, p. 92) and that talk about the place that members find themselves in together is a consistently appropriate topic of conversation. The importance that members place on the 'possessional relationship' between an environmental feature and a person are discussed where links between environmental features and members of society are viewed as a central concern for conversations and indicate an affiliative use of place orientation with the use of possessive pronouns, such as 'my' is used to demonstrate a possession over an environmental item (Sacks, 1992a).

Further links between people and place, or the way in which location is related to members, is discussed in relation to how people formulate their notions of place (Schegloff, 1972). Schegloff suggests that place names are often spoken with reference to geographical location (G) and people where the *relation to members* (Rm) is of utmost importance in securing a shared knowledge of the place being discussed. The speaker's orientation to place in Rm is thought to be a priority over mentioning a geographical feature, demonstrating the importance of social presence in everyday talk. These conversational features are used in the process of co-selecting topics of conversation, as an analysis of the activity tied to the mentioned place and people are discussed. When selecting a formulation of place it is suggested that,

> The selection of a 'right' term and the hearing of a term as adequate, appear to involve sensitivity to the respective locations of the participant and the referent (which can change over the course of the interaction); to the membership composition of the interaction, and the knowledge of the world seen by members to be organized by membership categories (where the composition can change over the course of the interaction); and to the topic or activity being done in the conversation at that point in its course. (Schegloff, 1972, p. 114–115)

This indicates the changing and evolving nature of the membership categories evident between the same members in their interactions with one another around the topic of location, suggesting that social relationships between the same people change fluidly throughout a sequence of interactions as they change their membership category compositions.

Schegloff (1972) suggests that 'names are to be used only when expectably recognized' (p. 92) where, if someone who is about to use a name is unsure whether the recipient will be able to recognise the person being talked about, they will either avoid using a specific name or enquire epistemic access to the recipient's knowledge of the name about to be given, 'do you know X?' Place names are used in a similar way where a shared knowledge of a place between interlocutors indicates a shared membership to a group of people who are 'in the know' about that specific location; when a person does not have a shared knowledge of a place they can be identified as 'strangers' (p. 93). This is linked to the work on 'insiders' and 'outsiders' where an outsider can be comparable to a 'stranger' due to their lack of 'insider' knowledge (Sacks, 1992a; Schegloff, 2007a). In relation to category R and K collections, an outsider is the dispreferred person to turn to for help as they do not have an emotional relationship and so bond of obligation as a member of the R collection would; but they can be the proper person to approach for knowledge (K), as identified in the work on suicide calls (e.g., Sacks, 1967).

A members' categorisation of others is evident on the way they approach talk about places with others, as the speaker will take into account the epistemological stance of the hearer's prior place knowledge when formulating their talk about that location (Schegloff, 1972). This is important for the everyday flow of conversation as a preferred response would be a mutual and shared understanding of the location, and trouble would be indicated by a failure of shared understanding. This lack of shared familiarity regarding a place can also demonstrate asymmetries of knowledge in everyday conversations where one person's knowledge is revealed through the sequences of turn-taking; the more knowledgeable person will often have a longer turn at talk to pass specific information on to the less knowledgeable person (Bateman and Waters, 2013). This particular conversational structure in the exchanging of knowledge is observable in teaching practice where teachers use informings to 'impart information from the informer to the recipient' (Gardner and Mushin, 2013, p. 63). However, although one would assume that informings would be prevalent in educational arenas where knowledge would be passed between teachers and students, Gardner and Mushin (2013) found that instances of such teacher informings were extremely rare.

Knowledge exchange around a relational problem about the environment

The following observations reveal how knowledge exchange is employed in the process of attending to relational problems in the outdoor environment between children and early childhood teachers. The first observation, Excerpt 1, takes place on one of the regular outdoor excursions to a local natural New Zealand bush environment that the early childhood teachers take the preschool children to.

Excerpt 1: Sam

Three preschool teachers and a group of preschool children arrive by minibus to a local bushland area. They gather together on a small bridge just in front of the forest entrance. After engaging in the routine of asking the Māori God of the forest, Tāne Mahuta, permission to enter the forest (see Bateman, Hohepa and Bennett, forthcoming, 2016 for analysis of this procedure) one of the preschool teachers asks the children to choose which way they would like to go, left or right. The majority of children stand to the left, but Matthew stands to the right on his own.

Learning Outside 105

The preschool teacher Sam (SAM) is holding hands with Aata (ATA) at the entrance of the forest. Matthew (MTW) is slightly ahead of them slowly stepping backwards to the right, away from the other children.

```
01 MTW:     ↑I'm- I'm sc↓a::red of that ((points to the forest
02          entrance on the left))
03          (0.4)
04 SAM:     ↑Ma:th:ew↓
05          (1.6)
06 MTW:     scared of go[ing in the::re
07 SAM:                 [are you going to come
08          (0.5)
09 SAM:     pardon
10 MTW:     *I'm (a bit) sca:red (to go in there)=there's
11          gho:sts in there↑*
12 SAM:     there's no gh↓osts in there Matthew↑
13 ATA:     there's Mahuta and there's ↑no:- Mah-=
14 SAM:                                            =come on we're
15          going to wash our fe↑et ((walks towards Matthew
16          whilst still holding Aata's hand))
17          (2.1)
18 SAM:     [come on
19 ATA:     [there's no ghostses in:: Mahuta's
20 SAM:     this way ((holds Matthew's hand))
21 ATA:     no [(                          )]
22 MTW:        [no it's not pointing that wa::y] it's pointing
23          ↑this way ((points to a sign that is pointing to
24          the right))
25 SAM:     cos that says to the log hauler point and we're
26          going to maybe see our hut or the waterfall .hh
27          that's th↑is way
28 MTW:     I don't want [to go to the waterfall] or your hut↓
29 ATA:                  [lets go to the waterfall]
30 SAM:     why not
31 MTW:     cos ↓I didn't make it with you::↑ two
32 SAM:     you didn't make it with us but that's o̅k:: (0.4)
33          most of the children who made it aren't in (place
34          name) anymore↓
35 MTW:     [(    )]
36 ATA:     [(    )]
37 SAM:     well that's true but you can still look at it
38 MTW:     I:: don't want to go up here: I don't want to-
39 SAM:     it's alright Matthew (0.5) I- I will make sure
40          nothing happens to you↓
```

As mentioned in the introduction, just prior to this sequence of actions the preschool teachers and children have come to a majority decision about which entrance of the forest to use, encouraging the children to have autonomy in their teaching and learning experiences as endorsed in the New Zealand national curriculum (MoE, 1996). However, Matthew was not part of the majority who decided to choose that particular entrance and he is now expressing his concerns about joining in the activity with the other children, stating that he is scared 'of that' and pointing to the forest entrance (lines 01–02). Through doing this Matthew shares knowledge about his perspective with Sam and his peers, both verbally and physically to maximise understanding (Bateman, 2012b) about his situation where he is the expert (Corsaro, 1997). Through sharing his knowledge, Matthew relates to his emotional feelings about the situation – that he is scared. There is a slight pause before and after Sam calls Matthew's name, and this is followed by Matthew reiterating his situation of being too scared to enter the forest (line 06).

Rather than immediately offering Matthew any relational help with his emotional upset, Sam overlaps Matthew's utterance by asking him if he is going to come (line 07). This is followed by a brief pause and Sam asking Matthew for clarification in his other-initiated repair, an action that is found to be the non-preferred strategy of repair due to it being less effective compared to self-correction, as it may take a number of turns to rectify (Schegloff, Jefferson and Sacks, 1977). This orientation to the repair of a shared understanding between the interlocutors suggests that, rather than ignoring Matthew's sharing of knowledge about his feelings of being scared, Sam needed further information from Matthew concerning his trouble.

Matthew replies by giving further explanation about his problem, but this time downgrades his trouble: 'I'm a bit scared' and offers a rationale for why he is scared of the place: because 'there's ghosts in there' (lines 10 – 11). Through this verbal action and non-verbal gesture of backing away from the entrance, Matthew demonstrates that he has a problem with this particular environmental feature as being associated with the negative emotion of being scary. Sam responds to this information from Matthew by providing a contrasting view of the environmental feature as he tells Matthew that there are 'no ghosts in there Matthew' (line 12). This could be heard in two different ways, either as a strategy to comfort Matthew's fear where Sam offers reassurance that no such trouble is apparent, or as an oppositional, dispreferred response to Matthew's knowledge about the current environment they are in.

This potential conflict situation arises from a competing demonstration of personal knowledge where Matthew states his knowledge about there being ghosts 'in there' and Sam asserting his knowledge that there are 'no ghosts in there'. This situation of two people offering their knowledge and neither assertion being accepted by the recipient was shown to co-produce a dispute in the prior chapter (Chapter 5). This current situation also suggests a possible trouble source over a K+/K+ position where neither recipient accepts the knowledge.

Matthew's telling to Sam and Aata that he is scared of going into that particular entrance of the forest because of ghosts can be linked to Schegloff (1972) where the geographical (G) location here is being linked to its relation to members (Rm), who are thought to be connected to that place. Matthew argues that as these residing members are scary, it is a good reason to avoid that particular geographical location. To counter this argument, Sam responds by suggesting that no such members live in that location (line 12); Sam does not suggest that ghosts do not exist, merely that they are not in the place where Matthew suggests they are. This is then followed by Aata, the child who Sam is holding hands with, joining in the conversation as he states that 'Mahuta' (the Māori God of the forest) is there (line 14) and then also that there are 'no ghosts in Mahuta's' (line 19), presenting his own knowledge about the place that supports Sam's stance. Further alignment with Schegloff's (1972) link between Rm and G can be observed in this utterance where Aata identifies the whole geographical location of the bushland as 'Mahuta's' (line 19), demonstrating that young preschool children also link a place with its relation to members.

Sam's utterances 'come on' and 'this way' (lines 14–20) try to persuade Matthew to enter the forest with directives (Goodwin, 2006; Kent, 2012). Such directives have been found in parental interactions with children where the parent tries to get the child to do something that the child is resisting to do (Kent, 2012). In such cases the parental directive is often responded to with a child's reluctance to comply, inevitably leading to a dispute. Sam's directive to Matthew to 'come on' is also coupled with a non-verbal gesture as he holds his hand and physically guides him towards the entrance of the forest that he has been resisting, an action otherwise known as 'shepherding' (Cekaite, 2010).

Matthew's next turn at talk asserts another conflicting statement towards Sam and another argument to support his reason for not entering the forest from that particular entrance; this time Matthew suggests that they are going in the opposite direction to a nearby signpost (lines 22–24). Matthew's orientation to this particular environmental feature works in support of his argument to go in the opposite direction as he makes the direction of the signpost 'noticeable' to everyone to stimulate a response (Schegloff, 1972). However, Sam shares his knowledge of this particular environmental feature as he explains that the hut and the waterfall are in the opposite direction to the sign, and therefore they do need to go that way (lines 25–27). As with the prior turns at talk between Sam and Matthew, these turns demonstrate how both participants provide their own knowledge about the environment to produce conflicting support for their oppositional stance.

In their next actions, both Matthew and Aata give opposing ideas about where to go in overlap of each other as Matthew suggests that he does not want to go to 'your hut' and Aata uses a collective preterm, *let's*, to suggest that they all go to the waterfall (line 28 and 29). Aata's *let's* works to create oppositional social dynamics to Matthew's *your hut* in that Aata's utterance connects the participants in a collective action and invites unity, whereas Matthew's identifies the specific environmental feature as belonging exclusively to Sam as an individual. Here, the 'possessional relationship' between the environmental feature of the hut and the people whom it belongs to is brought into play (Sacks, 1992a) where Matthew disaffiliates himself from the place by calling it 'your hut'.

Sam responds to Matthew's assertion about not wanting to go to the waterfall by further enquiring into the reason for this, initiating a why type question, indicating an asymmetry of knowledge between the asker and the answerer and also providing a challenging stance towards the answerer's accountability (Bolden and Robinson, 2011). Sam's direct question to Matthew about 'why' he does not want to go to the hut requires Matthew to produce an account, and he does so in his next turn as he suggests that he 'didn't make it with you two' (line 31). Matthew does not have a shared experience of building the hut with Sam and Aata and so does not have the same 'common sense geography' (Schegloff, 1972) or ownership over the environmental feature that the other members do, making Matthew the 'outsider' in this situation.

In this interaction Matthew offers three different reasons for why he does not want to enter the forest, initially with reference to (G) and (Rm) (Schegloff, 1972) by suggesting that there are ghosts in there, then that the sign is pointing in the opposite direction, and finally because he has not been part of the group that built the hut that they are going to see. Each time Matthew's assertions are responded to by Sam with direct conflicting utterances as he tells him that there are no ghosts, that they need to go in the opposite direction of the sign and that even though he did not help to make the hut he can still visit it. Through these sequences of knowledge exchange, Matthew also asserts an emotional problem of being scared and Sam's final response marks a more empathic stance towards this by offering some reassurance as he tells Matthew, 'I will make sure nothing happens to you' (lines 39–40).

Of significance here is the systematic way in which the participants attended to this trouble. The interaction began with an emotional upset being presented by one of the children, followed by knowledge exchange that worked to provide accounts for why the situation was perceived as problematic. The emotional upset is then sequentially responded to by the teacher following his accumulation of this new knowledge when he does attend to this trouble towards the end of the interaction in a way that makes demonstrable his rights and obligations to give help. Although most of the interaction demonstrates the co-production of a category K collection between Sam and Matthew, these interactions also work towards a more emotional giving and receiving of relational care where Matthew asserts his need for help with an emotional problem and Sam provides care for Matthew's safety and well-being in the co-production of a collection R SRP by offering his personal protection and reassurance.

Attending to the Safety of an Environmental Feature

Excerpt 2: Sam

During the walk through the bush, a teacher who is ahead of Sam on the trail stops to take a photograph of an environmental feature on the path. When Sam and the preschool child, Jenny (JEN), catch up to the teacher (TCH) and children the following occurs:

```
01 SAM:     ↓what were we looking a:t↑
02          1.7 ((teacher turns to look at Sam))
03 TCH:     ↓fungus (   ) ((points to the pathway))
04 SAM:     ↑a:h::↓ (1.4) >a=little=mushroom↓< (1.3) can you
05          see it↑ ((looks at Jenny. Crouches down and points
06          to the mushroom))
07          0.9
08 JEN:     is it ↓poi:↑son ((crouches down next to Sam and
09          looks closely at the mushroom))
10 SAM:     ↓probably (0.7) we don't normally ↑touch them: j-
11          incase they're poisonous
12 JEN:     how=bout <glu:bs>
13 SAM:     if we had gloves that would be alright↑ ((turns to
14          look at Jenny))
15 JEN:     how=bout $heaps of layers of glubs$ ((mimics the
16          action of putting on gloves and leans in towards
17          Sam smiling))
18 SAM:     well ↓you'd only ne↑ed ↓one::↑
```

Sam attends to a moment of interest around an environmental feature as he begins this interaction with the teacher who is looking at the ground with a group of children as he approaches. He initiates the interaction through displaying his lack of knowledge about the current situation as he asks the teacher 'what were we looking at' (line 01), using the collective proterm 'we' to produce a collective action between himself and the teacher (Bateman, 2011; Butler, 2008; Sacks, 1992a) and establishing joint attention around the noticing of an environmental feature (Kidwell and Zimmerman, 2007; Schegloff, 2007a). The teacher shares her knowledge with Sam as she gives him her first-hand experience information (Heritage and Raymond, 2005) as she explains that they have been looking at 'fungus' (line 03). Sam demonstrates that this new knowledge has been successfully received through his change of state response token (Heritage, 1984) with his 'ah' receipt (line 04). These initial knowledge exchange actions demonstrate that even though the teachers were not walking together on the path, they ensure that the children they are walking with experience a similar outdoor educational experience through systematically attending to each other's actions.

Once this new knowledge about the situation has been received, Sam goes on to relay the information to Jenny through a formulation of the environmental feature description. Here, Sam's formulation of 'fungus' (line 03) is 'a little mushroom' (line 04), spoken quickly as Sam becomes 'an active interpreter of the preceding talk' (Hutchby, 2005b, p. 310). Sam's interpretation of the prior teacher's talk makes the noticing of the environmental feature more specific and possibly more child friendly, making his knowledge distribution to Jenny more accessible through recipient design (Schegloff, 2007a). This display of joint understanding is imperative in the natural flow of everyday conversation where 'a basic normative assumption about talk is that, whatever else, it should be correctly interpretable in the special sense of conveying to the intended recipients what the sender more or less wanted to get across' (Goffman, 1981, p. 10).

A joint understanding is also imperative for successful knowledge exchange in teaching and learning moments where a range of verbal teaching strategies are used by teachers to maximise learning opportunities for children (Carr, 2011; Siraj-Blatchford and Manni, 2008). This type of factual informing, or 'telling' has occasionally been found within teaching and learning situations where a more knowledgeable person passes on information to a less knowledgeable person (Gardner and Mushin, 2013). There is a second brief pause, an opportunity for Jenny to respond which is not taken up, followed by Sam directing Jenny's attention to the feature as he asks Jenny if she can see it (lines 04–05), maximising the potential for joint attention through a 'showing' (Kidwell and Zimmerman, 2007).

There is a brief pause before Jenny responds to Sam's question, and when she does attend to the environmental feature she orients to the safety aspects of it as a primary interest, putting inflection on the word 'poison' (line 08), indicating that this is an important piece of knowledge that she needs here and now in this situation. Sam attends to this issue of safety that Jenny has raised by downgrading his information that the mushroom is 'probably' poisonous and follows this by orienting to the importance of not touching them as a collective action (line 09). This distribution of knowledge here is essential for the safety and well-being of the people involved. Here, Sam fulfils his obligation to provide help for the children he is caring for by telling Jenny not to touch the potentially harmful environmental feature, protecting her from physical harm.

Jenny then elaborates on how to protect from this potential poisoning harm as she suggests the wearing of gloves (pronounced 'glubs') (line 12) and Sam confirms this idea by agreeing that wearing gloves would alleviate the potential physical harm (line 13). Jenny works to upgrade this affirmed idea by suggesting that you could wear more than one pair of gloves for protection against poisoning whilst the smile talk could indicate that she is not serious (Jefferson, 2004). However, Sam returns to the seriousness of the situation with a second factual informing stating that you would really only need one pair of gloves to protect you.

The knowledge passed here is responsive to Jenny's concern about physical safety and is primarily related to the health and well-being of those interacting with the environmental feature rather than talk about other 'educational' aspects of the mushroom, such as how and/or why it grows in the bush location etc. As such, the orientation to physical care and well-being is observable as a priority item within the knowledge exchange here when engaging in an environmental noticing, suggesting the co-production of the category R collection as being of primary importance where members are obliged to give and receive relational care in such situations.

Teachers Attending to Priority Items during Knowledge Exchange about Environmental Features

These next excerpts extend on these prior ideas and demonstrate how teachers attend to a potentially problematic situation in relation to physical and emotional care-giving to the children and the omni-relevance of a collection R SRP in the everyday interactions between teachers and children.

Excerpt 3: Sam

Four preschool boys are playing in the sandpit while the teacher, Sam, is sitting nearby. Michael (MIC), Liam (LAM) and two other boys are digging around the same area with their spades. A hosepipe is running water in an area of the sandpit that is quite close to them. Some of the water runs into the hole they are digging.

```
01 MIC:        oh: lo↑ok ↓a wa↑terfall:: ((stops digging and looks
02             at the sand))
03 SAM:        ((walks towards the boys))
04             (5.2)
05 SAM:        loo::ks↓ good Michael↑
06 MIC:        look↑ ↓a wa↑terfall ↓down th↑[ere::: ((bends down
07             and points to a part of the sand))
08 SAM:                                     [it ↑is:::
09             ((two of the boys walk away towards the hosepipe))
10 MIC:        *it's ↓wobb↑ly↓ ↓wobb↑ly↓ ↑eh::*
11 SAM:        Urgh ((sits down on the sand opposite Michael))
12             (3.7)
13             ((Michael picks up handfuls of sand and sprinkles
14             them in another area of the sandpit))
15 SAM:        where's all ↑**this** sand coming from do you think↓
16→BOY:        °>sorry<° ((hits Sam's leg with his spade))
17→SAM:        >that's< alri:ght↑
18 MIC:        here comes- here comes the ra:::in↓= ((stands over
```

```
19                  the 'waterfall' and sprinkles sand onto it))
20  SAM:                                         =look all the
21                  sand is coming down↓ with the wa↑ter ((points to a
22                  place in the sand))
```

Sam is observing the preschool boys in the sandpit as they are digging holes and building things. Michael makes an environmental noticing 'oh look a waterfall' (line 01), and Sam responds to his noticing by walking over to him, making the situation one of important significance as he attends to Michael's interest in the environmental feature. The first few lines of this interaction show how one of the boys draws attention to a particular part of the sand and how Sam uses this environmental feature to support the educational concept of notice, recognise and respond (MoE, 1996), treating the event as a learning opportunity. This is demonstrated as the child mobilises an interest by talking it into being (Heritage, 1978; Bateman, 2011) and Sam noticing the child's interest and recognising it as an opportunity for a teaching and learning interaction as he approaches the children and orients his talk to the feature throughout the interaction.

Sam starts this teaching moment as he sits down next to the children and the sand (line 11) and begins a typical teaching enquiry as he asks the children where they think the sand is coming from (line 15). This type of verbal action is encouraged in early childhood teaching practice as it helps stimulate possibility thinking in young children (Burnard et al., 2006) and affords opportunities for developing working theories about the world (Bateman, 2013; Carr, 2011; Peters and Davies, 2011; Hargraves, 2013; Hedges, 2011). Through responding to Michael's interest in such a way, Sam is following the child's lead to realise a teachable moment (Hyun and Marshall, 2003). Sam then begins a typical teaching and learning episode as he uses an open question to prompt thinking about the construction of the 'waterfall' and makes explicit reference to Michael's epistemic state at the end of his utterance in tag position 'do you think'. Sam's use of 'do you think' (line 15) in tag position opens up an opportunity for the children to do some guess work and assert an opinion rather than be correct in their answer (Sacks, 1992a). Through each member contributing to the conversation around knowledge of the workings of the environment, their membership to the K collection category is co-produced.

Whilst this talk around the environmental feature of the waterfall progresses, one of the preschool boys walks past Sam and, as he does so, his spade hits Sam on the leg (line 16). As soon as this happens he immediately apologises to Sam, and Sam suspends his ongoing interaction to reassure the boy that 'that's all right' (line 17). In these initial turns and talk, Sam has responded to Michael's interest in an environmental feature and taken the opportunity to shape the talk into a teaching and learning episode until a very minor accident occurs that prioritises his attention. This abrupt shift from an interaction with one child to an interaction with another is not oriented to as problematic by any of the participants and so is accepted. Following this very brief insertion sequence Sam orients his attention back to Michael and the teaching and learning exchange.

Excerpt 4: Sam

Sam (SAM), the early childhood teacher, is in the garden of the early childhood centre. He is standing next to the outdoor climbing apparatus talking to two of the preschool children, Zion (ZIN) and Aata (ATA). Zion is sitting on a wooden plank situated across two large cubes like a bridge; Aata is sitting on one of the cubes and facing Zion.

```
01 ZIN:      ↓I can↑ sit- I can just hold onto the b↑ox↓ ((leans
02           across the plank of wood))
03 SAM:      ↓cool there's a little (0.3) pa↑ssion vine hopper↓
04           ((points to the insect on the plank of wood))
05 SAM:      ((both boys lean down to look at the insect))
06 ATA:      ↓Ah::↑
07 ZIN:      (      )
08 ATA:      ↓what is it
09 SAM:      That's a passion vine hopper=they're naughty=they
10           suck all the juice out of our erm vegetables↓
11 ZIN:      Sucks it aye= ((wobbles on the plank))
12→SAM:              =>↓yeah↓<=are you alri:ght↑ (0.3) ↓you
13→          ↑look like you might fall↓ off ((looks at Zion))
14 ZIN:      no
15 SAM:      no
```

Later in the interaction, Sam is still engaged in conversation
with Aata and Zion when his attention is turned to one of the
other children in the playground.

```
50→SAM:              =o::h↓ (2.5) you alright M↑i:ke
51           ((looks across the playground and walks towards a
52           child who has fallen off the apparatus))
```

From the beginning of this observation (line 01), Zion is observably interacting with the environment, orienting to how he wants to use it both verbally and physically as he lays on the plank of wood holding onto one of the cubes to steady himself. Zion demonstrates his knowledge of how to interact with the environment and his autonomy over the situation as he tells Sam about what he is able to do. This initial utterance by Zion demonstrates Zion's competencies as he chooses to share his knowledge about his abilities to interact with the apparatus with Sam and Aata.

Sam orients to another environmental feature as he draws the children's attention to the 'passion vine hopper' insect (line 03). The citing of a name of a person has been found to indicate the speaker's prior knowledge of the person being referred to (Sacks, 1992a) where the use of a specific name of an environmental feature can indicate that the speaker has prior knowledge of an environmental feature in the same way (Bateman and Waters, 2013; Schegloff, 1972). Schegloff (1972) discusses that names are only used by speakers when they are sure that interlocutors have a familiarity of that person or place in order to achieve a preferred response in the form of a shared knowledge; this way the conversation can move on in a more efficient way than if repairs were needed. However, in this interaction between Sam and Zion, Sam's use of the insect's name 'passion vine hopper' (line 03) leads to a failure of shared understanding when Aata indicates that he has no prior knowledge of the insect (line 08). Aata's use of a question to gain further information about the insect indicates an asymmetry of knowledge between Sam and Aata where Sam is the more knowledgeable in this situation (Bateman and Waters, 2013). Aata's lack of knowledge about the insect is noticed and responded to by Sam as he elaborates on what the insect is and does, in a possible informing (Gardner and Mushin, 2013), making it demonstrable that Sam does have more knowledge about the insect (lines 9–10).

In doing so Sam deals with this asymmetry of knowledge by proceeding to inform the children of further information about the insect, producing an educational interaction with conversational features similar to scaffolding (Waters and Bateman, 2013). With regard to teaching and learning, scaffolding is one way of increasing a person's knowledge about something in a way that demonstrates an informing from the more knowledgeable and possible asymmetries between the interlocutors; this is evident in lines 03–10. In this instance Sam and Aata co-produce a category K collection as Aata selects Sam as being the proper person to turn to for knowledge about identifying what the passion vine hopper was. Sam responds by showing himself as the more knowledgeable in the situation, initially through his production of a specific name for the insect and subsequently through his elaboration on the characteristics of the passion vine hopper. In this section of talk Sam is seen to be doing 'teaching' where he holds the floor to pass knowledge on to Aata as a less knowledgeable other.

Unlike Aata Zion demonstrates that he does have some prior knowledge of the insect as he adds his knowledge about the insect sucking (line 11). In doing so Zion shows a possible affiliation with Sam (Stivers, 2008; Waters and Bateman, 2013) as they have a shared knowledge and experience of the actions that the insect engages in, making them both 'insiders' as they share the same knowledge about that thing (Schegloff, 1972). Through demonstrating affiliation with someone, members assert themselves as being like that person who they are affiliated with by application of the consistency rule (Sacks, 1992a). Observations of children's talk-in-interaction in their social organisation show that children will make reference to membership and affiliation with certain people and in doing so make their relationships with one another relevant (Butler, 2008). Through assertion of a shared knowledge about an environmental feature, in this instance an insect, Zion demonstrates that he is a member of the category of people who are 'in the know' about this particular environmental thing (Schegloff, 1972).

When Zion demonstrates his knowledge about the passion vine hopper (line 11), he begins to wobble slightly on the plank of wood he is laying on. This non-verbal action is touched off and responded to by Sam immediately as he latches on to the end of Zion's utterance to ask if he is all right (lines 12–13). Sam's immediate orientation to Zion's safety and well-being demonstrates a direct shift from 'educational' talk about the task at hand, the exploration of an insect, to the relational care of one of the members present. Although this utterance asks for specific epistemic knowledge, putting Zion in the more knowledgeable position and presenting Zion as the person to turn to for advice about his personal situation, it also invokes Zion's personal safety as a priority over the ongoing interaction.

Through attending to the physical safety and well-being of Zion in such a way, Sam demonstrates his obligation to provide relational care for Zion as a priority item (Sacks, 1992a) over his 'educational teaching' activity. Sam's enquiry into Zion's safety is prioritised over the ongoing conversation about the insect and demonstrates the importance of the priority item as it overrules anything else being discussed in the ongoing interaction due to its significance at that time with those particular participants. Through enquiring about Zion's physical well-being Sam asserts himself as having a bond of obligation to offer this type of care for Zion in his role as a co-member of the SRP belonging to the R collection of members. The rights and obligations to give and receive relational help when issues of safety and well-being are jeopardised in situ aligns with addressing the goals of the New Zealand early childhood curriculum and positions these two members as belonging to the R category collection.

The omitted sequence of talk returned to the environment and how you have to be mindful of your actions when interacting with it. This interaction continues until Sam attends to a similar priority item concerning the well-being of another child in the playground as he notices a child falling off the apparatus they are climbing on (line 50). The immediacy of Sam's reference to the well-being of the children in his care overrules the ongoing 'teaching' interactions that constitute knowledge exchange, demonstrating the importance, or higher level hierarchy that the R collection has over the K collection in these instances. This excerpt also demonstrates how the membership category compositions change between the incumbents over the course of the interaction (Schegloff, 1972). As the relational utterance was inserted into the conversation in such a way, it could be observable as being omni-relevant, as omni-relevant devices 'do not follow any given last occurrence, but when they are appropriate, they have priority' (Sacks, 1992a, p. 313).

Excerpt 5: Jamilla

Jamilla (JAM) is sitting in the playroom with a group of toddlers. Two girls, Gemma (GMA) and Jenny (JEN), aged two and a half years are sitting in front of Jamilla. Jamilla has pictures of ducks on her t-shirt. Gemma points to the pictures and starts talking about them.

```
01  GMA:        ↑Why you got cats on ↓there↑ ((points to
02              Jamilla's t-shirt))
03  JAM:        Why I've got what on there
04              (0.4)
05  GMA:        cats↓
06  JAM:        ↑do they look like cats↓
07              (0.4)
08  GMA:        Like du↑cks↓
09  JAM:        du::cks yes they do look like ducks (0.3) why do
10              you think I have ducks on there↓
11  JEN:        those are duck=ducks↓ ((points at Jamilla's t-
12              shirt))
13  JAM:        >yep< (0.4) what are the ducks
14→             >doing<=<↑ca:reful::l> ((a boy, Joe, walks closely
15              between Jamilla and a chair and trips over.
16→             Jamilla looks at Joe and pushes the chair
17→             further away from him, then looks back at the
18              girls))
19  JOE:        ((stands up and rubs his knees then walks away))
20  JEN:        wap wap
21  JAM:        ↑what does a duck do↓ (0.8) what sound does a duck
22              make↓
```

Jamilla and the children are engaged in a conversation about the pictures on her t-shirt, initiated by one of the toddlers (Gemma) as she makes a noticing that they are animals and asks a 'why' type question to Jamilla about the pictures. Gemma's question about the pictures is supported with a non-verbal pointing, observed to help achieve joint attention and communicating her intentions (Filipi, 2009) and to help maximise shared understanding (Bateman, 2012b). Through these actions Gemma initiates an interaction with Jamilla as asking a question in a first pair part (FPP) requires the recipient to give an answer in a second pair part (SPP) response (Schegloff, 1992a). Gemma's use of a question about an environmental feature that has interested her indicates that she has less knowledge about the feature than the teacher in this instance, suggesting that she is currently in the K- position (Heritage, 2012a).

However, there is a dispreferred response by Jamilla as, rather than responding with a direct answer to Gemma's question, a failure of shared understanding is revealed and conversation repair is called for where Jamilla asks for clarification about the feature Gemma is asking about (line 03). Gemma replies by drawing attention to the animals on Jamilla's t-shirt, but incorrectly calls them cats, they are actually ducks. Jamilla attends to this discrepancy by asking if they 'look like cats', and therefore not directly correcting Gemma's identification but providing an opportunity for her to assert her opinion about what she thinks the animals look like. Sacks (1992a) suggests that an opinion can be asserted by a person when they do not have explicit knowledge about something, and therefore still providing them with an opportunity to engage in the ongoing conversation. Through being able to give an opinion about what she deems the pictures on Jamilla's t-shirt to look like, she can contribute to the interaction about the environmental feature without having any specific knowledge about it (Sacks, 1992a).

There is a slight pause before Gemma answers with her opinion that the pictures actually look like ducks (line 08). Jamilla gives a preferred response to this opinion as she agrees with Gemma, and then moves to extend the interaction further as she adds a question about the feature. This question seeks information from Gemma about her knowledge regarding the reason for why Jamilla has pictures of ducks on her t-shirt, affording the opportunity for a further opinion and the prolonging of the interaction between herself and Gemma through a question-answer sequence.

However, at this point a second toddler girl, Jenny, intervenes in the interaction as she identifies the pictures on Jamilla's t-shirt correctly. Jamilla then takes the opportunity to further extend the interaction by asking another question directly after positively confirming the answer to the prior question. This type of systematic questioning is found in early childhood education due to the endorsement of teachers using 'open-ended' questions to stimulate knowledge building in teaching and learning episodes (Bateman, 2013). This finding combined with insights from CA also suggests that questions are asked by teachers in order to sustain interactions with children, as the child will understand that a question requires an answer and reply in the turn allocation space, and therefore maintaining and extending the ongoing interaction. As 'sustained' interactions are also encouraged in early childhood education (Sylva et al., 2010) it is easy to see how question-answer sequences provide a way for teachers to be able to maintain teaching and learning episodes whilst attending to knowledge exchange. Through engaging in such K+ and K- turns at talk, the members can be seen to co-produce a category K collection from the start of this interaction.

Although the interaction so far has been co-produced through knowledge exchanges, and as such, asserting a category K collection as the members attend to each person's knowledge regarding the environmental feature, the interaction momentarily turns to a relational activity concerning the immediate well-being of a child when a toddler passes between Jamilla and a chair and trips over. During this part of the interaction (lines 14–17) Jamilla is asking a question to the girls when the incident happens. Jamilla finishes her utterance quickly when the boy trips, latching the end of her question to the utterance 'careful', speaking in a higher pitch, and placing emphasis and extending the word, indicating that the prosody of the utterance gives more attention to the word 'careful' (Schegloff, 1998).

When analysing talk-in-interaction, 'the rigor of our attention to *action* should not be less than that of our attention to *prosody*' (Schegloff, 1998, p. 254). The importance of synthesising talk, prosody and gesture when analysing interactions is recommended in order to provide insight into interactions in their totality (C. Goodwin, 2014; M. H. Goodwin, 2014; Ceite; 2014). In this instance Jamilla shifts all her attention to the problematic situation of a child tripping over a chair, not only by abruptly abandoning her current verbal interaction with two other children to suggest that the boy be 'careful', but by also by physically moving the chair out of the way in her reaction to the event. Through Jamilla's verbal and non-verbal actions the priority she is giving to the activity of caring for a child's safety and well-being in that interaction is demonstrated, making observable the rights and obligations tied to the giving and receiving of relational care to the people present (Sacks, 1972, 1992a) over knowledge exchange.

This display of verbal and physical help offered to the child during his accident is one that can describe the members as co-producing a category R collection as the teacher is obliged to give such help to a child who is in need of it, and the child has a right to receive such relational help. Through momentarily abandoning her child-initiated interaction regarding knowledge exchange about an environmental feature, attending to the relational care of the child is describable as overruling the current topic of talk. This action demonstrates the importance of the teacher attending to the relational care of children in that time and with those members and the omni-relevance of this relational activity. Once the boy stands up and walks away, Jamilla returns to the more 'educational' kind of talk expected in a teacher-child interaction as she asks the children about their knowledge regarding animal noises (lines 20–22).

Excerpt 6: Sarah

The preschool children have taken Chipmunk, the preschool duckling, out of his preschool habitat. The preschool children, including Stephen (STE) and Emma (EMMA), have filled up a large bucket with water and Chipmunk is now swimming in it. The children continue to pour small containers of water into the bucket whilst Chipmunk swims. Emma carries a particularly large container of water towards the preschool teacher Sarah (SAR) and the duckling.

```
09  SAR:       Shall we see if she wants a ↑swi:m↑
10  STE:       ↑>yep<↑
11  SAR:       ((Carries Chipmunk and places him in the bucket of
12             water))
13  STE:       Her needs it deep (0.8) yeah=her need
14             it↓deep↓(0.9) I'll make it deeper for her then she
15             can swim easily↓ ((pours water into the bucket))
16             now her can- now her- (0.4) °what's the black
17             things=↓sand↓°((uses a jug to transfer more water
18             to the bucket from a nearby water tray))
19  SAR:       ↓Well:: (1.3) here comes Emma with a who↓:le heap
20             of ↑wa:ter↓
21             (0.7)
22→            care::ful when you tip it in sw↑eet (0.3) that you
23→            don't- ((takes hold of the bucket))
```

At the start of this interaction, Sarah holds on to Chipmunk as the children fill up a bucket of water for the duck to swim in. Once the water reaches a particular level Sarah asks if they should see if she wants a swim (line 09). Stephen responds to Sarah's question by giving a preferred response, albeit a very quick one, as he agrees that they should see if the duck is ready for a swim (line 10). Responding to Stephen's agreement, Sarah carries the duck over to the bucket and places him into it gently (lines 11–12). Once Chipmunk is in the water, Stephen announces his actions of making the water deeper and a rationale to explain why he is doing it, as he demonstrates his knowledge about how to take care of a duck.

Stephen notices something black in the water and begins to ask a question about what it is, but quickly answers himself as he identifies the objects as sand (lines 16–17). During these initial exchanges Sarah offers the children an opportunity to contribute in the decision-making about what to do with the duck, implementing the early childhood curriculum strand 'Contribution' and principle of 'Empowerment' as she does so (MoE, 1996). This opportunity to contribute is taken up by Stephen as he demonstrates his expertise in duck husbandry. Each turn at talk here attends to knowledge about Chipmunk the duck.

Sarah then makes an environmental noticing as she watches Emma carry a container of water towards the bucket which Chipmunk is swimming in, and makes Emma aware that she has seen her through her verbal noticing about the observed activity (line 17). Sarah's noticing works in a number of ways here; it provides a way of letting Emma know Sarah's knowledge in the situation, and also as a way of affording the opportunity for the hearers (in this case the children in close proximity) to point out any discrepancies in her knowledge and misunderstandings that are in need of repair in their next conversational turn at talk (Eglin and Hester, 1999; Mondada, 2011).

As Emma has initiated this activity herself, Sarah's noticing could also be observable as a prompt for Emma to talk about what she is doing (Vehvilainen, 2011). As suggested by Schegloff (2007a), an environmental noticing in a FPP works to provoke a response about that thing in a preferred way by a SPP utterance also attending to the noticed environmental feature. Here, Sarah's announcement can be linked to both the giving and receiving of knowledge about the current situation regarding Emma and the bucket of water. However, there is a brief pause (line 21) where Emma passes the opportunity to respond to Sarah's announcement of her actions in an aligned or disaligned response (Mondada, 2011). Subsequently, in her next utterance, Sarah explicitly demonstrates that she suspects that Emma is going to pour the water into Chipmunk's bucket.

As well as making her understanding of the situation visible here, Sarah's utterance also demonstrates her concern for Emma's actions in the current situation as she breaks away from this knowledge exchange to tell Emma to be 'careful' and ends her utterance with 'sweet' (lines 22–23). Sarah's orientation to the safety and well-being of Emma is made significant here both verbally and with gesture where she offers her a cautious warning and then escalates her verbal action to a physical action as she takes hold of the bucket that Emma is holding (line 23), distributing its weight evenly between herself and Emma. Sarah's obligation to provide a safe environment for Emma is observable here in Sarah's actions through advising Emma to be careful, providing physical support and using the 'endearment term' (Jefferson, 1973, p. 82) 'sweet'. Through combining these actions, the caring relational work of the teacher is made observable (C. Goodwin, 2014; M.H. Goodwin, 2014; Ceite; 2014).

Even though this interaction was embedded within the context of a teaching and learning episode about how to care for animals, a teaching activity that is often seen in early childhood centres in New Zealand, there is also evidence of the ongoing importance of the teacher's role to care for the well-being of the children. The initial sequences of talk mark the activity of teaching and learning about caring for a duck, observable where the members co-produce a category K collection through offering specialised knowledge around an interesting environmental feature. The importance for Sarah to attend to the safety and well-being of Emma is then subsequently attended to as a priority item both verbally and non-verbally, demonstrating Sarah's obligation to provide relational care and Emma's for receiving it, situating them as members of the R category collection SRP and co-producing the activity as omni-relevant.

Excerpt 7: Sarah

Sarah (SAR) has been pushing a girl, Sara (SRA), on a swing. Sarah stops talking to Sara when she is approached by a second preschool girl, Katherine (KAT) who is crying and with her friend.

```
09  SAR:      holding on
10  SRA:      °mmm° () °
11  SAR:      ↑ee::k↑= ((Sarah pulls swing back and lets go))
12  SRA:            =higher than tha:t↑
13  SAR:      $higher then that↓$
14  SRA:      $ye↑ah hhh$
15            ((Sara continues swinging and starts to slow down))
16  SRA:      higher than that↓
17  SAR:      higher than ↑that↑ okay you ready:↑
18  SRA:      °yep°
19  SAR:      ↓you ready:↓ ((pulls swing back))
20  SRA:      °higher than that°
21  SAR:      as high as that ((lifts swing high in the air))
22  SRA:      >higher than that<
23  SAR:      $I can't get any higher$↓
24  SRA:      ((swings up to Sarah and reaches out to her
25            laughing))
26→SAR:      you alright **Kat**hrine↑ ((looks behind her twice))
27  ?         ((child speaks out of audio reach))
```

```
28→SAR:      you alright honey↑
29 KAT:      (~I banged my head on-~) ~I banged my head on he:r~
30           ((points to her friend))
31→SAR:      come here honey ((bends down, hugs Katherine and
32           rubs her head))
33 KAT:      ((hugs Sarah))
```

During the beginning of this observation (lines 09–25) Sarah and Sara are attending to the environmental feature of the swing that Sara is sitting on, where they are talking about how high Sara would like to be pushed. Sarah is asking questions that will help her to judge how high Sara would like to be lifted on the swing before she lets go. The importance of gaining a shared understanding between Sarah and Sara is of relevance here as lifting the swing too high could be unsafe and scare Sara and not lifting it high enough would result in disappointment. Sarah requires epistemic access to Sara's perception of the situation (Heritage, 2013; Stivers, Mondada and Steensig, 2011) in order to judge the height correctly and engages in knowledge exchange with Sara through a question-answer sequence to establish joint understanding. In this instance even though Sarah is officially the 'teacher', she is the less knowledgeable (K-), and Sara is the more knowledgeable (K+) (Heritage, 2013) regarding how high she wants to be pushed on the swing, which is 'higher than that' (lines 12, 16, 20 and 22). The category K collection is observably present through this knowledge exchange between Sara and Sarah through these initial turns at talk where Sarah seeks specialised knowledge that Sara has to inform the situation and progress the interaction successfully.

The interaction is abruptly abandoned as Sarah notices that one of the preschool girls, Katherine, is upset (line 26). Sarah makes her initial noticing of the situation by shouting out to Katherine to see if she is 'all right', using her name in tag position. The use of a name as an appended address term or 'final position address term' (Wootton, 1981, p. 143) provokes a situation where, rather than using a name to secure the attention of the person being called through a summoning, the appended address initiates the recipient to analyse the prior utterance and respond to the initiator accordingly (Baker and Freebody, 1986; Wootton, 1981). There is a possible response to Sarah's question (line 27), although the voice heard is out of range of the microphone and so the speech is inaudible.

Sarah continues by repeating the same question, but this time with the use of an 'endearment term' (Jefferson, 1973, p. 83): 'honey' in place of Katherine's name (line 28). As already mentioned the use of a name in tag position requires the recipient to analyse the prior utterance and provide a response; here, the use of an endearment term in tag position also works to provoke a response from the recipient with the addition of marking the utterance, and therefore interaction more generally, as more affective. Sarah's option of an endearment term to replace Katherine's name here provides a more personal, affiliative position when investigating the trouble. This time Katherine is heard clearly to give an account of the trouble as she explains that she bumped her head on her friend (line 29–30).

Sarah also attends to the trouble non-verbally as she moves her body so that she is turning her back on Sara who is still on the swing and bends down to Katherine's level, leaning in towards her to give her a hug, and Katherine responds by hugging Sarah back. This embrace is coupled with Sarah rubbing Katherine's head and, once again, using the endearment term 'honey'. Katherine responds in a preferred way to Sarah's actions as she reciprocates the hug in an affiliated way as she hugs her back in a full embrace (Goodwin, M. H., 2014). This action makes Katherine and Sarah observable as being engaged in a relational interaction together (Goodwin, 1981) as they both give and receive affection. In each of Sarah's turns of talk with Katherine she attends to the trouble in a relational way, verbally through the use of endearment terms and non-verbally by providing close physical contact through hugging her and rubbing her head.

Although the beginning of the interaction shows Sarah interacting with a child through knowledge exchange where the turns at talk co-produced a K category collection, Sarah's noticing of an upset child took priority over the interaction as Sarah responded to the upset child by abandoning her current interaction and attending to the trouble through activities that co-produced a collection R SRP where Sarah was the proper person to turn to about the emotional trouble. The way in which Sarah prioritised attending to the emotionally upset child by abandoning her current interaction was not attended to as problematic by any of the children present, and so can be observable as acceptable conduct. This acceptability of prioritising the giving and receiving of emotional care shows the omni-relevance of attending to an upset child in a relational way as having priority over an ongoing interaction.

Excerpt 8: Sam

Sam and the preschool children, Jenny (JEN) and Matthew (MTW) are walking along the bush trail during an outdoor excursion to a local forest. They are walking in a line along the narrow path when one of the children far ahead shouts back to Sam.

```
01 CH:      <Sa:::m↓>
02 SAM:     I <ca::n't> see you=I can see Michelle
03 CH:      come (do:wn) he::re::↓
04 SAM:     we're ↑coming
05 CH:      (hurry=up)↓
06 MTW:     <we::> are [↓coming::
07 SAM:                [we've gotta follow the pa:th
08          1.3
09 JEN:     where are we going
10 SAM:     o: we'll go ↑straight down↓
11          ((they approach a steep slope in the terrain))
12 MTW:     $↓wee:: (1.1) ↑wee:::$ ((jumps and walks quickly
```

```
13                    down the slope))
14→SAM:               Careful not to ru:n: because we don't want to sli:p
15                    Matthew
16 MTW:               $↑rock ↓n rol↑lin$=
17 SAM:                                   =Matthew
18 MTW:               $I ↑keep rock and rollin$↓ ((sways side to side))
19→SAM:               maybe holding on to the ↑rope would be a good idea↓
20                    (1.4)
21→                   .hhh coz if you start slipping you can hold
22→                   it tight and it can stop you from falling over .hhh
```

As Sam and the children are walking along the forest track one of the children who is out of visual range shouts his name very loudly (line 01) and Sam responds by telling her that he's coming (line 04). This position is subsequently mirrored by one of the preschool boys, Matthew, as he also responds by sharing knowledge about their position and telling them that they are coming (line 06). Sam overlaps the end of Matthew's utterance as he instructs that they have to 'follow the path', demonstrating his knowledge of the terrain and the route they are taking. Jenny subsequently attends to Sam's orientation to their position in the environment as she asks for further information about where they are going (line 09). Sam responds to Jenny's question by offering the information that she has requested as he tells her that they are heading straight down the immediate slope in front of them on the pathway.

This initial sequence of actions show how Sam asserts more knowledge about the terrain in the group's current environmental position as he tells them on two occasions where they are going, following the path (line 07) and going straight down (line 10). The way in which this interaction is co-constructed with the teacher owning the knowledge about the route the group will take and the children following the teacher's instructions demonstrates the conversational features of the teacher's authority as a practical action (Macbeth, 1991) even though the teacher and children are out of the usual school environment. The way in which teachers use instructions in the social organisation of a teaching and learning episode is acknowledged (Wells and Arauz, 2006) where teachers often have authority over children's actions. This is evident in the current interaction where the teacher shows his more knowledgeable (K+) position and the child shows their less knowledgeable (K-) position (Heritage, 2012) presenting a traditional 'teacher-pupil' interaction (Sacks, 1992a, 1992b).

Following these initial lines where Sam asserts his knowledge about the location, Matthew interacts with the terrain by taking the opportunity to jump and walk quickly down the slope, vocalising his actions (lines 12–13). The affordances of an outdoor terrain for encouraging children's development of risk-taking (Little, Wyver and Gibson, 2011; Tovey, 2007) and building resilience and a positive disposition towards learning (Ouvry, 2003) are well documented in childhood literature where such activities as running down hills are encouraged, as is observable throughout the 'bush' footage collected during this project. However, this current observation demonstrates how Sam attends to Matthew's quick walk down the steep slope as potentially problematic. This is demonstrated as Sam warns Matthew to be 'careful not to run' and gives an account for his warning 'because we don't want to slip' (lines 14–15).

Even though Matthew seems to be enjoying his experience marked by his 'smile talk' (lines 12, 16 and 18), Sam responds with the warning to be 'careful not to run' encouraging Matthew to be cautious of the terrain. Matthew responds by vocalising his physical movements (lines 16 and 18) rather than offering a response that is tied to Sam's warning, and so Sam quickly summons Matthew to ensure he is listening (Wooton, 1981), demonstrating the immediacy of the warning. However, Matthew continues with his action of 'rockin and rollin' and even upgrading these movements to be more observable (line 18), prompting Sam to offer further advice with an orientation to protection from the physical harm of falling over (lines 19–21).

This observation demonstrates how the teacher and children manage the outdoor location through exchanges about being knowledgeable about the environment or not, and how this exchange shifts when Sam gives caution regarding the physical safety of Matthew. These actions demonstrate how the child's safety is attended to as a priority item during the outdoor excursion when there is a distinct possibility of trouble, highlighting the relational aspects of care giving and receiving as having omni-relevance in the ongoing outdoor excursion.

Attending to an Emotional Trouble as a Priority in a Multi-party Interaction

The following observation demonstrates how the children and teacher attend to an emotional upset as a matter of priority during the ongoing conversation with a number of children whilst in the process of a teaching activity.

Excerpt 9: Sarah

Sarah, one of the preschool teachers, is crouching down on the patio area of the preschool with a group of children putting disposable plastic gloves on Chloe (CLO), Jenny (JEN) and Remi (RMI). One of the children, Kyla (KLA) is sitting on a tree stump holding Chipmunk, the preschool duckling. Emma (EMA) approaches.

```
01  EMA:        ↓Why are you guys pu↑tting gloves on:↓
02  SAR:        coz look in there ((points to Chipmunk's cage))
03              (0.7)
04  SAR:        and you ↓know what
05  EMA:        ↓what↓
06  SAR:        You're tak↓ing (0.8) that Mr Chipmunk home tonight
```

```
07              aren't you
08              ((A nearby child splashes water on Kyla))
09→KLA:         Argh He we:::t me:::↓
10 CLO:         well I want to [take Mr] Chipmunk (0.6) ho:me:
11→SAR:                        [ who:↓ ] ((looks at Kyla))
12→KLA:         Aa↑ta:::↓ ((points to Aata))
13 RMI:         [no=no=no ne:xt we:ek↓]
14→SAR:         [>ok<=so ↓what do you need to say to Aa↑ta:↓]
15 EMA:         but I want to:↓- (0.4) I wa↑nt some gl↓oves on::
16              ((Sarah looks at Kyla. Kyla looks at Aata))
17→KLA:         [<stop it Aa:ta:↓>]
18 JEN:         [can you put this glove on↓] (0.4) the glove on
19              [°ple:ase°] ((approaches Sarah with a glove))
20→SAR:         [ $Aata$ ] ((smiles and looks at Aata))
21 ATA:         ((drops the hosepipe downwards))
22 JEN:         can you put it on for-=with me::↓
23              (1.8)
24 SAR:         $loo↑k at Aata↓$
25              (1.5)
26 JEN:         °mmmm°
27 SAR:         he looks like he's just hopped out of a s↑wimming
28              pool↓
29              (5.8)
30 SAR:         So (0.4) we need to clean out that smelly cage
31              because you don't want to take that home do you↓
```

Sarah is involved in the activity of cleaning the cage of Chipmunk the preschool duckling, an activity that is used in early childhood centres to teach children the responsibility of owning and caring for an animal. Sarah goes about starting this event by distributing disposable gloves to the children who are interested in being involved in the activity. Whilst doing this Emma approaches Sarah and opens an interaction by asking why the children and Sarah are putting gloves on. This use of reference to an object as a legitimate way of starting an interaction with a desired person is acknowledged in prior CA research (Bateman and Church, forthcoming, 2015). In this situation Emma asks Sarah a question about the glove objects, making an answer from Sarah a preferred response; the use of a question-answer sequence and reference to a conversational 'object' is used by Emma to initiate the interaction with Sarah. Through this verbal action, Emma demonstrates her request for knowledge from Sarah, placing Emma in the K- position and Sarah in K+ position (Heritage, 2012a).

Sarah responds by directing Emma's attention to Chipmunk's cage, indicating that to 'look in there' would be enough to answer the question. This is then followed by a brief pause in talk (line 03) and Sarah using a conversational opening in her turn at talk, that being the 'you know what' technique Sacks

(1992a, p. 265) attributed to the talk of children who have restricted rights to speak to adults. This prompts the required response by Emma who asks a subsequent question 'what' (line 05), giving the turn of talk back to Sarah, who sequentially displays her knowledge about Emma taking the duckling home. Through this first section of interaction, Sarah and Emma make reference to knowledge initiated by Emma who turns to Sarah for information regarding the gloves and followed by Sarah asking Emma about her hosting of Chipmunk. Sarah uses a tag-question at the end of her utterance, 'aren't you' (line 07), ensuring the opportunity for further elaboration by Emma, either in agreement or disagreement to Sarah's suggestion. So far the interaction has presented Emma and Sarah orientating towards Chipmunk, as the surrounding children continue with the activity of cleaning the cage.

The next sequence of interaction (lines 09–26) shows how the group of children talk to Sarah about two different topics at the same time, and how Sarah manages this. Whilst Sarah is talking to Emma about taking Chipmunk home for the night, one of the nearby preschool boys, Aata, splashes Kyla with water as he plays with the hosepipe. This causes Kyla to shout out her disapproval (line 09) and become quite upset about the event. Although Chloe continues the discussion about the ongoing activity at hand in the next available talk space by telling about how she would like to take Chipmunk home (line 10), Sarah responds to Kyla rather than Chloe, overlapping Chloe's speech as she does so to find out who the 'he' is that sprayed Kyla (line 11).

The presence of two or more people speaking at the same time in conversational overlap can be problematic (Schegloff, 2000b) where, when members do not orient to an overlap as problematic, there are a number of reasons why; these include 'terminal overlaps' where the speaker is coming to the end of their sentence and 'continuers'. The latter are utterances such as 'mmhm', which show support and understanding of the speakers' utterances and are not seen as competition for the floor as they do not imply 'shift' in the turn of speech (see Jefferson, 1984 for more on this). 'Conditional access to the turn' where the speaker invites another member to interrupt their not-yet-complete utterance in order to support and/or extend what they are saying and 'choral' utterances that are done simultaneously not serially, such as laughter, greetings, congratulations etc., are also non-problematic overlaps. However, Sarah's overlap of Chloe's utterance does not align with any of these four legitimate reasons. It is suggested here that the reason the overlap is not oriented to as problematic is because the overlapping utterance is of immediate importance at that time for those people, where the action created by the overlap attended to an emotional problem as a matter of priority.

In response to Sarah's question, Kyla identifies the child as Aata (line 12) and this is followed by another preschool child, Remi, replying to Chloe's prior utterance (line 10) about wanting to take Chipmunk home. Rather than offering a reply that either aligns or disaligns with Remi in her next turn, Sarah continues to attend to Kyla's problem with Aata as she initially offers a summary 'ok' (line 14), which works to end that particular sequence of events as knowledge about the problem has been shared and the perpetrator has been identified. This prior sequence of actions has worked towards a shared understanding of the problem as knowledge about the event has been distributed and Sarah and Kyla now have more of a co-equal knowledge position.

Sarah then moves on to the next phase of dealing with this relational problem: how to solve it. She does this by asking Kyla a question about what she needs to 'say to Aata' (line 14), and in doing so offers Kyla the responsibility over her actions as a way of responding to the situation rather than giving her a direct instruction. Sarah encourages Kyla to resolve the situation herself by using her words (Church, 2009) and practice her agency (Mashford-Scott and Church, 2011), which she does in her response to Sarah's prompt by telling Aata to 'stop it' (line 17).

During Sarah's talk to Kyla (line 14), Emma joins in the talk about Chipmunk in overlap (line 15), but again this is not oriented to as a problem by any of the participants. Likewise, Kyla's assertion of 'stop it' (line 17) is overlapped by Jenny's talk asking for help putting her glove on (line 18). Although the activity that was set up by the teacher was aimed at taking care of Chipmunk, the impromptu event of Aata spraying Kyla with water and Kyla consequently becoming upset split the group into two separate conversations. The issue of two topics of talk running in parallel within the group was managed here by Sarah, giving priority to the relational activity of providing help for the emotionally upset child in this situation.

When Jenny approaches Sarah about putting a glove on, Sarah continues attending to the issue of Kyla and Aata as she calls Aata's name and smiles at him (line 20) rather than respond to Jenny. Jenny continues to ask Sarah for help with the practical matter of putting her glove on in her next utterance where she self-repairs her utterance from 'can you do this *for*' to '*with* me' (line 21). There is a slight pause as Sarah continues to smile and look at Aata before she finally does interact with Jenny, by giving her an instruction to 'look at Aata' (line 23). This action makes a transition between Sarah's interaction with Aata and Kyla, as the focus remains on Aata, and a return to her prior interaction with the other children as she now speaks directly to Jenny. There is a brief pause before Jenny gives a minimum response token 'mmm' in a quiet voice (line 25) and Sarah makes one last reference to Aata (lines 26–27) before a long pause and going back to the task of cleaning out the duckling cage.

Despite Sarah initiating the task of cleaning out the duckling cage as a teachable moment where she talks with the children about how to perform such a task involving specialised knowledge in the co-production of a collection K category, the event of an emotional upset co-produced a collection R SRP where Kyla turned to Sarah for emotional help and support, and Sarah provided that relational help as a matter of priority and in a way that suspended the knowledge-based activity.

Knowledge and Relationships in the Environment

These observations demonstrate how the environment is attended to as a way of exchanging knowledge between the members present. Through engaging in conversational exchanges around features of the environment, the teachers and children talk specific things into significance and omit others. The excerpts in this chapter demonstrates how asking for help regarding knowledge about an environmental feature (e.g., what a passion vine hopper is) coupled with the teacher's instructions and questions work together to co-produce a collection K of category members. Through the teachers providing names of environmental features, or offering information about the environment, it provides an opportunity to introduce new knowledge about a topic and establish teacher and child as being co-members of the same community who are in the know about that specific environmental feature (Schegloff, 1972).

Also, during the everyday activities between the young children and teachers, the orientation to preventing potential troubles through warnings of being careful were observable as priority items over the ongoing knowledge exchange that co-produced a teaching and learning activity. This was markedly achieved through teachers abandoning current interactions with children to attend to matters of relational caring for other children in quite abrupt ways. The systematic ways in which relational caring for children was prioritised by teachers through this abandonment, and by children through their immediate approach of a teacher when they were upset, can be observable as omni-relevant, that is, these relational interactions were immediately attended to with no prior build up to such an interaction (Sacks, 1992a). As noted in Chapter 2:

> There are, then, two tests for the omnirelevance of a social context. One is that the parties analyze each other as having produced category-bound activities bound to the categories comprising the collection parties to a particular context. The second test is that of anytime invocability. (Hester and Hester, 2012, p. 15)

In relation to the current excerpts, Hester and Hester's first 'test' reveals that the teachers in the present study are all observed engaging in the category-bound activities of prioritising a relational caring for a child demonstrated through their verbal and non-verbal actions; the second test of 'anytime invocability' is also observable.

When a relational trouble occurred it was attended to as a priority item by the teacher, marking the importance of attending to the physical and/or emotional needs of the child over the educational task-based conversations co-produced through knowledge exchange in the ongoing activity. This presented a shift from the co-production of an interaction through knowledge exchange to an SRP being co-produced through attending to an emotional or physical trouble. This relates to Schegloff's (1972) emphasis of the changing nature of membership categories during everyday interactions. These conversational features demonstrate how

SRPs are co-produced by the indexical and occasioned turns at talk, due to a 'bond of obligation' (Sacks, 1992a, p. 75). That early childhood teachers are obliged to help the children in their care, both educationally and relationally, is significant and unique within the arena of educational practices through various age-related educational settings; even more so when we consider the possibility of relational care taking precedence over what may be considered other 'educational' task activities. This is further explored in the subsequent chapter that investigates managing illness in early childhood education.

Chapter 7
Managing Illness: A Single Case Analysis

The prior chapters in this book have so far demonstrated how teachers, young children and toddlers co-produce an affiliated interaction through pretend play episodes (Chapter 4), how children's emotional upset in dispute situations are responded to as a priority by the teacher where knowledge is requested in the process of conflict resolution (Chapter 5), and how knowledge about an environmental feature can be tied to emotional feelings and prompt relational activities where safety and well-being are attended to as matters of priority (Chapter 6). Throughout these preceding chapters, relational activities are observable as a priority item between the children and their teachers, revealing the omni-relevance of such interactions during the mundane, everyday communications in early childhood education.

This phenomenon is now further revealed through the following single case analysis of an interaction between a child who has become ill and one of her teachers. Through the co-production of this interaction Sacks' collection R SRP is made observable through the child and teacher demonstrating their giving and receiving of relational care through the use of gesture and verbal activities. The category K collection is also brought into play through the teacher's professional capacity to deal with the trouble as she requests further knowledge around the trouble in order to provide the help.

Demonstrating and Identifying Illness

The following interaction between an early childhood teacher, Sarah, and a young four-year-old girl, Jenny, is now presented. During this interaction the sequences of events demonstrate how Jenny indicates a possible trouble to Sarah, and how Sarah attends to diagnosing and offering specific help for remedying the trouble. Although this observation occurred in a teaching and learning preschool environment, the similarities between this situation and Sacks' (1992a) 'therapy sessions' are evident in the conversation turn-taking process. Through using conversation analysis to explore the interaction, a better understanding of how such a situation is locally managed can be revealed.

The following analysis will demonstrate how caring for an ill child and being an ill child require access to knowledge and a shared understanding (Stivers, Mondada and Steensig, 2011) from the participants in order to provide relational care in a knowledgeable way. Even though one of the members verbally communicates infrequently, in this case Jenny, her actions also work towards the co-production of the interaction. The non-verbal contributions of young children are found to be of equal importance to their non-verbal where:

> By focusing on the next action as the locus for displaying how the preceding actions are understood, a very detailed picture has emerged of what these very young children are actually able to achieve with the non-verbal and limited verbal resources available to them. (Filipi, 2009, p. 241)

Much like the work by Filipi (2009), here the observation of Jenny's non-verbal responses to Sarah's questions in the form of an often slight movement of her head results in a subsequent action from Sarah, usually in the form of another question to secure further information. These turn-taking verbal and non-verbal sequences are managed through each member's contribution to the conversation.

A collection K category is co-produced through Sarah's professional approach to seeking knowledge about the problem from the more knowledgeable Jenny and where a fellow early childhood teacher, Sam, also helps. A possible solution to address the problem is then discussed in a sequential progression of the interaction based on the knowledge that Sarah has acquired towards the end of the interaction. However, Jenny and Sarah also engage in actions associated with a collection R SRP, as they make observable their close relational actions through intimate physical contact as Sarah cuddles Jenny, kisses her, sits Jenny on her lap and strokes her hair, as well as through Sarah's verbal reference to Jenny's emotional state as needing some 'love' at the end of the interaction. This priority of diagnosing and providing a specific type of help for Jenny in the everyday running of the early childhood centre, where there are many children to attend to, becomes observable as omni-relevant as Sarah systematically orients her attention towards Jenny during the morning tea session.

The single-case analysis reveals that, although membership to a K collection is demonstrated through Sarah requesting knowledge from Jenny, and Jenny providing the answers, the collection R category is also co-produced through category-bound activities (CBA) associated with giving and receiving of emotional care. This analysis demonstrates the complexities of teaching children of a young age where category K and R collections are co-produced during everyday interactions by the interlocutors.

The observation begins 2 minutes and 40 seconds into the video recording of the teacher, Sarah, for that day. Jenny, one of the four-year-old preschool children, has just arrived at preschool; she has her hood up and walks slowly whilst looking downwards. Sarah, the preschool teacher, is sitting at a table in the conservatory, chopping fruit for morning tea and talking to another four-year-old preschool girl, Dawn. Jenny approaches Sarah, picks up a chair and puts it next to the table then leaves the screenshot to get a drink.

What follows is the initial noticings of a problematic situation, where Sarah attempts to gain knowledge about the possible trouble in the subsequent interactions. The communicating of a trouble by Jenny and noticing of this communication by Sarah is initiated when Jenny returns to the table at 3 minutes and 33 seconds into the filming for that day.

3 minutes 33 seconds

The early childhood teacher Sarah (SAR) is sitting at the morning breakfast table with a four-year-old girl Dawn (DWN). A second four-year-old girl, Jenny (JEN), approaches the table holding a chair. Jenny puts the chair next to Sarah and leaves to get a drink. Zion, a four-year-old preschool boy, walks over to the table and sits in the chair that Jenny has just put at the table. Jenny approaches Zion:

```
01  JEN:    he::y I was sitting there↓ fi:rst↑ ((pushes Zion
02          with the side of her body but he remains in the
03          chair))
04          (0.7)
05  JEN:    [(                    )]
06  SAR:    [Zion↓ (0.2) up you ge:t↑]
07          (1.6)
08  DWN:    Zion didn't >wash=up< his ha:↓nds=
09  SAR:                                      =no you haven't
10          washed your ha:↑nds Zion↓ (0.7) >come=on< (2.3)
11          I'll hold your piece of apple for you:↑ . you wash
12          your hands and get a chair↓ ((stands up and moves
13          Zion gently out of the chair))
14  JEN:    ((immediately sits in the chair, but does not eat
15          anything))
16          ((Many more children approach the table))
```

This opening episode plays out a moral stance over who should be allowed to sit in the chair; lines 1–3 show the 'set-up' of this moral dilemma. Even though Jenny has located and positioned the chair, she then went away, making the chair available to others and, as such, it is taken by Zion. Jenny initiates the interaction with Zion as she approaches him and tells him that she was sitting in the chair first. This claim over first ownership of an environmental feature was observed in Chapter 5 Excerpt 3 and also in prior research (Church, 2009; Cobb-Moore, Danby and Farrell, 2008) where the *first possession rule* was accepted by children as a justification for ownership and exclusive rights to that feature. Here, Jenny's claim regarding her possession over the seat is supported with a physical gesture (Bateman, 2012b) as she uses her body to try to push Zion off the chair, making her intentions about the situation clear; Zion is in her seat and she is going to move him out of it. However, Zion does not accept this gesture as he remains seated.

There is a pause (line 4) followed by an inaudible utterance from Jenny (line 05) before the members present reveal their moral stance on the situation as Sarah tells Zion to get up, and therefore aligning with Jenny. Although Zion has now been asked to move out of the seat by two people, one being a figure of authority, the teacher, he still remains seated and there is a second hearable pause (line 7). Zion's action of remaining seated suggests that there has not been a legitimate enough reason given to justifiably suggest that he has to move; as an unacceptable request for an action to be done 'doesn't count' (Sacks, 1992a, p. 474), Zion does not have to do the requested action. Sarah's stance towards requesting Zion to move is subsequently responded to by Dawn, who also aligns with Sarah and Jenny. Dawn declares her stance by giving a reason for her alignment with Jenny and Sarah as she suggests that Zion should move because he has not washed his hands (line 8). The preschool rule of having to wash hands before sitting down to morning tea is one that is enforced every mealtime, and is oriented to here as a legitimate reason for Zion to move out of the chair.

This is then touched off by Sarah as she quickly latches on to Jenny's utterance and reiterates that Zion does have to move to wash his hands in a verbal directive 'you wash your hands' and embodied action as she shepherds him out of the chair (Cekaite, 2010) (lines 11–13). In doing so Sarah identifies the importance of the action of washing hands as an acceptable rule for joining the breakfast table. Sarah also adds that Zion has to 'get a chair' (line 12) at the end of her sentence, talking this object into importance for those people at that time and place, returning to the topic that initiated the interaction. This last part of Sarah's utterance demonstrates the group positioning now evident in the immediate social order, as it is now clear that Jenny, Sarah and Dawn are all aligned with each other. Zion subsequently responds to this social positioning by allowing Sarah to shepherd him out of the chair as he cooperates by moving willingly (Cekaite, 2010), leaving the present chair available.

Although Jenny displays her interest in sitting at the table through this first sequence of events, supported by Sarah and Dawn, when she does sit in 'her' chair at the morning tea table she does not eat (lines 14–15). By sitting at that table with people who are engaged in the activity of eating morning tea, Jenny joins a specific set of people who are engaging in the same CBA together. As Jenny is not eating, and so not joining in with the CBA displayed by all the other members in this situation, her *not* eating makes her observable as *not* being a member of the group she is sitting with, as she does not engage in the correct CBA for belonging to that group.

A category can be used to describe members involved in an explicit situation; in another situation at another time those people may be categorised differently (Lepper, 2000). In this instance the category of people involved in that location are those attending morning tea, involving the CBA of eating the food available at the morning tea table. When referring to some categories there are recognisable category contrasts, such as those members who are in a collection of people who are standing or, in contrast, those in a collection of people who are sitting (Sacks, 1992b). In this instance by sitting at the morning breakfast table, Jenny displays her willingness to engage with the members she has chosen to sit by (Goodwin, 1981), but by not engaging with the CBA of eating she is observably different to those members who she is sitting with.

The next section of the interaction goes on to reveal Sarah's initial orientation to Jenny's lack of eating as problematic.

6 minutes 38 seconds

Another four-year-old girl, Abby (ABY) is now sitting next to Dawn. Jenny is sitting opposite them. Sarah gives a quick glimpse in Jenny's direction and follows Jenny's line of vision towards the two girls, Abby and Dawn, who are chatting. Abby is holding the butter knife whilst engrossed in conversation with Dawn.

```
17 SAR:    °um° Abby:↑
18 ABY:    (0.6) ((makes eye contact with Sarah))
19 SAR:    ↓I think Jenny may be waiting for the bu↑tter↓
20 ABY:    ((looks at Jenny and then starts to butter her
21         bread))
22         ((more children come to sit at the table))
23 ABY:    there you go: <Je:nny↓> ((looks at Jenny and
24         holds the butter out towards her across the
25         table))
26 JEN:    ((looks at Abby and keeps her hands down))
27 SAR:    ↑thank you↓ Ab↑bs ((takes the butter off Abby and
28         passes it to Jenny)) ↑do you want that ↓Jenny
29 JEN:    ((shakes her head))
30 SAR:    ((slowly moves the butter away whilst looking at
31         Jenny))
32         ((more children approach the table. Sarah lays a
33         2nd table and sits at it cutting fruit for the
34         new children whilst talking to them. Jenny stays at
35         the 1st table))
```

Sarah attends to the situation of Jenny not eating by making reference to the possibility that she might be waiting for a specific food type, 'the butter' (line 19), indicating this to one of the children sitting at the table (Abby). As Jenny has made no such assertion verbally, Sarah hedges her suggestion with the downgrade about her knowledge position 'I think' (Stivers and Heritage, 2001). Sarah talks to several children while Jenny remains silent and sitting still and Abby uses the butter and then passes it on to Jenny.

Whilst holding the butter out to Jenny, Abby uses Jenny's name in a tag position as an appended address term; this form of address draws the recipient's attention to the prior utterance (Baker and Freebody, 1986; Wootton, 1981). However, Jenny's response is to look at Abby and not take the butter off her. Even though Abby offers the butter to Jenny both non-verbally and verbally, Jenny does not respond with a verbal or non-verbal utterance in reply. Sarah then intervenes as she also offers the butter to Jenny in her next action (lines 27–28). This time Jenny does respond with a non-verbal shaking of her head, prompting Sarah to slowly withdraw the butter, fixing her gaze on Jenny as she does so. As the other children continue to eat, Jenny still does not, instead she sits quite still, looking down at the table with her hood remaining up.

Jenny has now refused food using non-verbal gesture. Her silence followed by her shaking of her head in a 'no' movement indicates a problem as Jenny gives a dispreferred response to both Abby and Sarah when she declines both of their offers. Jenny's decline is systematically problematic as a dispreferred second turn hinders the progression of the conversation and so is problematic (Jefferson, 1974). Jenny's silence indicates a 'trouble spot' (Harris, 2006, p. 227) as it marks a possible trouble in the ongoing interaction with a dispreferred response.

Through observing Jenny's non-verbal cues of being silent and not eating, Sarah responds by making a downgraded 'next best guess' (Heritage, 2012a, p. 6) about what Jenny might want (line 19). However, Sarah's guess was proven incorrect as Jenny indicates that she does not want the item being offered, which Sarah double checks through an explicit question to Jenny 'do you want that' (line 28). This explicit knowledge seeking places Jenny in a more knowledgeable position, otherwise termed K+ (Heritage, 2012a), and in contrast places Sarah in the less knowledgeable position (K-). The asymmetries of knowledge between interlocutors have been explored where research concerning young children and teachers reveals knowledge inequity as a mundane activity in everyday interactions between young children and teachers (Bateman and Waters, 2013).

In relation to the current interaction, the asymmetries of knowledge continue to be present in the subsequent turns at talk, as Sarah continues to investigate Jenny's possible trouble in a K- position. These K+ and K- positioned categories demonstrate Sarah and Jenny's membership to the K collection of people who are proper to turn to for help with specialised knowledge about a trouble; here Jenny is more knowledgeable about her possible trouble than Sarah.

The interaction continues to progress as Sarah persists in seeking knowledge about the possible problem from Jenny, and Jenny begins to seek closer physical contact with Sarah.

The Co-production of Knowledge about illness

This next series of actions demonstrate how Sarah builds on the knowledge she has gained about Jenny so far during the interaction. Through the subsequent turns at talk, Sarah begins to attend to the possible trouble that Jenny is experiencing by attempting to gain knowledge about the problem. Jenny approaches Sarah and Sarah responds to Jenny's non-verbal actions by initiating talk about the possible problem.

12 minutes 48 seconds

Sarah is talking to two boys, one being Hamish (HAM), about a boat that they have made.

```
36 SAR:     what was the sai↑l made out of↓ ((eye contact with
37          the boys and talks to them about their boats))
38→JEN:     ((slowly approaches Sarah and leans in towards
39          her so that they are very close))
40→SAR:     ↑wha:t ↓is up with you: litt↓le miss Jenny:↓
41          ((looks at Jenny, puts her arm around Jenny and
42          pulls her in close))
43 JEN:     ((keeps her arms down in front of her and looks
44          downward))
45          (1.3)
46 HAM:     and paper (0.3) and it was made out of cardboard
47          (0.4) and (0.8) and >I'd=already=painted=it<
48          <bro::wn>↓ ((looks at Jenny and continues talking))
49 SAR:     wow it was a <bro:w↑n> boat↓ ((lifts Jenny up onto
50          her lap whilst keeping eye contact with the boys))
51          (1.4)
52→SAR:     what's↑ ↓going <on::>↑ (0.7) ↓don't you wanna↑ have
53          morning tea now:↓ ((rocks Jenny back and forth on
54          her knee))
55 JEN:     ((shakes head slightly))
56 SAR:     no: (1.3) are you fee:ling ok:
57 JEN:     ((shakes her head very slightly))
58 SAR:     you're **not** fee↑ling ok↓ (1.3) hmmm ((kisses
59          Jenny's head)) (0.3) what's the matter (9.0) um: is
60          your **be**lly ok
61 JEN:     ((shakes head slightly))
62 SAR:     your belly doesn't feel ok↓ (3.4) what do you n↑eed
63 JEN      ((remains silent and looking downwards))
64 HAM:     I w↑ant a jam sa:ndwich↓
65 SAR:     um you can get up . Hamish↓ and go round and get
66          the jam off this table
67 HAM:     what ((stands up))
68          (4.2)
69 HAM:     where↑'s the <ja:m>↓
70 SAR:     around here buddy↑
71          (1.7)
72 SAR:     do you just need **cuddles**↓
73          ((a teacher walks past and talks to Sarah. Sarah
74          talks to children at both tables whist rocking
75          Jenny on her lap and stoking her head))
```

This section of the interaction begins with Jenny approaching Sarah, who is now sitting at the second morning tea table and talking with two preschool boys in an 'educational' way as she asks questions about a boat project they have been working on, discussing how it was made and the materials used. Although Jenny still remains silent, she communicates to the adult non-verbally (Filipi, 2009) as she leans in very closely to Sarah. Although there has been no prior physical interaction between Jenny and Sarah, or Sarah and any other children, Jenny's approach to Sarah and leaning in towards her for close physical contact is not treated as problematic by any of the other children present. This lack of orientation to the close physical contact between Sarah and Jenny makes it observable as an everyday, mundane activity that is not significant to the other children where this relational activity of a teacher and child having such close physical proximity is accepted as the norm.

However, Sarah does respond to Jenny's approach as significant by demonstrating that Jenny's physical action is an indication of a problem, as Sarah begins to seek knowledge about the possible problem from the more knowledgeable Jenny with her question 'what is up with you' (line 40). Sarah does this by abandoning the 'educational' conversation that she is having with the boys about making their boats. Although Sarah's conversation involved stimulating discussion around a child's interest in an educational way where they were discussing materials and the process of construction, attending to a possibly troubled child takes priority. Sarah responds by mobilising talk about the possible problem, attending to the problem as a topic of conversation (Bateman, Danby and Howard, 2013a).

Sarah makes her first verbal orientation to Jenny having a possible trouble. In her question she also uses an 'endearment term' (Jefferson, 1973, p. 83) 'little miss Jenny', in a tag-position at the end of her question. Jefferson's exploration of endearment terms in tag positions sheds light on how these types of endearment terms help shape an interaction:

> That the particular TYPE of address term occurring in these fragments are 'endearment' terms may be sequence-specifiable (within the constraints of relational requirements). That is, at call beginnings and endings, they provide expressions of 'glad to (have) hear(d) from you', and may, for endings in particular, be involved in work which, independently of the particulars of a given interaction, formulates it now as a happy and satisfying one. (Jefferson, 1973, p. 83 fn)

Jenny initiates a close embrace as she approaches Sarah and leans in closely to her so that they have close physical contact (lines 38–39). Sarah responds in a preferred way as she returns the gesture by putting her arms around Jenny in a close embrace. Whilst requesting knowledge from Jenny and using an endearment term in doing so, Sarah also responds to her approach physically as she puts her arms around Jenny and holds her close (lines 41–42). Even though Jenny has initiated this close physical action, she responds to Sarah's embrace by keeping her arms down by her sides and avoids eye contact with Sarah (lines 43–44). This type of response has been observed as a way of children disaffiliating themselves from the ongoing interaction as they do the activity of engaging in restricted second pair part utterances to a prior first pair part (Bateman, 2010). This verbal and non-verbal silence, like the action of not eating at the breakfast table (lines 26–35), is problematic as it hinders the progress of the interaction and, as such, is a dispreferred action and further indicates a problem (Jefferson, 1974).

There is a brief pause as Hamish stops talking while Sarah and Jenny interact and then he returns to the topic of boat making (lines 46–48). Although Jenny does not hug Sarah back in an affiliated response (M. H. Goodwin, 2014), Jenny does willingly receive Sarah's hug as she continues to lean in and makes no verbal or non-verbal assertion to move away. Sarah responds to Hamish's talk about his boat with the use of an assessment (line 49), which works to bring the conversation to a close (Pomerantz, 1984). Whilst doing this Sarah also lifts Jenny on to her knee in an action to transition from one topic with one person to another with a different person. This change is further evidenced in Sarah's next action as, when Hamish has finished talking, there is a pause followed by Sarah looking at Jenny and asking her for further information about 'what's going on' (line 52).

By attending to Jenny rather than following up the interaction with the boys, Sarah makes interacting with Jenny at that time in that place as having priority. This further mobilising of the problem is known to elicit accounts of trouble from young children by teachers in early childhood education settings so that teachers can gain shared knowledge with a child about their problem (Bateman, Danby and Howard, 2013a). There is a brief pause following Sarah's question, leaving space for Jenny to answer, but she remains silent and so Sarah continues, using a 'next best guess' (Heritage, 2012a, p. 8) again, found to be used by a less knowledgeable other when the required information is elusive (Bateman and Waters, 2013). The guess that is used here supports the prior observation of Sarah attending to Jenny's lack of eating at the breakfast table as problematic as Sarah returns the topic back to the earlier interaction (lines 17–35) by saying 'don't you want to have morning tea now' (lines 52–53).

This question initiates a sequence of question-answer exchanges (lines 52–62 and 72) between Sarah and Jenny where they engage in diagnosing Jenny's problem, as Sarah asks questions and Jenny answers them non-verbally. Sarah initially starts with the 'next best guess' indicated above (lines 52–53), which elicits a response from Jenny as she shakes her head indicating that she does not want food. Sarah's question directly links back to Jenny's action of refusing to eat when handed the butter, suggesting that Sarah did deem Jenny's refusal of the butter as significant. When Jenny shakes her head to indicate that she does not want food, Sarah verbally repeats Jenny's answer by saying 'no' and leaving a pause for Jenny to answer (line 56).

Jenny does not answer and so Sarah continues her enquiry as she asks her if she is feeling ok, to which Jenny replies 'no', again non-verbally by shaking her head. Sarah's second utterance here links Jenny's declaration that she does not want food to her feelings of not being 'ok'. Again, Sarah summarises Jenny's answer by clarifying 'you're not feeling very well', with emphasis on the word 'not', again leaving a space for a reply and then Sarah muttering 'hmmm'. Sarah then offers a question that is more exact about the specific reason Jenny is not feeling ok, by referring to a specific part of her anatomy, her 'belly' (line 60). Jenny's response suggests that Sarah has correctly identified the problem as Jenny shakes her head to indicate that her belly does not feel ok.

This sequence of actions involving an early childhood teacher asking questions and directly repeating or formulating a version of the child's answer in reply is acknowledged as aligning with talk in therapy sessions (Bateman, 2013) where a formulation or direct repeat of an answer does the role of acknowledging the persons answer without giving premature assessment or judgment. Sarah's use of questions here work to elicit knowledge from the more knowledgeable Jenny, as she competently offers answers regarding her physical state, helping Sarah to gain sufficient information regarding Jenny's trouble. This sequence of actions co-produce a category K collection where the interaction progresses through knowledge exchange regarding the specialised knowledge that Jenny has about her feelings, and what she needs (line 62).

When Sarah asks her next question 'what do you need' (line 62) one of the preschool children (Hamish) uses this turn space to interact with Sarah as he informs that he wants a jam sandwich (line 64), bringing the conversation back to the mealtime activity. Following this, Sarah links back to her utterance on line 62, as she offers a suggestion about what Jenny could possibly need as she says 'do you just need cuddles' (line 72).

In the morning tea episode so far, the interactions between Jenny and Sarah (lines 38–45 and 52–63) can be observed as insertion sequences (Schegloff, 1972) as they mark brief interludes in the ongoing task of 'doing morning tea', which continues in parallel to Jenny and Sarah's interactions. Sacks (1992a) suggests that insertion sequences have the character of being a priority in the ongoing conversation as members attend to the inserted topic as a non-problematic break in the sequence of the ongoing conversation. Insertion sequences are seen as omni-relevant as they can appear at any point in the conversation (Sacks, 1992a).

In relation to this ongoing interaction between Sarah and Jenny, a possible trouble with Jenny was identified early on at the beginning of the observation when Jenny had a problem with the ownership of the chair (line 1). Throughout the subsequent turns at talk, Sarah is observed as attempting to elicit knowledge from Jenny concerning her problem, putting Sarah in the position of less knowledgeable (K-) whereas Jenny is in the more knowledgeable (K+) position (Heritage, 2012a) about what is troubling her. These sequences of interaction work to co-produce a collection K category that is centered around knowledge access, as Sarah attempts to diagnose Jenny's trouble.

However, Jenny's approach of Sarah that showed close physical proximity as she leaned in towards Sarah (lines 38–39), and Sarah's response of putting her arms around Jenny in an embrace, her use of a term of endearment (line 40), lifting her on to her lap (lines 49–50) rocking her back and forth in a soothing motion (lines 53–54 and 74–75) as well as kissing (lines 58–59), verbally identifying her need for cuddles (line 72) and stroking her head (lines 74–75) are all relational CBAs that co-produce a collection R SRP. These relational actions of close body contact, kisses, cuddles and stroking demonstrate how the collection category R is co-produced through CBA and its 'anytime invocability' (Hester and Hester, 2012, p. 15) making the collection category R observable (Hester and Hester, 2012; Sacks, 1992a).

This series of actions presents the complex relationship between young children and early childhood teachers where the members can belong to a collection K category where the interactions often progress around knowledge distribution in the co-production of the educational context, as well as belonging to the category set of people who provide relational help in a category R collection. Here, the way in which such a complex situation is achieved is observable through the use of insertion sequences where relational activities take priority in an omni-relevant way. This sequence of events is further developed in the subsequent progression of the interaction.

17 minutes 57 seconds

Sarah is still seated at the morning tea table with Jenny on her lap when Hamish asks for more drinks.

```
76 HAM:     Sarah (0.4) Sarah (0.6) we need more drinks↓
77 SAR:     oh my goodness (0.6) we do (1.0) where are we going
78          to put you (1.2) ((looks at Jenny)) where would
79          you like to sit↓ (0.8) do you just want to wait for
80          me to come back from the microwave (0.4) or do you
81          want to go and sit on the couch↓
82 JEN:     ((lifts her head up slightly and then drops it
83          again))
84 SAR:     hmmm (0.5) you're a bit out of sorts aren't you↓
85 SAM:     even we need more apples
86 SAR:     we- even we- oh I need to cut up some apple ((moves
87          Jenny off her lap)) here (0.6) you sit on my seat↓
88          (0.9) I'm going to check the bread that I forgot I
89          put in the microwave ((walks over to microwave))
90 JEN:     ((sits in Sarah's chair))
```

This series of actions poses the problem of what to do with Jenny now that it has been established that she is not feeling very well; this is mobilised by Sarah as she makes the problem explicit (lines 77–81). Sarah then looks at Jenny and there is a noticeable pause; the gaze makes certain who Sarah is addressing and the pause allows a space for Jenny to answer (Filipi, 2009). There is no response from Jenny though, and so Sarah goes on to give Jenny the opportunity to decide where she wants to sit (lines 78–81), giving her some autonomy over the next sequence of actions to be performed. Jenny does not answer Sarah's question though and so Sarah, again, offers a next best guess (Heritage, 2012a) as she suggests two options that Jenny may possibly want to pursue. The first option offered by Sarah involves her giving Jenny continued care where Jenny could wait for Sarah to go to the microwave and then return; the second option involves a noted progression from the ongoing interaction where Jenny becomes more independent and moves away from Sarah. However, neither option is taken as Jenny remains silent and does not indicate a choice verbally or non-verbally.

This lack of response from Jenny is responded to as problematic by Sarah as she offers an account for Jenny's lack of response (line 84). In doing so Sarah demonstrates that she now has some knowledge of why Jenny may be acting in this dispreferred way and affirms Jenny's lack of response as acceptable in the current situation due to her not feeling very well. Sarah adds a tag question to the end of her account, which gives Jenny another opportunity to align with Sarah through a preferred answer, but Jenny does not take this up either. By taking time to attend to Jenny, Sarah displays that this is a priority over the CBA of providing morning tea at the morning tea table, even when the members have identified that they need more drinks (line 76).

A second child (Samuel) then addresses Sarah to ask for more apples (line 85), bringing the attention back to the morning tea activity once more. In order to attend to providing more food and drinks, Sarah no longer asks Jenny's opinion, but physically moves Jenny off her lap and sits her in her chair, explaining to Jenny what she is doing as she moves away. This action allows Sarah to move away from the ill child to attend to the requests of the other children around the morning tea table (line 89) whilst also ensuring that Jenny is comfortably positioned on one of the chairs.

29 minutes 38 seconds

Once Sarah has provided more food for the children sitting around the morning tea table she sits down next to Jenny. Sarah is holding some apples to cut up for the children.

```
91  JEN:      ((leans in towards Sarah with her head down))
92  SAR:      °↑are=you=ok↑° ((leans down towards Jenny and puts
93            her arm around her shoulders))
94            (1.5)
95  SAR:      ↓I'll cut the apple and then you can po↑p up for a
96            snuggle↓ ok↑
97  JEN:      ((nods her head))
98            (2.4)
99  SAR:      your bel↑ly not (0.4) feel good↓ ((cuts apple))
100 JEN:      ((shakes her head))
101           (80.7) ((other children talk to Sarah. Sarah walks
102           away from the table and then returns, sits down and
103           talks to the children around the table))
104 JEN:      ((moves slowly onto Sarah's lap))
105 SAR:      ((lifts Jenny more securely onto her lap whilst
106           talking to a passing teacher))
```

```
107            (59.1) ((Sarah rocks Jenny whilst talking to
108            others. Jenny leans into Sarah with her head down))
109  SAR:     °↑what are we gonna↓ d↑o with you↓° ((leans down
110            towards Jenny))
111            (82.8) ((Sarah talks to others whilst Jenny
112            remains on her lap))
113  SAR:     just p↑op. your legs around ↓the:re:↑ ((lifts Jenny
114            up whilst still seated))
115  JEN:     ((places her legs around Sarah's waist and puts
116            her head on Sarah's shoulder))
117  SAR:     ↓there we go and then I can ↑cut some ↓more ↑apple
118            up (2.9) °↑might just put that on this plate↑°
119            ((uses one hand to cut apple and move plates whilst
120            the other is across Jenny's back))
121  JEN:     ((pulls her hood down and turns to watch what
122            Sarah is doing at the table then places her head
123            back on Sarah's shoulder))
124            (9.6)((a preschool girl, Bliss, approaches Sarah))
125  SAR:     >would=you< like some more apple↑ (1.2) or are you
126            ↓done ((speaks to Bliss))
127  BLI:     °↓done↓°
128  SAR:     ↑ok↓ (0.5)      are you going to Nga↑here
129  BLI:     °↓yes↓°
130  SAR:     yep (0.4) cool↓ (1.6) must be almost time to go:
131  BLI:     ((walks away))
132            (5.6)
133  SAR:     ((places hand on Jenny's forehead))°↑hmmm:°(1.3)
134            >have=↑to< ↓take your tempe↑rature I think↓ ((talks
135            to other children around the table about their
136            food whilst rocking Jenny))
137            (51.8)
138  JEN:     ((puts her arms up around Sarah's neck and pulls
139            her close. Rubs her head on Sarah))
140            (23.1)((Sarah cuddles Jenny closely and continues
141            talking to the other children))
142  SAR:     ↓just move this out the way a bit eh↑ ((moves the
143            microphone over towards her shoulder)) ↓there we
144            go↓
145  JEN:     ((puts her head back on Sarah's other shoulder))
146  SAR:     morning Ryland↑ (1.8) good morn↓ing↑ (3.8) ((looks
147            over towards the door)) hold on Jenn:y (1.4) come
148            with me: ((lifts Jenny up and stands up. Walks
149            towards the door carrying Jenny. Returns to the
150            table with Jenny a couple of minutes later))
```

Sarah is now sitting next to Jenny and talking to other children about the food. Jenny initiates the next series of actions, again non-verbally, as she leans in towards Sarah with her head down and offering no eye contact. Although she does not engage in eye contact with Sarah, her embodied action of leaning in towards Sarah is responded to as a communication that there is still a problem, as Sarah asks her if she is ok quickly and quietly (line 92). Sarah's request for information regarding Jenny's welfare is coupled with an affiliated embodied action as she leans towards Jenny and puts her arms around her in an embrace. Again, Jenny remains silent and motionless.

Sarah's next utterance demonstrates that she has some knowledge about what Jenny might want, even though Jenny has not explicitly told her, as she tells Jenny that she can 'pop up for a snuggle' once she has finished cutting the apple (lines 95–96). This physical closeness and reference to a relational activity suggests Sarah and Jenny's co-production of a collection R SRP, where the members are observable as engaging in the activity of sharing a close embrace as souse-spouse or friend-friend in an action of 'loving contact' (Goodwin and Cekaite, 2012, p. 129). The relational activity of 'snuggling' is one that would not ordinarily be observed in an educational setting as the members that make up such an institution are teachers (professionals) and students (laypersons), suggesting a category collection K. However, it is the actions of the members present that co-produce the social relationships and context of institutions. Unlike the concept of context being a physical environmental space, this ethnomethodological perspective offers the perception of context as being co-constructed by the participants through their immediate interactions (Goodwin and Duranti, 1992). Here, as with the prior three chapters, the relational activity of close physical contact and talking of snuggling together works to co-produce a much more relational social order between the teacher and young child.

Jenny responds in a positive way to Sarah's embrace and suggestion of a 'snuggle' as she nods her head in agreement with Sarah, suggesting that this is an activity that is acceptable at this time, in this place, by these participants. The next utterance provides a possible account for why the activity of snuggling is acceptable as Sarah reiterates the problem located earlier (line 99) as she suggests to Jenny that her belly doesn't feel good, and Jenny agrees with this statement (line 100). These turns at talk make Sarah's actions observable as accountable; if a child is feeling unwell then Sarah is accountable to make her feel better, in this instance through the use of a 'snuggle'. The collection R SRP is therefore further observable through Sarah's demonstration of her 'rights and obligations concerning the activity of giving help' (Sacks, 1972, p. 37). The programmatic relevance of providing such help is also demonstrable here where an ill child in a category R collection would require an adult to take care of them where the non-incumbency, or absence of a person to take care of an ill child, would be observable (Sacks, 1972).

There is a brief interlude for 80 seconds as Sarah moves away from the morning tea table and then talks to other children seated around the table once she sits down again (lines 101–103). Once Sarah is seated, Jenny does not wait for an invitation, but rather initiates the action of moving closer to Sarah as she slowly moves on to her lap (line 104). Sarah reacts, also non-verbally, as she settles Jenny more securely onto her lap. This brief moment demonstrates Jenny's willingness to have a close physical engagement with Sarah, taking the opportunity to redeem the previously mentioned 'snuggle' (lines 95–96) and Sarah responds by attending to the organisation of the 'snuggle' (lines 105–106) as she begins rocking Jenny back and forth.

This rocking motion continues throughout Sarah's subsequent conversations with other children present and a passing teacher, providing consistent relational care for Jenny whilst also attending to her other daily activities. Once more Sarah makes reference to the well-being of Jenny in the conversation, this time with a single utterance, as Sarah abandons her ongoing conversation with the other children present to insert the utterance (line 109) before immediately returning to her conversation with the other children present. A temporary solution of what to do with Jenny is found (lines 113–123) as Sarah arranges Jenny in way that ensures she can still perform her routine duties of providing morning tea for the many children around the table, whilst also attending to caring for an ill child as a priority through her continuous interaction with her.

Jenny is now sitting on Sarah's lap, facing her, and Sarah is cutting fruit and talking to the other children when another preschool girl, Bliss, approaches Sarah (lines 124–131). Sarah interacts with her only briefly in a series of pre-closings (Schegloff and Sacks, 1973) demonstrated in the talk where 'pre-closings provide a space in which new mentionables may be inserted, they do not always lead to closings and are never more than *possible* pre-closings' (Liddicoat, 2011, p. 297). In each of her three turns at talk with Bliss, Sarah gives the opportunity to close the current interaction as she offers Bliss some fruit and then adds 'or are you done' (line 125), which Bliss replies with 'done', closing that line of topic. Sarah then continues by marking the close of the interaction with 'ok' (Schegloff and Sacks, 1973) and moves on to another topic by asking Bliss if she is going on the bush walk (line 128), to which Bliss affirms that she is but gives no further remark. Sarah then makes another marked close with an assessment 'cool' and a prompt for Bliss to leave as Sarah tells her it 'must be almost time to go' (line 130). Following this co-production of a closing, there is a pause in talk as Bliss exits.

Once Bliss has left, Sarah returns to caring for Jenny again as she touches Jenny's forehead to retrieve first-hand knowledge about Jenny in a sensory way in what can be likened to a 'haptic sense to construct the action in progress' (Goodwin and Cekaite, 2012, p. 136). In doing so Jenny draws all her attention back to caring for Jenny, disengaging from the other children present at the morning tea table. Sarah follows this action with a suggestion that she may need to take Jenny's temperature, making her caring for Jenny observable through her embodied actions and her verbal assessment of the situation. The non-verbal action of touching Jenny's forehead followed by a suggestion to take Jenny's temperature indicates that Jenny's forehead may have been hot enough to warrant further investigation. This suggestion upgrades the problem from Jenny feeling 'out of sorts' (line 84) to the need to employ professional medical diagnostic equipment.

Through employing this piece of medical equipment, Sarah adds a resource in her attempt to diagnose the problem with Jenny, indicating that as yet, there has been an insufficient diagnosis made, as Sarah is only aware that there is a problem with Jenny's 'belly' (line 99). However, Sarah does not show any urgency in locating the thermometer or in taking Jenny's temperature. Instead there is more non-verbal relational interaction between Jenny and Sarah as Jenny cuddles in closer to Sarah and Sarah picks Jenny up and carries her when she has to move away from the table. These non-verbal actions also demonstrate an upgrade for caring for Jenny as earlier, when Sarah had to move away from the table she gave Jenny options to wait for her or move away, now Jenny is physically picked up and carried with Sarah, ensuring consistency in their close proximity.

37 minutes 56 seconds

Jenny is still sitting on Sarah's lap when another early childhood teacher, Sam, approaches.

```
151  SAR:    hey: (0.4) will you get the thermometer↑ (1.2)
152          >↓please↓< ((talks to Sam who is out of camera
153          shot))
154  SAM:    (she came in with) (              )
155  SAR:    ah she di:d didn't >she=she=had=her<
156          <immunizations::> (1.6) <tha::t> would be why
157          you're not <fe:el>ing grea:t (0.3) coz you had an
158          in↑jection:↓
159  JEN:    ((nods slightly))
160  SAR:    I for↑got about tha:t↓
161          (18.7)
162  SAR:    °↑oh↑° Michael's having a ↓ja::m sandwich this
163          morning↑ ((looks at the preschool child Michael))
164          (9.3)
165  SAM:    (    ) ((sits on a chair close to Sarah))
166  SAR:    might have to have a little sl↑eep today↓ ((strokes
167          Jenny's hair))
168  SAM:    ((passes Sarah the thermometer))
169  SAR:    ↑uh↑ (7.9) ((places the thermometer in Jenny's
170          ear and looks at Jenny))
171          °↓yeah↓° (0.9) th↑irty-seven point t↓wo (1.9) just
172          feeling yu:cky↓ (1.2) shall we do your other ear
173  JEN:    ((nods head and turns head around so that her other
174          ear is exposed))
175  SAR:    ↑Okay↓ (1.6) >Oh< $I can't see it where's it gone$
176          ((reaches around Jenny and tries to put the
177          thermometer in her ear))
```

```
178 SAM:        $.hhh$ ((laughs quietly))
179 SAR:        $Do I ha↓ve it↑$ (0.6) ↓no↑
180 SAM:        $°↓let me have a go↓°$=
181 SAR:                                =↓Sam can do it ↑I ↓can't see
182             ((passes the thermometer to Sam))
183             (9.5) ((Sam places the thermometer in Jenny's ear
184             then removes it and looks at the reading. Jenny
185             remains still with her head on Sarah's shoulder))
186 SAM:        >thirty< eight:↓
187             (5.9) ((Sam and Sarah hold each others gaze and
188             nod their heads))
189 - 192      ((Sarah and Sam share some discussion around
                medication and then Sam walks away))
```

These next turns at talk reveal how a second early childhood teacher (Sam) assists with finding an answer to the diagnosis of Jenny's problem, and the systematic ways in which a next course of action is taken once the problem is identified.

Sarah looks at Sam and involves him in the interaction she is having with Jenny (lines 151–152). By initiating an interaction with Sam, asking him to get the thermometer, Sarah immediately orients to her need for access to medical diagnostic equipment, the purpose of this particular item is to provide information about a possible raised temperature, which would confirm the presence of an illness. Sam's response is partly inaudible, but the beginning of his utterance can be heard as providing Sarah with his knowledge about Jenny, indicating that Sarah's call for a thermometer was heard by Sam as a need to know more about the state of Jenny's health. Sarah's response clearly marks a change of state token (Heritage, 1984) indicating that her knowledge position about Jenny's problem is changing. To make her understanding explicit, she goes on to verbally state her new knowledge regarding Jenny's actions (lines 155–157) 'because she had her immunisations'. Sarah then pauses before directing her speech to Jenny with an assertion of this 'having immunisations' as being a legitimate reason for Jenny to 'feel not great'.

Sarah follows this by making her knowledge of Jenny's situation visible to Jenny as she remarks 'coz you had an injection'. Up until this point, there has been much guess work involved in the interaction where Sarah has demonstrated her K- position with regard to Jenny's state of health. Even though Sarah managed to ascertain that Jenny had an upset stomach through her non-verbal cues of talk, Sarah continued diagnosing Jenny's trouble in her subsequent orientation to Jenny, as a priority over her interactions with other children present around the morning tea table. This further investigation has now led to Sarah gaining the same knowledge as Jenny about the situation. Although it has been suggested that there can never be a fully co-equal K+/K+ or K-/K- relationship (Enfield, 2011), this situation implies that Sarah has similar knowledge as to the root of the problem as Jenny now.

Jenny subsequently acknowledges Sarah's realisation as she nods slightly, affirming Sarah's new knowledge. This is followed by Sarah stating that she had 'forgotten' about that information, indicating that she did have prior knowledge of Jenny's situation, but that this knowledge was temporarily inaccessible. Following a pause Sarah makes a noticing about one of the children sitting at the table with her, as she momentarily places her attention back onto the morning tea activity as she orients to Michael eating a jam sandwich, marking that the ongoing activity is still to be attended to. There is then another moment of silence as Sam approaches Sarah followed by Sarah offering a possible solution for Jenny's problem as she suggests that Jenny might need to have a sleep. This marks a shift in Sarah's interaction sequence with Jenny as she progresses from no longer eliciting knowledge from Jenny to a possible way of fixing the problem. A similar systematic process as was observed in Chapter 5 where the teachers initially needed knowledge about a dispute situation prior to suggesting a possible way to resolve the matter.

Once Sam has reached Sarah and Jenny he sits down in a chair next to them and passes the thermometer to Sarah, making himself available as a member of the ongoing interaction through his proximal engagement (Goodwin, 1981). Sarah does the activity of taking Jenny's temperature and reading the result of the test out loud 'thirty-seven point two'. This new knowledge allows Sarah to make the subsequent assessment, that the raised temperature is making Jenny feel 'yucky' (line 172).

Once Jenny's slight raise in temperature has been established, giving more knowledge about Jenny's condition to Sarah and now Sam, Sarah attempts to take a further reading from Jenny's other ear. This situation now takes on a humorous role as Sarah struggles to find Jenny's ear and Sam laughs quietly at the attempt. Sarah smiles and asks Sam if she 'has it' and Sam, still smiling, offers his help. This collaborative interaction of taking an ill child's temperature between Sam and Sarah has similar interactional features to collaborative sentences. This begins with Sarah latching on to the end of Sam's utterance (line 179–180) where Sam takes over the temperature taking as Sarah is finding it difficult. The collaborative action resonates with a collaborative utterance where 'one person produces an almost complete sentence and finds him-self searching for a last word or a last phrase which he can't find' (Sacks, 1992a, p. 321). As Sarah struggles to complete her physical task, Sam intervenes and completes the physical action for her, co-producing a collaborative embodied action.

Further affiliation is then shown between Sam and Sarah as Sam reads out a similar, yet slightly higher, temperature reading from Jenny's other ear and both Sam and Sarah hold each other's gaze and nod their heads (lines 186–188). This affiliation in nodding has been found in prior research (Stivers, 2008) where an affiliative stance is shared by the members through this action in receipt of some telling. Through engaging in these actions, the affiliative stance towards a collaborative caring for Jenny is co-produced between the two teachers and this now progresses in the next series of actions (lines 188–192) where Sarah and Sam discuss possible medication and then Sam disaffiliates himself from the current situation by walking away.

The prior sequences of actions between Jenny and Sarah have demonstrated Jenny playing out a problem through embodied action as she leans in closely to Sarah and Sarah responded by providing relational care, co-producing CBA aligning with a collection R category. Within the systematic unfolding of this interaction was also the knowledge exchange shared between both members, both verbally and non-verbally, as Sarah requested knowledge and Jenny answered in the process of diagnosing the problem. Sarah then investigated the reason for Jenny's trouble by eliciting help from another early childhood teacher, Sam, and professional diagnostic medical equipment, the thermometer. During the next few lines of observation, Sarah works to bring this interaction to a close.

Sarah is sitting at the morning tea table cutting apple for two boys; Jenny is sitting on her lap. Sarah stops cutting and puts her hands down by her sides. Jenny reaches for Sarah's arms and lifts them around her. Sarah cuddles Jenny.

41 minutes 37 seconds

```
193  SAR:   .hhh <↓We:ll↓> (1.9) ↑morning tea's done for
194         ↓an↑other day↓ tsk
195         (1.3)
196  BOY:   hhh. ((giggles))
197  SAR:   <↑ti:me> to pack it up↓
198         (1.5)
199  BOY:   hhh. ((giggles))
200  SAR:   where would you like to be ↑miss (1.7) while I pack
201         up morning tea (1.7) would you like to be inside on
202         the c↑ou:ch=
203  JEN:   =((shakes her head))
204  SAR:   would you just like to sit here on the ch↑air
205  JEN:   ((shakes her head))
206  SAR:   no (0.4) would you like to be outside $in the ↓rain
207  JEN:   ((looks outside))
208  SAR:   what about over in the family area↓ with
209         Jessica=
210  JEN:   =((shakes her head))=
211  SAR:                        =↑oh=my=goodness where
212         we gonna put you then
213         (3.6)
214  SAR:   would you like to go see Eva↓ ((feels
215         Jenny's forehead and strokes her hair))
216  JEN:   ((nods her head))
217  SAR:   mmm=yeah shall I take you to Eva (0.2) for some
218         more <↑lo:ves>
219  JEN:   ((nods her head))
```

```
220 SAR:        ↑come on then↓ ((lifts Jenny up and carries her
221             away))
```

Sarah begins this sequence of actions with 'well' (line 193) to mark the closing of a prior topic and the opening of the next (Heritage, 1984). Sarah then identifies the episode that she has just engaged in with the children as 'morning tea' as she explicitly states that that particular episode is being closed for 'another day'. This marks the episode as morning tea and does not orient to the prior sequences of action as being about caring for an ill child; even though the conversation exchanges that co-produced this episode demonstrated that this more relational activity was also being co-produced as a priority.

Although this action demonstrates that Sarah has marked this moment as an accurate place for a closing to occur (Schegloff and Sacks, 1973), it has to be touched off and accepted by the other participants in order for the closing to be co-produced in a systematic way. Here, the mark to close the sequence of morning tea is responded to by one of the children who is present as he giggles (line 196). Sarah moves on to provide a stepwise action (Jefferson, 1984) as she moves from her reference to ending morning tea to suggesting that it is time to 'pack up'. This move supports the closing of morning tea as both packing up and the end of morning tea both have co-class membership (Sacks, 1972) to 'the closing of an activity'.

Sarah subsequently brings the two activities together in her next turn at talk where she returns to the problem of where to put Jenny as she continues in her everyday work of closing the morning tea routine. This is accomplished by Sarah asking Jenny where she would like to go and giving the packing up of morning tea as a reason for Jenny having to be moved (lines 200–202). Through these actions Sarah prepares the children for a pending transition from what is happening currently to the next sequence of actions as she begins drawing the morning tea to a close. Here, Sarah's actions are produced in a similar way to Sacks' (1972) therapy sessions, as the action of closing can only be initiated by the professional in the professional/layperson interaction.

Lines 201–212 involve Sarah making a series of suggestions about where Jenny could possibly go and declines from Jenny for each suggestion, demonstrating the importance of the two interlocutors' agreement before the transition of Jenny can progress. Sarah then changes her approach of offering environmental features as possibilities to move to, to offering Jenny the name of another person. Although the knowledge transfer is important in the co-production of this transition, where Jenny has to agree to being moved to a particular place suggested by Sarah, relationships are also brought into play. This relationship between geographical location (G) and its relation to members (Rm) (Schegloff, 1972) was further explored in Chapter 6 and is significant here as, when another staff member is suggested in connection to moving to another place, Jenny agrees to be moved to her (line 216).

During this naming of a possible other carer, Sarah also strokes Jenny's hair adding further attention to their relational interaction. This relational interaction is then further progressed as Sarah suggests that Jenny can go to the other staff member 'for some more loves' (line 218). Sarah's utterance of 'more' indicates that Jenny has already been engaged in an interaction that has involved love, further attending to the co-production of being members of the category R collection.

Rights to Request and Provide Help

Sacks' famous works on suicide calls offers insight into people's right to ask for help from a spouse or family member through their co-membership to the category R collection, and when these people are not available they turn to a person from the K collection, as was the case in the suicide calls. Here we see that a four-year-old child, Jenny, turned to her teacher Sarah for help when she was feeling unwell. The teacher Sarah then engages in CBA conducive to members of the category R collection by giving cuddles and kisses and by being physically reassuring. It is observable here that although Sarah and Jenny belong to the MCD teacher/pupil who are members of the K collection of people who interact around knowledge exchange in teaching and learning episodes, when deemed appropriate by both parties they also engage in the CBA of being in a category R collection. In this instance Jenny has the right to request help in the form of relational care from her teacher and this is shown through the teacher's reciprocal response to Jenny as they co-produce the situation.

Although, in this interaction, Jenny does not communicate verbally, which could mark a problem in the ongoing flow of conversation and a possible disaffiliation from Sarah; she replaces her verbal actions with physical gestures to communicate her need to be close to Sarah and her desire to be in an interaction with her. This aligns with the work of Fillipi (2009) as it demonstrates the importance of non-verbal gesture as communication in a turn-taking sequence in early childhood. None of this activity is turned to as problematic in a third position repair when a verbal action of providing relational help for Jenny is attended to by Sarah and Sam. Likewise, when Sarah provides the physical response of cuddling Jenny, stroking Jenny's hair and kissing her, it is accepted as an everyday action in that place at that time with those members due to it not being touched off as problematic and in need of repair in a next action.

Knowledge and Relationships in Managing Illness

This chapter has demonstrated how a single case analysis of an interaction between a four-year-old child and their early childhood teacher reveals their co-production of membership to both K and R collections. Throughout the everyday activity of morning tea, the teacher attended to the ongoing process of providing food and drink for all children present at the morning tea table, but also abandoned this ongoing interaction several times to attend to the exclusive relational caring of Jenny. Through attending to Jenny in such a way, Sarah made observable the importance of providing relational care in the form of hugs, kisses, stroking, rocking and talking of love and snuggles, as a matter of priority and omni-relevance. The systematic way in which these priority sequences were inserted into the ongoing morning tea activity reveals how the trouble was initially communicated, the diagnosis of the trouble and possible treatments for the trouble, all co-produced between Jenny and Sarah.

Sarah and Jenny co-produce a collection K category through the knowledge exchange around their approach to the diagnosis of the problem through asking questions to gain knowledge about the trouble, solution and providing a possible treatment. In this instance K- and K+ positioned categories were evident where Sarah was the less knowledgeable about Jenny's trouble, and Jenny was the more knowledgeable with her first-hand experience. However, there is also evidence of Jenny and Sarah being members of the collection R SRP through the interlocutors requesting and providing relational help throughout the interaction. CBAs involving close physical contact, stroking, kissing and rocking are attended to, co-producing membership to the category R collection.

This single case observation demonstrates that, although Sarah is doing general teaching for all of the children in her care during morning tea, she pays explicit attention to Jenny in a way that diagnoses her problem, organises context specific solutions and possible further treatment through talk inserted into the ongoing morning tea activity. This observation aligns with other findings in this book that suggest that the way in which collection R categories are brought in to play involve the insertion of priority items, making these specific activities around category R collections omni-relevant, that is, having the utmost importance during daily activity between early childhood teachers and young children.

Chapter 8
Knowledge and Relationships in Early Childhood Education

This book presented an analysis of interactions between children aged two and a half to five years and their early childhood teachers during their daily activities inside and outside of their early childhood education centre. The children and teachers were observed engaging in pretend play, engaging with the environment, dispute situations and attending to illness. Through observing and analysing these interactions as they unfold in situ, a unique insight into teaching and learning episodes in early years education is afforded. The research, in its attempts to reveal real life teaching and learning processes, deliberately avoided the confinement of predefined hypotheses that are often associated with research exploring 'educational' activity. In doing so the conversational turn-taking evident in each teacher-child episode made observable how knowledge exchange and relationships were managed between the participants as a members matter.

Although a more general labelling of the participants and place of research can be described as teachers, pupils and an early childhood education setting, this book alerts the reader to the usefulness of a data-driven approach to observing and analysing the everyday conversations that co-produced the social interactions. This perspective avoids predefined ideas about these people and what might be expected to be found, and allows the participants to speak for themselves.

As discussed in Chapter 2, research in the area of early years education has shifted somewhat from viewing the child as an empty vessel or passive recipient of knowledge passed on from a more knowing teacher, to understanding teaching and learning as a collaborative and social process. Although this is the case, there still remains to be limited information available that provides insight into the ways in which teaching and learning is co-produced in this social way. Chapters 4, 5, 6 and 7 have attempted to shed more light on this process by providing examples of interactions between teachers and children in their everyday activities with each other.

The Usefulness of CA in Early Childhood Education Research

Through employing ethnomethodology, conversation analysis and membership categorisation analysis to the study of teacher-child interactions, this book has revealed the ways in which teachers and children work together to initiate and maintain the co-production of knowledge and relationships through the various activities they engage in on a daily basis with each other, verbally and with gesture. The underpinning concept in conversation analysis of a shared understanding being pivotal to the natural progression of everyday interactions lends itself well to the socio-cultural approach to teaching and learning within the New Zealand early childhood curriculum. This child-led approach to teaching and learning in early childhood settings affords opportunities for children to initiate interactions with their teachers about the things that they find interesting, attending to some things and not others. The orientation to specific features of conversation is recognised as significant in CA where the question of *why that there and now* is attempted to be answered through looking at the turn-taking sequences in talk-in-interaction (Schegloff, 1991; Schegloff and Sacks, 1973).

This book provides instances of how knowledge exchange is oriented to as significant by the participants where they request and provide information for each other in systematic and responsive ways; a social action that would probably be expected in an education setting. However, the interactions documented here also demonstrate how the participants collaboratively attend to the request and provision of physical and emotional caring, a social action that may not be so expected in an education setting. On discovering members' systematic orientation to, and co-production of R and K collections, this book offers further insight into early childhood research regarding the significance of emotions and relationships in early childhood education, to explain more fully how this aspect of teaching is managed in everyday practice (Elfer, 2012; David, 1996; Page and Elfer, 2013; Stephen, 2010). As emotional attachments and holistic well-being are increasingly significant aspects of global policy concerning early childhood provision (see Page and Elfer, 2013 for an overview), the ways in which such relational care is co-produced in everyday early childhood education is of paramount importance. It is argued here that CA affords ways of revealing such interaction in situ.

The Omni-relevance of Relational Activity in Early Childhood Education

Throughout this book the systematic ways in which knowledge exchange is co-produced is demonstrated as a mundane feature of everyday practice between young children and their teachers where one person's talk is shown to be understood in the response of the recipient, and new knowledge is given and received. Whilst these episodes of teaching and learning were progressing, there were also moments when children demonstrated signs of an emotional upset, sometimes caused by physical troubles. When these incidents occurred, the teachers were found to orient to the upset as a priority, often abruptly abandoning their ongoing interaction with a different child. This finding that relational activities consistently took priority over other interactions was unexpected and was a key finding from the research project.

The unexpected nature of the use of priority items in daily activities is mirrored in the work of Sacks (1992a):

> I was working on these things without any intention of dealing with the issue of omni-relevance, not much was happening. It was when I was working on the priority character of those insertable sequences, and asked, 'how is that priority invoked, and what allows this one or that one to do it?' that it became apparent that it was material which was very much related to the phenomenon of omni-relevance. (p. 316)

That teachers and children attend to relational issues in such an omni-relevant way was observable to the members present, in situ and was therefore also observable to the researcher where the finding emanated from the iterative viewing of the interactions over time. Hester and Hester (2012) also provide an insight into how omni-relevance is observable in everyday interactions by making reference to the CBA that are displayed in their talk-in-interaction coupled with the 'anytime invocability' (p.15).

The empirical Chapters 4, 5, 6 and 7 work in such a way as to build on each other to gradually demonstrate the ways in which relational activities are exhibited by teachers and children. Relational activities are increasingly observable in the chapters where, initially through pretend play activities in Chapter 4, the teachers and children either align or affiliate with each other by fully engaging in pretend play, or not. The final excerpts in Chapter 4 demonstrate how attending to issues of safety and well-being were attended to as having omni-relevance over engaging in pretence when the *actual* eating of pretend play objects (stones in Excerpt 7 and sand in Excerpt 8) was of issue. In Chapter 5 the teachers were observed abandoning their ongoing interactions with other children to attend to an upset child (Excerpts 1–4), children who were upset by a dispute approached a teacher (Excerpts 5 and 6) and teachers orientated to promoting relational activities to resolve disputes (Excerpts 7–9). Building on these ideas, Chapter 6 shows how emotions (Excerpt 1) and issues of physical safety and well-being (Excerpt 2) are linked to the environment, where the excerpts increasingly demonstrate how category R collection is made omni-relevant as these relational issues are attended to as a priority by the members present. The omni-relevance of managing illness in relational ways is then demonstrated through a single case analysis of an ill child in Chapter 7.

Within these chapters the 'anytime invocability' (Hester and Hester, 2012, p.15) of the relational R category collection was both talked into being and co-produced physically by both teachers and children in their requests and provision of help with emotional and physical troubles. When managing these relational issues, the importance of knowledge exchange was significant in order for the members present to achieve a shared understanding of the situation. The teachers demonstrate their joint interest in children's tellings where they explicitly prompt a telling from a child; this prompting is evidenced in prior work on relationships in storytelling (Goodwin, 1981; Mandlebaum, 1989), in formal psychotherapy interactions (Hutchby, 2005b) and less formal situations where teachers prompt children's emotional tellings about difficult situations (Bateman, Danby and Howard, 2013a, 2013b; Bateman and Danby, 2013).

The interactions show how the 'members enact incumbency in particular relationship categories by engaging in actions and practices that are recognizably appropriate for incumbents of that relationship category' (Pomerantz and Mandlebaum, 2005, p. 155). During their co-production of an interaction the participants demonstrated their incumbency to a collection R category through their CBA. The findings here show how the activity of problem sharing and the receipt and acknowledgement of an interlocutor's problems marks a relationship category as both members show their joint interest and attend to the problem as a matter of priority.

A Child's Search for Help in an Educational Institution

When exploring the interactions, the omni-relevance of Sacks' collection R category was evident. In relation to this, the *programmatic relevance* was also significant where 'if R is relevant, then the non-incumbency of any of its pair positions is an observable' (Sacks, 1972, p. 39). In relation to the teacher-child interactions presented in this book, if a child showed signs of emotional trouble, the absence of an adult to comfort that upset child was observable. This was demonstrated as the teachers responded immediately to such troubles where they worked to fill the gap of an otherwise noticeably absent adult carer. The children's actions also worked to co-produce the collection R category with the teachers as they accepted the teacher's giving of help, and explicitly approached teachers for help with an emotional trouble.

Throughout the chapters when a relational trouble was made observable, either initiated by a child or teacher, the teacher and child attended to it as a priority over the ongoing interaction. This priority sequence suggests the bond of obligation that the teacher has to provide relational care for young children, and the children's rights to request and receive it. The teachers and children are observed engaging in such CBA as hugging, kissing and stroking, presenting a shift from the usual teacher-child CBA engaged in through teaching and learning activities about task-based issues. These shifts in the co-production of membership categories are acknowledged as part of everyday interactions (Schegloff, 1972) and observable here where the category R and K collections were not stagnant, but were co-produced through physical gesture and talk-in-interaction.

Sacks (1972) suggests that within the category R collection there is a first position that includes those in the relational category who are proper to turn to for emotional support, Rp; and those in second position who would be improper to turn to, Ri. The child-parent SRP demonstrates one Rp collection of members where the parent has a set of rights and obligations to give emotional help and support to their child in a first-position. A teacher-pupil category set would ordinarily belong to the category K collection as they distribute specialised knowledge and so would be in first position of this knowledge category, Kp. However, in the absence of a parent (first-position Rp) it is possible that the teacher-child SRP offers similar opportunities for Rp in early childhood when children are still in need of emotional help and support when their parent is absent. In the early childhood educational setting in this book, the adults that do provide such relational help for children experiencing trouble are the teachers, positioning them as being active participants in both Kp and Rp collections.

Although the members who attend educational institutions can be categorised as 'teacher-pupil' or 'lecturer-student' through the membership inference-rich representative (MIR) device (Sacks, 1992a), these people could also be given other identities, depending on which is the most relevant at that time and in that place. When considering the hierarchy of relevance in relation to the interactions discussed in this book, the order of relevancy implies that the most important category be used to describe them (Sacks, 1992a), so that a troubled child would need a compassionate adult. In terms of cover devices, here the identities of 'teacher-pupil' could act as a 'cover' identity for, more simply, 'adult-child'. This can be linked to *partitioning constancy* (Sacks, 1992a, p. 317, original italics) where the members of one population (teacher) can also belong to another population (adult).

Through a better understanding of the social relationships evident in early childhood education between teachers and children, we see that, when searching for help in early childhood education, it is possible that there is *always* someone to turn to. The observations and analysis presented in this book demonstrate how a young child's search for help can always found, whether through a collection K category or collection R. This is evident through analysing young children's interactions with their toddler and preschool teachers where emotional help and knowledge exchange were co-produced. These observations demonstrate the co-production of collection categories during everyday mundane activity in early childhood education where the activity of the co-production of category collections was both occasioned and indexical (Hester and Francis, 1997).

The activities that the early childhood teachers and children engaged in together demonstrate the ways in which they are obliged to provide and request for help from each other, educationally and relationally. This relational giving and receiving of care in early childhood education situations has elsewhere been fittingly termed 'professional love' (Page, 2011, p. 313). Within educational institutions the interactional exchanges that privilege such a term are significant and unique, making early childhood education an educational institution and the work of early childhood teachers recognisable as multifaceted and complex.

The Complex Work of Early Childhood Teachers

The priority given to attending to emotional troubles is systematically produced whenever a child shows signs of needing relational help during everyday activity. As such it is describable as having systematic importance in daily activities in early childhood education. Children attend to relational activities as having priority as they call for help from the teachers and ask them to attend to such help giving. Teachers attend to relational activities as priority through their orientation to it, not directly linking it to an ongoing activity, but as an event that takes precedence over current interactions (Sacks, 1992a).

We have seen through the contents of this book that, in early childhood education, children's cries for help, whether they are requiring knowledge or relational support, are noticed, recognised and responded to by their early childhood teachers. The interactions analysed here speak to the 'emotional complexity of the work' (Page and Elfer, 2013, p. 8) of early childhood teachers and young children. In their everyday activities teachers and children work together to co-produce knowledge exchange involving task problems, recognised in *sustained shared thinking* (Siraj-Blatchford and Manni 2008; Sylva et al., 2010) when exploring working theories (Bateman, 2013; Carr, 2011; Peters and Davies, 2011; Hargraves, 2013; Hedges, 2011) and possibility thinking (Burnard et al., 2006). In the excerpts presented in this book, knowledge exchange around relational troubles is also co-produced where the teachers asked for information from the more knowledgeable children before making an informed decision about how to respond.

This co-production of knowledge and relational activities is observed here as a mundane part of early childhood education and is demonstrated as such by the children and teachers in this book through their actions, as they allow relational activities to take priority without orienting to such an action as problematic. The sequential organisation of doing both teaching, learning and caring for each other in early childhood education can be seen as 'business as usual' (Jefferson, 1980, p. 153) as emotional upset and troubles are dealt with saliently (Page and Elfer, 2013). The interactions here demonstrate the orderly way in which the activity of teaching and learning can also incorporate the essential interactional features of providing emotional and physical care and well-being for very young children on a daily basis.

Through engaging in such activities, the 'balancing' involved in early childhood teaching is observable where aspects such as providing content/topic knowledge, behaviour management and emotional support are all attended to in everyday interactions with children. This is a unique feature of teachers' conversations and actions in early childhood education with very young children and offers insight into the daily lives of teachers where they make deliberate noticing, recognising and responding decisions in order to achieve what seems to be an appropriate balance.

Early childhood education in New Zealand involves educating teachers to notice, recognise and respond to opportunities where teaching and learning moments could occur by following the child's interests. This book has presented some episodes where teaching and learning was noticed as such by the participating teachers. As such, the systematic ways in which the early childhood curriculum framework, *Te Whāriki*, was implemented is revealed. By attending to 'educational' as well as 'relational' needs in their everyday work, the teachers are successfully implementing the strands of 'contribution' and 'well-being' as well as the principles 'empowerment' and 'relationships'. This is done through effective verbal and non-verbal communication, implementing the 'communication' strand and ensures the holistic care of the children, making observable the 'holistic' principle embedded throughout their everyday practice.

Providing such a framework offers opportunities for relational as well as educational interactions to be attended to as a members matter and with the saliency of evolving category collections. It is argued here that the importance of an early childhood curriculum framework that supports the holistic well-being of the child as well as stimulating possibility thinking and wider social learning about the world is imperative. Only through such guidance can the impromptu needs of a child be attended to in such ways. Although there is interest in employing a more formal structure to early childhood education through literacy and numeracy strategies, a holistic curriculum (as in New Zealand) affords teachers and children opportunities to engage in multifaceted, personal and emotional interactions where each members' interests are attended to during the co-construction of everyday interactions.

Also, of significance here is how an ethnomethodological approach to the study of teaching and learning interactions afforded a unique insight into the everyday, mundane activities that occurred there. Conversation analysis enabled the systematic and orderly features of knowledge exchange and social stances to be revealed through the turns at verbal and non-verbal actions engaged in by the participants. Membership categorisation analysis afforded an understanding about how relational and knowledge category collections were co-produced by these members in situ. It is hoped that the findings in this book can contribute to the important research that is already available in the areas of early childhood education and EM, CA and MCA.

Appendix: CA Transcription Conventions

The conversation analysis symbols used to transcribe the data are adapted from Jefferson's conventions described in Sacks, Schegloff and Jefferson (1974).

[	the beginning of an overlap.
]	the end of an overlap.
=	the equals sign at the end of one utterance and the beginning of the next utterance marks the latching of speech between the speakers. When used in-between words it marks the latching of the words spoken in an utterance with no break.
(0.4)	the time of a pause in seconds.
::	lengthening of the prior sound. More or less colons are used to represent the longer or shorter lengthening.
↑	a rising intonation in speech.
↓	a falling intonation in speech.
-	abrupt break from speech.
Underscore	marks an emphasis placed on the underscored sound.
Bold	underscored words in bold indicate heavy emphasis or shouting.
°degree sign°	either side of a word indicates that it is spoken in a quiet, soft tone.
(brackets)	utterance could not be deciphered.
((*brackets*))	double brackets with words in italics indicate unspoken actions.
$dollar$	Dollar signs indicate the talk was in a smile voice.
creaky	Asterisks indicate the talk was in creaky voice.
~wavy line~	Wavy lines indicates a wobbly voice.
>arrows<	utterance spoken quickly.

Reference

Sacks, H., Schegloff, E. A and Jefferson, G. (1974) A Simplest Systematics for the Organisation of Turn-Taking for Conversation, *Language*, Volume 50, pp. 696–735.

References

Aarsand, P.A and Aronsson, K. (2009). Response cries and other gaming moves – Building intersubjectivity in gaming. *Journal of Pragmatics*, 41, 1557–1575.

Antaki, C. and Widdicombe, S. (1998). Identity as an achievement and as a tool. In C. Anataki and S. Widdicombe (eds), *Identities in Talk* (pp. 1–14). London: Sage.

Atewell, P. (1974). Ethnomethodology since Garfinkel. *Theory and Society*, 1(2), 179–210.

Atkinson, J.M. and Drew, P. (1979). *Order in Court: The Organisation of Verbal Interaction in Judicial Settings*. London: Macmillan.

Baker, C.D. (2000). Locating culture in action: Membership categorization in texts and talk. In A. Lee and C. Poynton (eds), *Culture and Text: Discourse and Methodology in Social Research and Cultural Studies* (pp. 99–113). St Leonards, New South Wales: Allen and Unwin.

Baker, C.D. and Freebody, P. (1986). Representations of questioning and answering in children's first school books, *Language and Society*, 15(4), 451–483.

Bateman, A. (2010). *Children's Co-construction of Context; Prosocial and Antisocial Revisited* Unpublished PhD Thesis. University of Wales Swansea, Wales.

Bateman, A. (2011). Huts and heartache: The affordance of playground huts for legal debate, *Journal of Pragmatics*, 43, 3111–3121.

Bateman, A. (2012a). *Pedagogical Intersubjectivity: Teaching and Learning Conversations Between Children and Teachers*. Wellington, New Zealand: NZCER.

Bateman, A. (2012b). When verbal disputes get physical. In S. Danby and M. Theobald (eds), *Disputes in Everyday Life: Social and Moral Orders of Children and Young People* (*Sociological Studies of Children and Youth*, 15) (pp. 267–296). Bradford: Emerald.

Bateman, A. (2012c). Forging friendships: The use of collective pro-terms by pre-school children, *Discourse Studies*, 14(1), 165–180.

Bateman, A. (2013). Responding to children's answers: questions embedded in the social context of early childhood education, *Early Years: An International Research Journal*, 33(3), 275–289.

Bateman, A. and Church, A. (2014). Objects as social access tools in the primary school playground. Paper presented at International Conference on Conversation Analysis (ICCA) June 23rd – 29th, 2014. UCLA, California.

Bateman, A. and Church, A. (in press, 2015). Children's use of objects in an early years playground, European Early Childhood Education Research Journal.

Bateman, A. and Danby, S. (2013). Recovering from the earthquake: Early childhood teachers and children collaboratively telling stories about their experiences, *Disaster Management and Prevention Journal*, 22(5), 467–479.

Bateman, A., Hohepa, M. and Bennett, T. (forthcoming, 2016). 'Indigenising outdoor play with young children in New Zealand' in T. Waller (ed.) *Outdoor environments and learning in early childhood*. Sage Handbook

Bateman, A. and Waters, J. (2013). Asymmetries of knowledge between children and teachers on a New Zealand bush walk, *Australian Journal of Communication*, 40(2), 19–32.

Bateman, A., Danby, S. and Howard, J. (2013a). Everyday preschool talk about Christchurch earthquakes, *Australia Journal of Communication*, 40(1), 103–123.

Bateman, A., Danby, S. and Howard, J. (2013b). Living in a broken world: How young children's well-being is supported through playing out their earthquake experiences, *International Journal of Play*, 2(3), 202–219.

Bateman, A., Hohepa, M., and Bennett, T. (forthcoming, 2016). Indigenising outdoor play in New Zealand. In T. Waller (ed.), *International Handbook of Outdoor Play and Learning*. London: Sage.

Benwell, B and Stokoe, E (2006). *Discourse and Identity*. Edinburgh, Edinburgh University Press.

Berk, L.E. and Winsler, A. (1995). *Scaffolding Children's Learning: Vygotsky and early childhood education*. Washington: NAEYC.

Bilton, H. (2010). *Outdoor Learning in the Early Years: Management and Innovation (third edition)*. London: Routledge.

Birdwhistell, R.L (1970). *Kinesics and Context: Essays on Body–Motion Communication*. London: Penguin Press.

Bjork-Willen, P. (2012). Being Doggy: Disputes embedded in preschoolers' family role-play. In S. Danby and M. Theobald (eds), *Disputes in Everyday Life: Social and Moral Orders of Children and Young People (Sociological Studies of Children and Youth*, 15) (pp. 119–140). Bradford: Emerald Insight.

Bolden, G.B., and J.D. Robinson. (2011). Soliciting accounts with why-interrogatives in conversation, *Journal of Communication*, 61, 94–119.

Bruner, J., Jolly, A., and Sylva, K. (1976). *Play: Its Role in Development and Evolution*. New York: Penguin Books.

Burdelski, M. (2010). Socializing politeness routines: Action, other-orientation, and embodiment in a Japanese preschool, *Journal of Pragmatics*, 42(6), 1606–1621

Burnard, P., Craft, A., Cremin, T., Duffy, B., Hanson, R., Keene, J., Haynes, L. and Burns, D. (2006). Documenting 'possibility thinking': a journey of collaborative enquiry, *International Journal of Early Years Education*, 14(3), 243–262

Busch, G. (2012). 'Will, you've got to share': Disputes during family mealtime. In S. Danby and M. Theobald (eds), *Disputes in Everyday Life: Social and Moral*

Orders of Children and Young People (Sociological Studies of Children and Youth, 15) (pp. 27–56). Bradford: Emerald Insight.

Butler, C.W. (2008). *Talk and Social Interaction in the Playground.* Hampshire: Ashgate.

Butler, C.W. and Weatherall, A. (2006). 'No We're Not Playing Families': Membership Categorization in Children's Play, *Research on Language and Social Interaction*, 39(4), 441–470.

Butler, C.W., Fitzgerald, R. and Gardner, R. (2009). Branching out: Ethnomethodological approaches to communication. *Australian Journal of Communication*, 36(3), 1–14.

Carr, M. (2007). *Learning Wisdom.* Wellington, New Zealand: NZCER.

Carr, M. (2011). Young children reflecting on their learning: Teachers' conversation strategies, *Early Years: An International Journal of Research and Development*, 31(3), 257–270.

Carr, M., Lee, W. and Jones, C. (2004). *Kei tua o te pae. Assessment for Learning: Early childhood Exemplars. Book 2: Sociocultural Assessment, Book 4: Children Contributing to Their Own Assessment.* Wellington: Learning Media.

Carr, M., Peters, S., Davis, K., Bartlett, C., Bashford, N., Berry, P., and Wilson-Tukaki, A. (2008). *Key Learning Competencies across Place and Time: Kimihia te ara tōtika, hei oranga mō to ao.* Wellington, New Zealand: NZCER.

Cazden, C. (2001). *Classroom Discourse: The Language of Teaching and Learning.* Portsmouth: Heinemann.

Cekaite, A. (2010). Shepherding the child: embodied directive sequences in parent-child interactions, *Text and Talk*, 30(1), 1–25.

Cekaite, A. (2012). Tattling and Dispute Resolution: Moral order, emotions and embodiment in the teacher-mediated disputes of young second language learners. In S. Danby and M. Theobald (eds), *Disputes in Everyday Life: Social and Moral Orders of Children and Young People* (Sociological Studies of Children and Youth, 15) (pp. 165–192). Bradford: Emerald Insight.

Cekaite, A. (2014). Embodied directive sequences: Timing and coordinating of talk and touch in adult-child interactions. Paper presented at International Conference on Conversation Analysis (ICCA) June 23rd – 29th, 2014. UCLA, California.

Church, A. (2007). Conversation analysis in early childhood research, *Journal of Australian Research in Early Childhood Education*, 14(2), 1–10.

Church, A. (2009). *Preference Organisation and Peer Disputes: How Young Children Resolve Conflict.* Aldershot: Ashgate.

Church, A. (2010). Opportunities for learning during storybook reading at preschool. In L. Wei (ed.), *Applied Linguistics Review* (pp. 225–251). Berlin, Germany: De Gruyter Mouton.

Cobb-Moore, C. (2012). 'Pretend I was Mummy': Children's production of authority and subordination in their pretend play interaction during disputes. In S. Danby and M. Theobald (eds), *Disputes in Everyday Life: Social and Moral*

Orders of Children and Young People (*Sociological Studies of Children and Youth*, 15) (pp. 85–118). Bradford: Emerald Insight.

Cobb-Moore, C., Danby, S. and Farrell, A. (2008). 'I told you so': justification used in disputes in young children's interactions in an early childhood classroom, *Discourse Studies*, 10(5), 595–614.

Corsaro, W.A. (1979). 'We're friends right?': Children's use of access rituals in a nursery school, *Language in Society*, 8(3), 315–336.

Corsaro, W.A. (1985). *Friendship and Peer Culture in the Early Years*. Ablex Publishing Corporation, Norwood, N.J, U.S.

Corsaro, W.A. (1997). *The Sociology of Childhood*. London: Sage Publications.

Corsaro, W.A. (2014). *The Sociology of Childhood* (4th edition). London: Sage Publications.

Cromdal, J. (2001). *Can I be with?*: Negotiating play entry in a bilingual school, *Journal of Pragmatics*, 33, 515–543.

Cromdal, J. (2004). Building bilingual oppositions: Code-switching in children's disputes. *Language in Society*, 33, 33–58.

Cromdal, J. (2009). Childhood and social interaction in everyday life: Introduction to the special issue. *Journal of Pragmatics*, 41, 1473–1476.

Danby, S. (1996). Constituting social membership: Two readings of talk in an early childhood classroom, *Language and Education,* 10 (2 and 3), 151–170.

Danby, S. (2002). The communicative competence of young children, *Australian Journal of Early Childhood*, 27(3), 25–30.

Danby, S. (2005). Preschool girls, conflict and repair. In J. Mason and T. Fattore (eds), *Children Taken Seriously: In Theory, Policy and Practice* (pp. 172–181). London: Jessica Kingsley Publishers.

Danby, S. and Baker, C. (1998b). How to be masculine in the block area. *Childhood*, 5(2), 151–175.

Danby, S. and Baker, C. (2000). Unravelling the fabric of social order in block area. In S. Hester and D. Francis (eds), *Local Educational Order: Ethnomethodological Studies of Knowledge in Action* (pp. 91–140). Amsterdam: John Benjamins.

Danby, S. and Baker, C.D. (1998a). What's the Problem? Restoring Social Order in the Preschool Classroom. In I. Hutchby and J. Moran-Ellis (eds), *Children and Social Competence: Arenas of Action* (pp. 157–86). London: Falmer.

Danby, S. and Theobald, M. (2012). *Disputes in Everyday Life: Social and Moral Orders of Children and Young People* (*Sociological Studies of Children and Youth*, 15) Bradford: Emerald Insight.

Danby, S., and Baker, C. (2001). Escalating terror: Communicative strategies in a preschool classroom dispute. *Early Education and Development*, 12(3), 343–358.

Danby. S. (2009). Childhood and social interaction in everyday life: An epilogue, *Journal of Pragmatics*, 41, 1596–1599.

David, T. (1996). Their Right to Play. In C. Nutbrown (ed), *Respectful Educators – Capable Learners: Children's Rights and Early Education* (pp. 90–98). London: Paul Chapman Publishing.

Davis, K. and Peters, S. (2008). *Moments of Wonder, Everyday Events: How are Young Children Theorising and Making Sense of their World?* Wellington, New Zealand: NZCER.

Deniz-Tarum, S. and Kyratzis, A. (2012). Challenging and orienting to monolingual school norms in Turkish American children's peer disputes and classroom negotiations at a U.S. Turkish Saturday school. In S. Danby and M. Theobald (eds), *Disputes in Everyday Life: Social and Moral Orders of Children and Young People* (*Sociological Studies of Children and Youth*, 15) (pp. 193–120). Bradford: Emerald Insight.

Dowling, M. (2007). Ethnomethodology: Time for a revisit? A discussion paper, *International Journal of Nursing Studies*, 44, 826–833.

Drew, P. and Heritage, J. (1992). Analyzing talk at work: an introduction. In P. Drew and J. Heritage (eds), *Talk at Work: Interaction in Institutional Settings* (pp. 3–67). Cambridge: Cambridge University Press.

Dupret, B. and Ferrie, J-N. (2008). Legislating at the shopfloor level: Background knowledge and relevant context of parliamentary debates, *Journal of Pragmatics*, 40, 960–978.

Durden, T., and Dangel, J. R. (2008). Teacher-involved conversations with young children during small group activity, *Early Years*, 28(3), 251–266.

Eglin, P. and Hester, S. (1999). 'You're all a bunch of feminists'. Categorization and the politics of terror in the Montreal Massacre, *Human Studies*, 22, 253–272.

Eglin, P. (2002). Member's gendering work: 'women', 'feminists' and membership categorization analysis. *Discourse & Society*, 13(6), 819–825.

Elfer, P. (2012). Emotion in nursery work: Work Discussion as a model of critical professional reflection, *Early Years: An International Journal of Research and Development*, 32(2), 129–141.

Elfer, P. (2013). Emotional aspects of nursery policy and practice – progress and prospect, *European Early Childhood Education Research Journal*, 4, 1–16.

Emmison, M. (forthcoming, 2015). Conversation Analysis. In J. Manza (ed.), *Oxford Bibliographies in Sociology*. New York: Oxford University Press.

Enfield, N.J. (2011). Sources of asymmetry in human interaction: Enchrony, status, knowledge and agency. In T. Stivers, L. Mondada and J. Steensig (eds), *The Morality of Knowledge in Conversation* (pp. 285–312). Cambridge: Cambridge University Press.

Evaldsson, A.-C. (2005). Staging insults and mobilizing categorizations in a multiethnic peer group, *Discourse & Society*, 16, 763–786.

Evaldsson, A.-C. (2007). Accounting for friendship: Moral ordering and category membership in preadolescent girls' relational talk, *Research on Language and Social Interaction*, 40(4), 377–404.

Filipi, A. (2009). *Toddler and Parent Interaction: The Organisation of Gaze, Pointing and Vocalisation.* Amsterdam: John Benjamins Publishing Company.

Fitzgerald, R. (2012). Membership categorization analysis: Wild and promiscuous or simply the joy of Sacks?, *Discourse Studies*, 14(3), 305–311.

Fitzgerald, R., Housley, W. and Butler, C. (2009). Omni-relevance and interactional context. *Australian Journal of Communication*, 36(3), pp. 45-64.

Fjørtoft, I. (2004). Landscape as playscape: The effects of natural environments on children's play and motor development. *Children, Youth and Environments*, 14 (2), 21–44.

Francis, D and Hester, S. (2004). *An Invitation to Ethnomethodology*, London: Sage.

Gardner, R. (2012). Enriching CA through MCA? Stokoe's MCA keys, *Discourse Studies*, 14(3), 313–319.

Gardner, R. and Mushin, I. (2013). Teachers telling: Informings in an early years classroom, *Australian Journal of Communication*, 40(2), 63–82.

Gardner, R. and Mushin, I. (2014). *An Investigation into Factual Informings*. Paper presented at International Conference on Conversation Analysis (ICCA) June 23rd – 29th, 2014. UCLA, California.

Garfinkel, H. (1967). *Studies in Ethnomethodology*, Oxford: Prentice-Hall.

Goffman, E. (1981). *Forms of Talk*. Pennsylvania: University of Pennsylvania.

Göncü, A and Gaskins, S. (2011). Comparing and extending Piaget and Vygotsky's understandings of play: Symbolic play as individual, sociocultural and educational interpretation'. In A.D. Pellegrini (ed), *The Oxford Handbook of the Development of Play* (pp. 48–58). Oxford: Oxford University Press.

Goodwin M.H. (1990). He-Said-She-Said: Talk as Social Organisation among Black Children. Indiana University Press: Bloomington, IN.

Goodwin, C. (1979). The interactive construction of a sentence in natural conversation. In G. Psathas (ed), *Everyday Language: Studies in Ethnomethodology* (pp. 97–121). New York, NY: Irvington Publishers.

Goodwin, C. (1981). *Conversational Organisation: Interaction Between Speakers and Hearers*. New York: Academic Press.

Goodwin, C. (2000). Action and embodiment within situated human interaction, *Journal of Pragmatics*, 32, 1489–1522.

Goodwin, C. (in press). Narrative as talk-in-interaction. In A. de Fina and A. Georgakopoulou (eds), *Handbook of Narrative Analysis*. Malden, MA: Wiley-Blackwell.

Goodwin, C. (2014). *Grasping the World*. Paper presented at International Conference on Conversation Analysis (ICCA) June 23rd – 29th, 2014. UCLA, California.

Goodwin, C. and Duranti, A. (1992). Rethinking Context: An Introduction. In A. Duranti and C. Goodwin (eds), *Rethinking Context: Language as an Interactive Phenomenon* (pp. 1–42). Cambridge: Cambridge University Press.

Goodwin, C. and Goodwin, M.H. (1992). Assessments and the construction of context. In A. Duranti and C. Goodwin (eds), *Rethinking Context: Language as an Interactive Phenomenon* (pp. 147–190). Cambridge University Press: Cambridge.

Goodwin, C. and Goodwin, M.H. (2000). Emotion within Situated Activity. In A. Duranti (ed.), *Linguistic Anthropology: A Reader* (pp. 239–57). Malden, MA: Blackwell.

Goodwin, C. and Heritage, J. (1990). Conversation analysis, *Annual Review of Anthropology*, 19, 283–307.

Goodwin, M.H. (1998). 'Games of Stance: Conflict and Footing in Hopscotch'. In S. Hoyle and C. Temple Adger (eds), *Kids' Talk: Strategic Language Use in Later Childhood* (pp. 23–46). New York: Oxford University Press.

Goodwin, M.H. (2002). Building power asymmetries in girls' interaction, *Discourse Society*, 13, 715–730.

Goodwin, M.H. (2006). *The Hidden Life of Girls: Games of Stance, Status and Exclusion*. London: Wiley Blackwell.

Goodwin, M.H. (2014). *Concurrent Operations in Hugs: Embodied Intimate Interaction in the Family*. Paper presented at International Conference on Conversation Analysis (ICCA) June 23rd – 29th, 2014. UCLA, California.

Goodwin, M.H. and Cekaite, A. (2012). Calibration in directive/response sequences in family interaction, *Journal of Pragmatics*, 46, 122–138.

Goodwin, M.H. and Goodwin, C. (1987). Children's Arguing. In S.U. Philips, S. Steele and C. Tanz (eds), *Language, Gender and Sex in Comparative Perspective* (pp. 200–248). Cambridge: Cambridge University Press.

Goodwin, M.H. and Kyratzis, A. (2007). Children socializing children: Practices for negotiating the social order among peers, *Research on Language and Social Interaction*, 40(4), 279–289.

Goodwin, M.H., Goodwin, C. and Yaeger-Dror, M. (2002). Multi-modality in girls' game disputes, *Journal of Pragmatics*, 34, 1621–1649.

Goodwin, M., Cekaite, A. and Goodwin, C. (2012). Emotion as stance. In M. Sorjonen and A. Perakyla (eds), *Emotion in Interaction* (pp. 16–41). Oxford: Oxford University Press.

Hargraves, V. (2013). What Are Working Theories? And What Can We Do to Support Them?, *Early Education*, 54, 34–37

Harris, J. (2006). The interactional significance of tears: A conversation analytic study. Unpublished PhD thesis, University of Queensland.

Hassard, J. (1990). Ethnomethodology and organisational research: An introduction. In J. Hassard and D. Pym (eds), *The Theory and Philosophy of Organisations: Critical Issues and New Perspectives* (pp. 97–108). New York: Routledge.

Hayano, K. (2011). Claiming epistemic primacy: yo-marked assessments in Japanese. In T. Stivers, L. Mondada and J. Steensig (eds), *The Morality of Knowledge in Conversation* (pp. 58–81). Cambridge: Cambridge University Press.

Hedges, H. (2011). Connecting 'snippets of knowledge': Teachers' understandings of the concept of working theories. *Early Years: An International Journal of Research and Practice*, 31(3), 271–284.

Hepburn, A. (2004). Crying: Notes on description, transcription and interaction, *Research on Language and Social Interaction*, 37(3), 251–290.

Hepburn, A. and Potter, J. (2007). Crying receipts: Time, empathy and institutional practice, *Research on Language and Social Interaction*, 40(1), 89–116.

Heritage, J. (1978). Aspects of the flexibilities of natural language use, *Sociology*, 12, 79–103.

Heritage, J. (1984). A change-of-state token and aspects of its sequential placement. In J.M. Atkinson and J. Heritage (eds), *Structures of Social Action* (pp. 299–345). Cambridge, UK: Cambridge University Press.

Heritage, J. (2011). Territories of knowledge, territories of experience: Empathic moments in interaction. In T. Stivers, L. Mondada and J. Steensig (eds), *The Morality of Knowledge in Conversation* (pp. 159–183). Cambridge: Cambridge University Press.

Heritage, J. (2012a). Epistemics in action: Action formation and territories of knowledge, *Research on Language and Social Interaction*, 45(1), 1–29.

Heritage, J. (2012b). The epistemic engine: Sequence organization and territories of knowledge, *Research on Language and Social Interaction*, 45(1), 30–52.

Heritage, J. (2013). Epistemics in Conversation. In J. Sidnell and T. Stivers (eds), *The Handbook of Conversation Anaysis* (pp. 370–394). Chichester: Wiley-Blackwell.

Heritage, J. (2014). *Turn-initial Position and One of its Occupants: The Case of 'Well'*. Paper presented at International Conference on Conversation Analysis (ICCA) June 23rd – 29th, 2014. UCLA, California.

Heritage, J. and Raymond, G. (2005). The terms of agreement: Indexing epistemic authority and subordination in assessment sequences, *Social Psychology Quarterly*, 68(1), 15–38.

Hester, S. and Francis, D. (1997). Reality analysis in a classroom storytelling, *The British Journal of Sociology*, 48(1), 95–112.

Hester, S. and Francis, D. (2000). Ethnomethodology and Local Educational Order. In S. Hester and D. Francis (eds), *Local Education Order. Ethnomethodological Studies of Knowledge in Action* (pp. 1–19). Philadelphia: John Benjamins Publishing Company.

Hester, S. and Hester, S. (2012). Category Relations, omnirelevance, and children's disputes. In S. Danby and M. Theobald (eds), *Disputes in Everyday Life: Social and Moral Orders of Children and Young People* (Sociological Studies of Children and Youth, 15) (pp. 1–25). Bingley: Emerald.

Housley, W. and Fitzgerald, R. (2002). The reconsidered model of membership categorization analysis, *Qualitative Research*, 2(1), 59–83.

Hutchby, I. (2001). Resisting the incitement to talk in child counselling: Aspects of the utterance 'I don't know', *Discourse Studies*, 4, 147–168.

Hutchby, I. (2005). Children's talk and social competence, *Children & Society*, 19, 66–73.

Hutchby, I. (2005b). 'Active listening': Formulations and the elicitation of feelings – talk in child counselling, *Research on Language and Social Interaction*, 38:3, 303–329

Hutchby, I. and Woofit, R. (1998). *Conversation Analysis: Principles, Practices and Applications*. Cambridge: Blackwell.

Hyun. E. and Marshall. J.D. (2003). Teachable-moment-oriented curriculum practice in early childhood education, *Journal of Curriculum Studies*, 35(1), 111–127.

Jacoby, S. and Ochs, E. (1995). Co-construction: An introduction, *Research on Language and Social Interaction*, 28(3), 171–183.

Jefferson, G. (1973). A case of precision timing in ordinary conversation: Overlapped tag-positioned address terms in closing sequences, *Semiotica*, 9(1), 47–96.

Jefferson, G. (1974). Error correction as an interactional resource, *Language in Society*, 3(2), 181–199.

Jefferson, G. (1979). A technique for inviting laughter and its subsequent acceptance/declination. In G. Psathas (ed.), *Everyday Language: Studies in Ethnomethodology* (pp. 79–96). New York: Irvington Publishers.

Jefferson, G. (1980). On 'Trouble-Premonitory' Response to Inquiry, *Sociological Inquiry*, 50, 153–85.

Jefferson, G. (1984). On stepwise transition from talk about a trouble to inappropriately next-positioned matters. In J.M. Atkinson and J.C. Heritage (eds), *Structures of Social Action: Studies in Conversation Analysis* (pp. 191–222). Cambridge: Cambridge University Press.

Jefferson, G. (2004). Glossary of transcript symbols with an introduction. In G.H. Lerner (ed.), *Conversation Analysis: Studies from the First Generation* (pp. 13–31). Amsterdam: John Benjamins.

Kent, A. (2012). Compliance, resistance and incipient compliance when responding to directives, *Discourse Studies*, 14(6), 711–730.

Kidwell, M. (2011). Epistemics and embodiment in the interactions of very young children. In T. Stivers, L. Mondada and J. Steensig (eds), *The Morality of Knowledge in Conversation* (pp. 257–284). Cambridge: Cambridge University Press.

Kidwell, M. (2005). Gaze as Social Control: How Very Young Children Differentiate "The Look" From a "Mere Look" by Their Adult Caregivers, *Research on Language and Social Interaction*, 38(4), 417–449.

Kidwell, M. and Zimmerman, D.H. (2007). Joint attention as action, *Journal of Pragmatics*, 39, 592–611.

Kitson, N. (2010). Children's fantasy role play – why adults should join in. In J. Myles (ed.), *The Excellence of Play* (pp. 108–120). Milton Keynes: Open University Press.

Koschmann, T. (2011). Understanding understanding in action, *Journal of Pragmatics*, 43(2), 435–437.

Kyratzis, A. (2004). Talk and interaction among children and the co-construction of peer groups and peer culture, *Annual Review of Anthropology*, 33, 625–649.

Kyratzis, A. (2007). Using the social organisational affordances of pretend play in American preschool girls' interactions, *Research on Language and Social Interaction*, 40(4), 321–352.

Labov, W. and Fanshel, D. (1977). *Therapeutic Discourse*. New York: Academic.

Lepper, G. (2000). *Categories in Text and Talk*. London: Sage Publications.

Lerner, G.H. and Zimmerman, D.H. (2003). Action and the appearance of action in the conduct of very young children. In P.I. Glenn, C.D. LeBaron and J.

Mandelbaum (eds), *Studies in Language and Social Interaction* (pp. 441–457). London: Routledge.

Leung, S. (2002). Conflict talk: A discourse analytical perspective, *Columbia University Working Papers in TESOL & Applied Linguistics*, 2(3), 1–19.

Liddicoat, A.J. (2011). *An Introduction to Conversation Analysis*. London: Continuum International Publishing Group.

Lindström, A and Sorjonen, M.J. (2013). Affiliation in conversation. In J. Sidnell and T. Stivers (eds), *The Handbook of Conversation Analysis* (pp. 350–369). Oxford: Blackwell Publishing.

Little, H., Wyver, S. and Gibson, F. (2011). The influence of play context and adult attitudes on young children's physical risk-taking during outdoor play, *European Early Childhood Education Research Journal*, 19(1), 113–131.

Macbeth, D. (1991). Teacher authority as practical action, *Linguistics and Education*, 3, 281–314.

Macbeth, D. (2011). Understanding understanding as an instructional matter, *Journal of Pragmatics*, 43(2), 438–451.

Mandelbaum, J. (1989). Interpersonal activities in conversational storytelling, *Western Journal of Speech Communication*, 53, 114–126.

Markman, E.M. (1989). *Categorization and Naming in Children: Problems of Induction*. London. The MIT Press.

Mashford-Scott, A. and Church, A. (2011). Promoting Children's Agency in Early Childhood Education, *Research on Youth and Language*, 5(1), 15–38.

Maynard, D.W. (1985). How children start arguments. *Language and Society*, 14(1), 1–30.

Maynard, D.W. and Clayman, S.E. (1991). The diversity of ethnomethodology. *Annual Review of Sociology*, 17, 385–418.

Maynard, D.W. and Zimmerman. D.H. (1984). Topical talk, ritual and the social organization of relationships, *Social Psychology Quarterly*, 47(4), 301–316.

Maynard, T. and Thomas, N. (2004). Introduction. In T. Maynard and N. Thomas (eds), *An Introduction to Early Childhood Studies* (pp. 1–4). London: Sage.

Maynard, T. (2007). Special issue: Outdoor play and learning, education 3–13, *International Journal of Primary, Elementry and Early Years Education*, 35(4), 305–407.

Maynard, T. and Waters, J. (2007). Learning in the outdoor environment: a missed opportunity? *Early Years: An International Research Journal*, 27(3), 255–265.

Maynard, T., Waters, J. and Clements, J. (2013). Child-initiated learning, the outdoor environment and the 'underachieving' child, *Early Years: An International Research Journal*, 33(3), 212–225.

McHoul, A. and Rapley, M. (2005). A case of attention-deficit/hyperactivity disorder diagnosis: Sir Karl and Francis B. slug it out on the consulting room floor, *Discourse and Society*, 16(3), 419–449.

McHoul, A., Rapley, M. and Antaki, C. (2008). You gotta light? On the luxury of context for understanding talk in interaction, *Journal of Pragmatics*, 40, 827–839.

McWhinney, B. (2007). *The CHILDES Project: Tools for Analyzing Talk – electronic edition*. Mahwah, NJ: Lawrence Erlbaum Associates

Mehan, H. (1979). *Learning Lessons: Social Organization in the Classroom*. Cambridge, MA: Harvard University Press.

Ministry of Education. (1996). *Te Whāriki. He Whāriki Mātauranga mō ngā Mokopuna o Aotearoa. Early Childhood Curriculum*. Wellington, New Zealand: Learning Media.

Mitchell, L., and Cubey, P. (2003). *Characteristics of Professional Development Linked to Enhanced Pedagogy and Children's Learning in Early Childhood Settings: Best Evidence Synthesis*. Wellington. New Zealand: Ministry of Education.

Mondada, L. (2011). The management of knowledge discrepancies and of epistemic changes in institutional interactions. In T. Stivers, L. Mondada and J. Steensig (eds), *The Morality of Knowledge in Conversation* (pp. 27–58). Cambridge: Cambridge University Press.

Mooij, T. (1999a). Promoting prosocial pupil behaviour: 1 – A multilevel theoretical model, *British Journal of Educational Psychology*, 69, 469–478

Mooij, T. (1999b). Promoting prosocial pupil behaviour: 2 – Secondary school intervention and pupil effects, *British Journal of Educational Psychology*, 69, 479–504.

Ochs, E. (1979). Transcription as theory. In E. Ochs and B. Schieffelin (eds), *Developmental Pragmatics* (pp. 43–72). New York, NY: Academic Press.

Ouvry, M. (2003). *Exercising Muscles and Minds*. London: National Children's Bureau.

Page, J and Elfer, P. (2013). The emotional complexity of attachment interactions in nursery, *European Early Childhood Education Research Journal*, 21(4), 553–567.

Page, J. (2008). Permission to love them. In C. Nutbrown and J. Page (eds), *Working With Babies and Children From Birth to Three* (pp. 181–187). London: Sage.

Page, J. (2011). Do mothers want professional carers to love their babies?, *Journal of Early Childhood Research*, 9 (3), 310–323.

Pepler, D.J and Craig, W.M. (1995). A peek behind the fence: Naturalistic observations of aggressive children with remote audiovisual recording, *Developmental Psychology*, 31(4), 548–553.

Perakyla, A. (2004). Validity in Research on Naturally Occurring Social Interaction. In D. Silverman (ed.), *Qualitative Research: Theory, Method and Practice* (pp. 365–382). London, England: Sage.

Peräkylä, A. (2005). Active listening and the formulation of concerns. In I. Hutchby (ed), *The Discourse of Child Counselling* (pp. 79–99). Amsterdam: John Benjamins.

Peters, S. and Davis, K. (2011). Fostering children's working theories: Pedagogic issues and dilemmas in New Zealand, *Early Years*, 31(1), 5–17.

Piaget, J. (1976). Symbolic Play. In J. Bruner, A. Jolly, and K. Sylva. (eds), *Play: Its Role in Development and Evolution* (pp. 555–569). New York: Penguin Books.

Pike, C. (2010). Intersubjectivity and misunderstanding in adult-child learning conversations. In H. Gardner and M.A. Forrester (eds), *Analysing Interactions in Childhood: Insights from Conversation Analysis* (pp. 3–23). Chichester: Wiley-Blackwell.

Pollner, M. and Emerson, R. (2001). Ethnomethodology and Ethnography. In P. Atkinson, A. Coffey, S. Delamont, J. Lofland and L. Lofland (eds), *Handbook of Ethnography* (pp. 118–135). London: Sage.

Pomerantz, A and Fehr, B.J. (1997). Conversation analysis: An approach to the study of social action as sense making practices. In Teun A. van Dijk (ed.), *Discourse as Social Interaction* (pp. 65–91). London: Sage.

Pomerantz, A. (1984). Agreeing and disagreeing with assessments: Some features of preferred/dispreferred turn shapes. In J.M. Atkinson and J. Heritage (eds), *Structures of Social Action: Studies in Conversation Analysis* (pp. 57–101). Cambridge: Cambridge University Press.

Pomerantz, A. and Mandlebaum, J. (2005). Conversation analytic approaches to the relevance and uses of relationship categories in interaction. In K.L. Fitch and R.E. Sanders (eds), *Handbook on Language and Social Interaction* (pp. 149–171). Mahwah, NJ: Lawrence Erlbaum Associates.

Pomerantz, A.M. (1980). Telling my side: 'Limited access' as a 'fishing' device. *Sociological Inquiry*, 50, 186–198.

Psathas, G. (1990). *Interactional Competence*. Washington D.C.: University Press of America.

Psathas, G. (1999). Studying the organisation in action: Membership categorization and interaction analysis, *Human Studies*, 22, 139–162.

Rapley, T. (2012). Order, order: A 'modest' response to Stokoe, *Discourse Studies*, 14(3), 321–328.

Rendle-Short, J. (2014). *Knowledge Management in Children's Spontaneous Activities*. Paper presented at International Conference on Conversation Analysis (ICCA) June 23rd – 29th, 2014. UCLA, California.

Rogoff, B. (2003). *The Cultural Nature of Human Development*. Oxford; Oxford University Press.

Ruusuvuori, J. (2013). Emotion, Affect and Conversation. In J. Sidnell and T. Stivers (eds) *The Handbook of Conversation Analysis* (pp. 330–349). Oxford: Blackwell Publishing.

Sacks, H and Schegloff, E.A. (1979). Two preferences in the organisation of reference to persons in conversation and their interaction. In G. Psathas (ed.), *Everyday Language: Studies in Ethnomethodology* (pp. 15–21). New York: Irvington Press.

Sacks, H. (1972). An initial investigation of the usability of conversational data for doing sociology. In D. Sudnow (ed.), *Studies in Social Interaction* (pp. 31–75). London: Collier-Macmillan.

Sacks, H. (1973). On some puns: With some intimations. In R.W. Shuy (ed.), *Report of the Twenty- third Annual Round Table Meeting of Linguistics and Language Studies* (pp. 135–144). Washington, D.C: Georgetown University Press.

Sacks, H. (1984a). On doing 'being ordinary'. In J.M. Atkinson and J. Heritage (eds), *Structures of Social action* (pp. 413–429). Cambridge, UK: Cambridge University Press.

Sacks, H. (1984b). Notes on Methodology. In J.M. Atkinson and J. Heritage (eds), *Structures in Social Action: Studies in Conversation Analysis* (pp. 2–27). Cambridge: Cambridge University Press.

Sacks, H. (1992a). *Lectures on conversation (Vol. I)*. Oxford: Blackwell.

Sacks, H. (1992b). *Lectures on conversation (Vol. II)*. Oxford: Blackwell.

Sacks, H., Schegloff, E.A. and Jefferson, G. (1974). A simplest systematics for the organisation of turn-taking for conversation, *Language*, 50, 696–735.

Sacks, H., Schegloff, E.A. and Jefferson, G. (1974). A simplest systematics for the organisation of turn-taking for conversation, *Language*, 50, 696–735.

Schegloff, E.A. (1996a). Confirming allusions: Toward an empirical account of action, *The American Journal of Sociology*, 102(1), 161–216.

Schegloff, E.A. (2007a). *Sequence Organisation in Interaction: A Primer in Conversational Analysis (Volume 1)*, Cambridge: Cambridge University Press.

Schegloff, E.A. (1968). Sequencing in conversational openings, *American Anthropologist*, 70(6), 1075–1095.

Schegloff, E.A. (1972). Notes on a Conversational Practice: Formulating Place. In D. Sudnow (ed.), *Studies in Social Interaction* (pp. 75–120). New York: Free Press.

Schegloff, E.A. (1991). Reflections on talk and social structure. In D. Boden and D.H. Zimmerman (eds), *Talk and Social Structure: Studies in Ethnomethodology and Conversation Analysis* (pp. 44–70). Cambridge: Polity Press.

Schegloff, E.A. (1992a). Repair after next turn: The last structurally provided defense of intersubjectivity in conversation, *The American Journal of Sociology*, 97(5), 1295–1345.

Schegloff, E.A. (1992b). In another context. In A. Duranti and C. Goodwin (eds), *Rethinking Context: Language as an Interactive Phenomenon* (pp. 191–228). Cambridge: Cambridge University Press.

Schegloff, E.A. (1998). Reflections on studying prosody in talk-in-interaction, *Language and Speech*, 41(3–4), 235–263.

Schegloff, E.A. (2000a). Getting serious: Joke – serious 'no', *Journal of Pragmatics*, 33, 1947–1955.

Schegloff, E.A. (2000b). Overlapping talk and the organisation of turn-taking for conversation, *Language in Society*, 29(1), 1–63.

Schegloff, E.A. (2007b). A tutorial on membership categorization. *Journal of Pragmatics*, 39, 462–482.

Schegloff, E.A. and Sacks, H. (1973). Opening up closings. *Semiotica*, 7, 289–327.

Schegloff, E.A. and Sacks, H. (1973). Opening up closings. *Semiotica*, 8(4), 289–327.

Schegloff, E.A., Jefferson, G. and Sacks, H. (1977). The Preference for self-correction in the organisation of repair in conversation, *Language*, 53(2), 361–382.

Seedhouse, P. (2005a). Conversation analysis as research methodology. In K. Richards and P. Seedhouse (eds), *Applying Conversation Analysis* (pp. 251–265). Hampshire: Palgrave Macmillan.

Sidnell, J. (2010). *Conversation Analysis: An Introduction*. Oxford: Wiley-Blackwell.

Sidnell, J. (2011). The epistemics of make-believe. In T. Stivers, L. Mondada and J. Steensig (eds), *The Morality of Knowledge in Conversation* (pp. 131–158). Cambridge: Cambridge University Press.

Silverman, D. (1998). *Harvey Sacks; Social Science and Conversation Analysis*. Oxford: Blackwell Publishers Ltd.

Silverman, D. (2006). *Interpreting Qualitative Data: Methods for Analyzing Talk, Text and Interaction*. London: Sage.

Silverman, D. (2012). Beyond armed camps: A response to Stokoe, *Discourse Studies*, 14(3), 329–336.

Sinclair, J.M., and Coulthard, M. (1975). *Towards an Analysis of Discourse: The English Used by Teachers and Pupils*. London: Oxford University Press.

Siraj-Blatchford, I. and Manni, L. (2008). 'Would you like to tidy up now?': An analysis of adult questioning in the English foundation stage, *Early Years*, 28(1), 5–22.

Siraj-Blatchford, I., Sylva, K., Muttock. S., Gilden, R. and Bell, D. (2002). *Researching Effective Pedagogy in the Early Years*. DfES Research Report 365. London, England: HMSO Queens Printer.

Siraj-Blatchford, I., Sylva, K., Taggart, B., Sammons, P., Melhuish, E. and Elliot, K. (2003). Intensive studies of practice across the foundation stage. *The Effective Provision of Pre-School Education (EPPE) Project. Technical Paper 10*. London, England: Institute of Education, University of London.

Siraj-Blatchford, I. and Sylva, K. (2004). Researching pedagogy in English pre-schools, *British Educational Research Journal*, 30(5), 713–730.

Stephen, C. (2012). Learning in early childhood. In P. Jarvis and M. Watts (eds), *The Routledge International Handbook of Learning* (pp. 103–111). Abingdon: Routledge.

Stephen, C. (2010). Pedagogy: The silent partner in early years learning. *Early Years*, 30(3), 15–28.

Stivers, T. (2008). Stance, alignment, and affiliation during storytelling: When nodding is a token of affiliation, *Research on Language and Social Interaction*, 41(1), 31–57.

Stivers, T. and Heritage, J. (2001). Breaking the sequential mold: Answering 'more than the question' during comprehensive history taking, *Text*, 21(1/2), 151–185.

Stivers, T., Mondada, L. and Steensig, J. (2011). *The Morality of Knowledge in Conversation*. Cambridge: Cambridge University Press.

Stokoe, E. (2012a). Moving forward with membership categorization analysis: Methods for systematic analysis, *Discourse Studies*, 14(3), 277–303.

Stokoe, E. (2012b). Categorial systematics, *Discourse Studies*, 14(3), 344–354.

Sylva, K., Melhuish, E., Sammons, P., Siraj-Blatchford, I. and Taggart, B. (2010). *Early Childhood Matters: Evidence from the Effective Pre-School and Primary Education Project*. London, England: Routledge.

Sylva, K., Melhuish, E.C., Sammons, P., Siraj-Blatchford, I. and Taggart, B. (2004). The effective provision of pre-school education (EPPE) Project: *Technical Paper 12 – The Final Report: Effective Pre-School Education*. London, England: DfES / Institute of Education, University of London.

Tapper, K. and Boulton, M.J. (2002). Studying aggression in school children: The use of wireless microphone and micro video camera, *Aggressive Behaviour*, 28, 356–365.

Tarplee, C. (2010). Next Turn and Intersubjectivity in children's Language Acquisition. In H. Gardner and M. Forrester (eds) *Analysing Interactions in Childhood: Insights from Conversation Analysis* (pp. 3–22). Sussex: Wiley.

ten Have, P. (2000). *Doing Conversation Analysis: A Practical Guide*. London, England: Sage.

ten Have, P. (2004). *Understanding Qualitative Research and Ethnomethodology*. London: Sage.

Theobald, M., and Danby, S.J. (2012). 'A problem of versions': Laying down the law in the school playground. In S. Danby and M. Theobald (eds), *Disputes in Everyday Life: Social and Moral Orders of Children and Young People* (*Sociological Studies of Children and Youth*, 15) (pp. 221–241). Bradford, GBR: Emerald Insight.

Theobald, M. (2013). Ideas as 'possessitives': Claims and counter claims in a playground dispute, *Journal of Pragmatics*, 45, 1–12.

Theobald, M.A., and Kultti, A. (2012). Investigating child participation in the everyday talk of teacher and children in a preparatory year, *Contemporary Issues in Early Childhood*, 13(3), 210–225.

Tobin, J.J., Wu, D.Y.H. and Davidson, D.H. (1989). *Preschool in Three Cultures*. Yale: Yale University Press.

Tobin, J.J., Hsueh, Y. and Karasawa, M. (2009). *Preschool in Three Cultures Revisited*. Chicago: Chicago University Press.

Tovey, H. (2007). *Playing Outdoors: Spaces and Places, Risk and Challenge*. Maidenhead: McGraw Hill.

Vehvilainen, S. (2011). Identifying and managing resistance in psychoanalytic interaction. In A. Perakyla, C. Antaki, S. Vehvilainen and I. Leudar (eds), *Conversation Analysis and Psychotherapy* (pp. 120–138). Cambridge: Cambridge University Press.

Vygotsky, L. (1976). Play and its role in the mental development of the child. In J. Bruner, A. Jolly, and K. Sylva. (eds), *Play: Its Role in Development and Evolution* (pp. 537–554). New York: Penguin Books.

Waller, T. (2005). International Perspectives. In T. Waller (ed.), *An Introduction to Early Childhood: A Multidisciplinary Approach* (pp. 63–80). London: Sage.

Waller, T. (2007). The trampoline tree and the swamp monster with 18 heads: Outdoor play in the foundation stage and foundation phase, *Education 3–13:*

International Journal of Primary, Elementry and Early Years Education, 35(4), 393–407.

Waters, J. and Bateman, A. (2013a). Revealing the interactional features of learning and teaching moments in outdoor activity, *European Early Childhood Education Research Journal*, 21(3), 1–13.

Waters, J. and Bateman, A. (2013b). *Scaffolded and Co-constructed Interactions in Outdoor Experiences in Wales and NZ*. Paper presented at EECERA conference, Tallin, Estonia; August 28th – 31st 2013

Waters, J., and Maynard, T. (2010). What elements of the natural outdoor environment do children of 4–7 years attend to in their child-initiated interactions with teachers?, *European Early Childhood Education Research Journal*, 18(4), 473–83.

Wells, G and Arauz, R.M (2006). Dialogue in the classroom, *The Journal of the Learning Sciences*, 15(3), 379–428.

Whitehead, K. A. (2012). Moving forward by doing analysis, *Discourse Studies*, 14(3), 337–343.

Wood, D.J. and Middleton, D. (1975). A study of assisted problem solving, *Journal of Psychology*, 66, 181–91.

Wood, D.J., Bruner. J. and Ross, G. (1976). The role of tutoring in problem solving, *Journal of Child Psychology and Psychiatry*. 17, 89–100.

Wootton, A.J. (1981). Children's use of address terms. In P. French and M. MacLure (eds), *Adult–Child Conversation* (pp. 142–58). New York, NY: St Martins.

Index

affiliation 19, 41, 42–43, 44–46, 47, 50, 54, 64–65, 72–73, 87–88, 98, 114, 122, 148, 155
  affective 26, 85
  –alignment distinction 19
  co-production of 59, 60, 62, 65, 102, 131
  dis- 27, 49, 51, 54, 75, 108, 168
alignment 19, 41, 42–43, 48, 50, 80, 134, 149, 155
  –affiliation distinction 19
  co-production of 41
  social 19
asymmetries of knowledge 13, 102, 104, 108, 114, 136
  –morality link 19

Butler, Carly 6, 8, 16, 19, 20–21, 23, 24, 28, 34, 42, 45, 54, 72, 109

Carr Margaret 3, 14, 32, 37, 52, 59, 110, 112, 158
category bound activities (CBA) 26, 29, 45, 61–62, 65, 98, 132, 156 *see also* collection K; collection R; membership categorisation
  emotional upset, and 70
  pretend play, in 45, 47–48, 54, 57–58, 59, 60, 61
  relational 140–141, 151, 152, 155, 156
  shared 45–46, 47, 54, 57–58, 60, 94, 134
children 1–2, 6, 11–12, 26–27, 39
  conversation repair, and 18, 53, 106 *see also* conversation
  deficit model of 2, 12
  disputes among 67, 79, 98–99 *see also* disputes
  initiating interaction 17–18, 19, 56, 154 *see also* interaction
  pretend play 41–43, 72 *see also* pretend play
  socially competent model of 6, 12, 19, 23, 72 *see also* social competencies
  working with 34–35
co-construction/production 6, 12
  affiliation, of 58 *see also* affiliation
  closing, of 145
  context, of 12, 17, 21–22, 24, 27 *see also* turn-taking
  conversation, of 12 *see also* conversation
  disputes, of 67, 98 *see also* disputes
  interactions, of 2, 4, 5, 6, 9, 11, 12, 26–27, 123, 128, 159 *see also* interaction
  institutions, of 20, 21
  knowledge, of 6, 14, 27, 81, 94, 136, 153–154, 158
  exchange 68, 76, 84
  moral order, of 24 *see also* moral stance
  omni-relevant devices in *see* membership categorisation
  peer cultures, of 12
  pretend play, of 43, 62 *see also* pretend play
  reciprocal nature of 12
  relational activities, of 6, 27 *see also* relational care
  relationships, of 153–154 *see also* relational care
  shared understanding in 3, 6, 154 *see also* shared understanding
  social organisation, of 23
  social order, of 13, 22, 23
  SRPs, of 72, 73, 85, 98, 108, 111, 127, 144, 152, 156 *see also* standard relational pair
  teaching and learning moments 4, 32
  turn-by-turn 6, 12 *see also* turn-taking

collaborative knowledge exchange 2, 6, 15
see also knowledge exchange
collection K 7, 27–28, 29, 48, 73, 76,
81–82, 131, 151 see membership
categorisation; also standard
relational pair
co-producing 51, 53, 54, 72, 96, 108,
112, 114, 117, 120, 122, 128, 132,
140, 152, 154, 156–157
K+ 18, 72, 83,
/K+ relationship 75–76, 78, 91–92,
94, 95, 106, 147
/K- relationship 78, 84, 87, 96, 98,
117, 121, 123, 125, 136, 140,
152
K- 18, 72, 77, 83, 94, 116, 147
/K+ relationship 78, 84, 87, 94, 96,
98, 117, 121, 123, 125, 136,
140, 152
/K- relationship 147
Ki (knowledge improper) 28–29
Kp (knowledge proper) 28, 29, 157
rights and responsibilities within 48,
77, 151
collection R 7, 25, 27–28, 29, 48, 70,
78, 132 see also membership
categorisation; standard relational
pair
anytime invocability 155–156
co-producing 29, 72, 73, 81, 82, 85,
94, 98, 108, 111, 118, 122, 128,
131, 140–141, 151, 154
first position 28
higher level hierarchy of 115
omni-relevance 9, 90, 152, 155, 156
Ri (relationship improper) 28, 29, 70,
156
right and responsibilities within 25,
48, 70, 87, 96–97, 115, 144, 151
Rp (relationship proper) 29, 70,
156–157
communication 12, 15, 34
everyday 1, 3, 4
mis- 18
non-verbal 8–9, 18, 27, 39, 41, 43, 54,
57, 72, 83–84, 95, 98, 132, 144,
151, 159

verbal 21, 39, 54, 72, 83, 95, 98, 110,
112, 132, 159 see also conversation
analysis
conversation 3, 4, 13, 17, 52, 53, 103,
128–129, 158
-al openings 17, 44, 126
analysis see conversation analysis
co-construction of 12, 103
cognitively challenging talk 4
closings 17, 139
Error Correction Format 18
joint understanding in 110, 114
knowledge exchange, and 6, 104 see
also knowledge exchange
reciprocal 4
repair 18, 53, 106, 116, 119
repeat utterances 18, 49, 50, 52, 53,
54, 61, 72–73, 78, 79–80, 86–87,
92, 94, 121, 140
turn-taking in 25, 42, 49, 54, 126 see
also turn-taking
conversation analysis (CA) 2, 5–7, 17–20,
37–39, 42, 159
CBA and 26–27 see also category
bound activities
context in 21
dispreferred responses 49, 54, 57, 63,
65, 71, 75, 77, 80, 81, 102, 106,
116, 136
disputes, of 67, 68, 73, 78, 90 see also
disputes
emotional trouble, of 73, 82, 120–122,
124–127
endearment terms 120, 121–122, 138,
140
feelings talk 69, 73, 77
illness, of 131 see also illness
initiating 44, 125
knowledge exchange 2, 6, 14, 18,
107, 113–115, 111–112 see also
knowledge exchange
MCA and 22 see also membership
categorisation
multi-party interaction, of 124–127
noticing, of 102–104, 111–112,
118–120 see also noticing
oppositional responses 95, 106, 107

orientation, of 122–124 *see also* orientation
preferred responses 53, 56, 57, 63–64, 71, 80, 81, 96, 102, 104, 114, 117, 119, 125, 138, 142
priorities within 111–112, 117–118, 120–122 *see also* priorities
relational problem, of 104–108
repeat utterances *see* repeat utterances
safety, of 109–111
shared understandings in 18 *see also* shared understanding
failure of 115–118
spouse talk 47
talk-in-interaction 117 *see also* interaction
teacher-child interactions in 15–16, 153–154
transitions 150–151
trouble spots 136
turn-taking in 17–20 *see also* turn-taking
unmotivated looking 5, 36, 37, 38
usefulness of 153–154

decision-making 84, 94, 158
children's 106, 119
disputes 8, 67, 68, 73, 78, 82, 85, 88, 90, 93, 94
affiliation in 87–88
co-production of 78, 79
emotional upset in 69, 70, 73, 74–75, 78–79, 80–81, 83, 89, 95, 97
first possession rule 79, 80, 133–134
knowledge exchange in 70–71, 72–73, 76, 81, 82, 83–84, 88, 89, 93–94, 96, 98
mobilising problems 69
omni-relevant devices in 24 *see also* membership categorisation
repeat utterances in 80, 95 *see also* conversation
resolution 71–72, 78, 81, 85, 86–87, 90, 92

early childhood curriculum 2, 98, 15, 115, 154, 159 *see also* Te Whāriki
child-led approach 154

communication 159
contribution 119
empowerment 119, 159
five strands of 15, 97, 119, 159
four principles of 15, 97, 159
framework 2, 159
implementation 3, 159
relationships 159
starting point 2
early childhood education 2, 12, 117, 159
conversation analysis, and 6, 7, 15–16, 153–154 *see also* conversation analysis
ethnomethodology, and 7, 16–17 *see also* ethnomethodology
exceptional institution, as 98
open-ended questions in 5, 13, 19, 52, 117 *see also* open-ended questions
outdoor environment and 101 *see also* environment
pretend play in 39, 58 *see also* pretend play
primary focus of 14
priorities within 139, 158 *see also* priority
relational care in 14–15, 87–88, 97, 98, 131, 153–156, 157, 158
social processes within 13–14
effective pedagogy 3, 5, 13
Effective Provision of Preschool Education (EPPE) study 4–5, 13–14, 31, 32
embodied actions 26, 27, 72, 134, 144, 145, 148, 149
emotional receipts (ER) 97
endearment terms 120, 121–122, 138, 140
environment 8, 101, 128–129
conversation, and 21, 104, 109 *see also* conversation analysis
noticing 102–104, 111–112, 116
orientation within 102–103, 113–114, 124 *see also* orientation
pedagogical tool, as 101–102
recipient-designed 102
scaffolding, and 13 *see also* scaffolding
social 12, 21
epistemic primacy 45, 64, 65

ethnomethodology (EM) 5, 7, 16–17, 42, 159
  context in 144

Heritage, John 8, 18, 20, 21, 47, 50, 52, 59, 72, 84, 88, 91, 92, 95, 96, 102, 109, 112, 116, 121, 123, 125, 136, 139, 140, 141, 147, 150

illness 8–9, 131
  identifying 133–136, 145–147
  co-production of knowledge about 136–140, 151–152
    non-verbal communication in 141–146
  managing 131, 148, 149–150, 151–152
  priority, as 138, 141–142
institutional talk 20–22
  interactional practice, as 21
  rules of conduct 20–21
  turn-taking in 20 see also turn-taking
interaction 23, 31, 32, 97, 154
  closing 54, 59, 77, 87, 92, 139, 145, 149, 150
  co-construction of 2, 4, 5, 6, 11, 12, 19, 26, 123, 131–132, 153, 156 see also co-construction
  collaborative 148 see also affiliation; alignment
  cultural differences and 13
  educational 159
  embodied actions in 26, 27, 72, 134, 144, 145, 148, 149
  initiating 17, 44, 125, 133, 137, 147
  institutional talk 20 see also institutional talk
  knowledge in 18
  prosody in 26, 79, 80, 92, 95, 97, 117
  relational 122, 131, 154–156, 159
  repeat utterances 18, 49, 50, 52, 53, 54, 61, 72–73, 78, 79–80, 86–87, 92, 94, 121, 140
  social 17, 22, 27, 42
  talk-in- 5, 7, 8, 16, 36, 98, 114, 154 see also talk-in-action

teacher-child 12, 13, 15–16, 17, 20–22, 156–157 see also learning; teaching
turn-by-turn 6, 12, 154 see also turn-taking

knowledge exchange 2, 6, 14, 18, 51, 54, 60, 67, 70, 104, 108, 110, 111, 122, 154, 157 see also conversation analysis
  asymmetry in 19, 108, 114 see also asymmetries of knowledge
  collaborative 2, 6, 15
  co-production of 6, 68, 158 see also co-construction/production
  question-answer sequences in 13–14, 18, 47, 117, 121, 139 see also question-answer sequences
  relational problems, and 39, 104–108
  shared understanding in 110, 114–115, 116 see also shared understanding
    breakdown of 72, 114, 116
  social process, as 4, 15, 29

learning 11, 14 see also teaching
  co-construction of 12, 37, 128, 153 see also co-construction/production
  context specific 2
  –emotional relationship link 14, 15, 158
  episodes 2, 6, 14, 20, 32, 36–37, 102, 112, 117, 120, 123, 151
  interaction 5, 11–14, 31, 156–157 see also interaction
  knowledge exchange see knowledge exchange
  natural environment and 101
  open-ended questions 5, 13–14, 92, 112, 117
  moments 2, 3, 4, 6, 32, 33, 37–38, 59, 110
  scaffolding 13, 102 see also scaffolding
  social process, as 11, 13–14, 15, 153
Learning Story books 20
Learning Wisdom project 3–4
loving contact 144

membership categorisation 21, 23, 28, 103–104, 156, 159
   affiliation 26 *see also* affiliation
   CA and 22 *see also* conversation analysis
   CBA and 26–27, 29, 45, 61–62, 65, 98, 132, 156 *see also* category bound activities
   category sets 157 *see also* collection K; collection R
   co-production of 156 *see also* co-construction/production
   analysis (MCA) 3–4, 5, 22–24, 37, 38, 159
   devices (MCD) 23–24, 26, 48
      consistency rule 23
      cover 25–26, 157
      doing description 23
      mapping to 48
      membership inference-rich representative (MIR) 23, 157
      omni-relevance 24–26, 115, 155
   hierarchy of relevance in 23, 157
   identity 3–4, 21, 23, 57, 87, 157
   insiders 15, 28, 43, 104, 114
   outsiders 28, 43, 70, 104, 108
   positioned categories 21–22, 23–24, 136, 152
   ratification 21, 26, 57
   relational 29 *see also* turn-taking
   Rm 103, 107, 108, 150
moral stance 72, 73, 75, 76, 84, 87, 89, 133

noticing 3, 32, 38, 116, 119, 122, 132–133, 158–159
   environmental 102–104, 109, 110–112, 116, 119
   verbal 83, 116, 119, 121

open-ended questions 5, 13–14, 92, 112, 117
orientation 8, 18, 20, 37–38, 39, 45, 54, 64, 87, 138, 154
   categories, to 22, 23
   conversation analysis of 122–124, 154 *see also* conversation analysis
   environment, to 20, 21, 102–103, 113–114, 123, 124
   non-verbal 37
   omni-relevant devices, to 24 *see also* membership categorisation
   priority items, to 25, 69, 115, 119, 124, 128, 132, 147
   relational activities 39, 155, 158
   verbal 21, 138

pretend play 8, 39, 41, 72
   activities 41–43
   adults in 41–42
   adjacency pairs 45, 46, 49
   affiliation in 42–43, 44–45, 49, 54, 57, 62, 63, 64, 65–66 *see also* affiliation
      dis- 51, 54
   alignment in 42–43, 48 *see also* alignment
   CA and 42 *see also* conversation analysis
   CBA in 45, 47–48, 54, 57–58, 59, 60, 61
   co-players 48, 54
   co-production of 43, 57, 59, 60, 65–66 *see also* co-construction/production
   imaginative transformation 46
   initiating 43, 46, 48, 51, 60
   knowledge 48, 51, 54, 65–66 *see also* knowledge exchange
      transfer 46, 47, 48, 49–50, 53, 61, 65
   MCA and 42 *see also* membership categorisation
   mapping 65
   non-verbal action in 43, 52, 53, 56 *see also* communication
   reality in 60, 62, 63, 64–65
   relationships in 65–66
   suspending 62, 63, 64–65
   turn-taking in 41–42 *see also* turn-taking
priority 8, 25, 111, 115, 154–155
   collection R 9, 25 *see also* collection R
   emotional trouble as 78, 79, 83, 85, 89, 122, 124–127, 154, 158
   illness as 132, 138, 142, 145, 147, 152

omni-relevant devices, of 24, 122
reality, of 60
relational 68, 78, 97–98, 128–129, 152, 155, 156, 158
  safety as 60, 62, 65–66, 84, 85, 111, 115, 118, 120, 124, 128
  sequences 152, 156
professional love 15, 157
prosody 26, 79, 80, 92, 95, 97, 117

question-answer sequences 13–14, 17–18, 47, 117, 121, 139
  initiation-response-evaluation (IRE) 14, 19
  initiation-response-feedback (IRF) 14, 19

relational care 14–15, 84–85, 108, 111, 115, 118, 120, 129, 131, 145, 149, 151, 152, 154–155, 156
repeat utterances 18, 49, 50, 52, 53, 54, 61, 72–73, 78, 79–80, 86–87, 92, 94, 121, 140 *see also* conversation; disputes
research 1–2, 3, 31
  data analysis 37–39
  data collection 35–36
  design 35
  ethics 34–35
  participants 32–34
  teaching and learning episodes 36–37
Researching Effective Pedagogy in the Early Years (REPEY) study 5, 13–14, 31, 32
  possibility thinking 5, 32, 52, 112, 158, 159

scaffolding 13, 14, 98, 102, 114
shared understanding 3, 5–6, 18, 19, 22, 27, 52, 62, 104, 116, 121, 127, 131, 154, 155 *see also* conversation analysis; knowledge exchange
  breakdown of 49, 53–54, 61, 64, 65, 72, 104, 114, 116
  co-production of 3, 6, 29, 57 *see also* co-construction; interaction
  repair of 49, 51, 57, 106
smile talk 110, 124

social competencies 1, 19, 23, 72
spouse talk 47
standard relational pair (SRP) 20, 25, 27–29, 50, 60 *see also* turn-taking
  child-parent 156–157
  collection K 27–28, 29 *see also* collection K
  collection R 25, 27–28, 69, 73, 78, 132 *see also* collection R
  insider 28
  obligations within 115, 120, 144
  outsider 28–29
  rights within 144, 150–151
  teacher-child 131, 157
storytelling 19–20, 26, 42, 155–156
sustained shared thinking 3, 4, 13, 158

'take your time' (TYT) 97
talk-in-interaction 5, 7, 8, 16, 98, 114, 117, 155
  co-production of 101, 156
  turn-taking sequences in 154
Tāne Mahuta 104
teaching 14, 104, 117, 158–159 *see also* learning
  context specific 2
  co-production of 4, 5, 6, 12
  –emotion connection 14–15
  interaction in 5, 7, 11–14, 156–157 *see also* interaction
  scaffolding 13, 102, 114 *see also* scaffolding
  moments 6, 31, 33, 36–37, 110, 112
  social process, as 11, 15, 18
Teaching and Learning Research Initiative (TLRI) projects 31–32, 37
telling 18, 19–20, 29, 52, 59, 81–82, 83–84, 87, 93, 102, 110, 126, 148, 155–156
  story- 19–20, 26, 42, 155–156
  troubles 89, 98, 107
Te Whāriki 1, 2, 3, 4, 15 *see also* early childhood curriculum
  implementation 3, 159
  strands 34, 97, 159
turn-taking 6, 12, 17, 25, 41, 52, 57, 62, 125–126, 154 *see also* conversation analysis

turn-taking (cont.)
   allocation of 20, 54, 80
   co-construction of context, and 21 *see also* co-construction
   communication, in *see* communication
   conditional access 126
   dispreferred turn shapes 50, 106
   first pair part (FPP) 17–18, 52, 102, 116, 119
   preferred turn shapes 61
   priority in 25
   second pair part (SPP) 17, 18, 52, 102, 116, 119
   restricted 138
   standard relational pair (SRP) 20, 27 *see also* standard relational pair

unmotivated looking 5, 36, 37, 38 *see also* conversation analysis